Falconry in Mews and Field

Falconry in Mews and Field

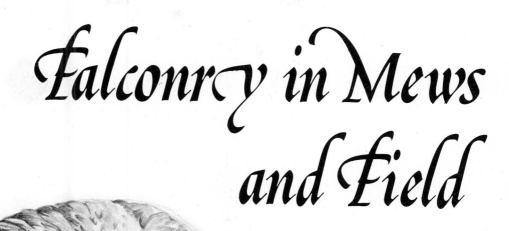

Emma Ford

B. T. BATSFORD LTD. LONDON

I would like to dedicate this book to my mother,
who gave me my first hawk, and without whose
long-suffering support I would never have
become a falconer

ISBN 0 7134 4047 3

Typeset and printed in Great Britain by
Butler & Tanner Ltd
Frome and London
for the publishers
B. T. Batsford Ltd.
4 Fitzhardinge Street
London W1H 0AH

Frontispiece: Peregrine Falcon

Title page: Common Buzzard

Contents

List of colour photographs

Red-tailed Buzzard	Lugger Falcon
Bateleur Eagle	Pallas's Sea Eagle
Changeable Hawk Eagle	Prairie Falcon
Goshawk	Peregrine Falcon
Philippine Eagle	Merlin
Lanner Falcon	Sparrowhawk

Acknowledgments

I would like to express my grateful thanks for their contributions particularly to Robin Haigh, and also to Robert Hallmann, Charles Jardine, Mac Cook and the Northern England Falconry Club, Robert Boucher, Warren Earp, Peter Asborno, Ron Krupa, Frank Porcari, J. B. Platt, Ph.D., Bernard Prevost, Michael J. Johnson, Ronald Stevens, Erik Rundhvist, R. R. Hartley, Kevin C. Carson, Dr Alan Kemp, Scott Keniston, Heinz Pils, Rick Morant, John Ashton, Jim Plainson, Jon James and to my father and my husband, Steve, for his tremendous enthusiasm and encouragement.

Photographs 108 and 109 are reproduced by permission of John Curtis. The remaining photographs were taken by Robert Hallmann. The line illustrations are by Charles Jardine and Stephen Ford.

NOTE

Measurements have been given in imperial throughout the text for convenience, but metric equivalents for the flying weights will be found in the table on page 176.

Preface

Falconry is the art of taking quarry with trained hawks. To achieve this end, all falconers have their own methods of training and managing hawks, and consequently some will disagree with parts of this book. I have tried, however, to the best of my ability, to make the information in this text both accurate and helpful by going into as much depth as possible, particularly in the chapters on the training of the individual species.

European Eagle Owl

1 The History of Hawking

There is no record of when the first hawk was trained by man, but falconry probably originated in the East. It was almost certainly devised as a method of obtaining food, rather than as a sporting pastime. One of the earliest pieces of documentary evidence concerned with falconry was supplied by Henry Layard who, while visiting the ruins of Khorsabad, came across a bas-relief which apparently depicted a hawk on the wrist of a falconer. This may well have dated from as early as 1700 BC. Aristotle, Pliny and Ctasias make reference to the use of hawks but it is unclear if the hawks are actually trained, for it seems likely that the methods of training would have been described or documented in some way. Jameson in *The Hawking of Japan* gives an account of some trained goshawks entering Japan from

1 A cadge of falcons

China in the 47th year of the reign of Empress Jingu (AD 244) but the art was not established in Japan until AD 355 when the Emporor Nontoku had a strange hawk, which was perhaps a goshawk, presented to him and it was trained and caught many pheasants. Presumably encouraged by this success, he established a 'hawk office' for the care and training of hawks. Falconry gradually spread westwards, and although it is hard to trace its exact path, it possibly reached the British Isles in about AD 860. King Ethelbert II was the first English monarch to become proficient in the art of falconry. Hunting in Anglo-Saxon times was apparently a rather casual affair; men hunted whenever game was plentiful, wherever it was to be found, as private land was virtually unknown. It is widely thought that hawking was restricted during this period to the upper classes and royalty, but this is probably a misconception arising from the fact that the pastimes of the gentry were more widely documented than those of the lower classes. With the arrival of the Normans, however, land ceased to be common property, and the right to hunt became more of a class privilege. Falconry quickly became an art which was taught, like archery and riding, to the sons of gentry as a matter of course. From this time originates the kind of hawking scene with which most people are familiar. A day of sport would commence with reports coming in from the forester to the hawking party concerning the whereabouts of the quarry. A decision would be taken as to the best area, and the party would set forth on horseback to enjoy a day's sport. The hawks were trained, not by their aristocratic owners, but by a residential falconer, who then handed over the fully trained hawk to its handler for the day. If the day's hawking was successful, the falconer was highly praised and *vice versa*. The office of Royal Falconer was created. This person was treated with great respect and was, in certain reigns, considered to be fourth in line of seniority at court. The post was very well paid and highly respected.

In 1486 *The Boke of St Albans* was published. This work explains that a man would own a certain species of hawk according to his social rank. The list is written as follows:

An Emperor—the eagle, the vulture and the 'melowne' [possibly a kite or a general term to cover many species]

A King—the gyrfalcon or the tiercel gyr

A Prince—the falcon gentill or tiercel gentill [a much-used name for the peregrine]

A Duke—the falcon of the rock [another name for a peregrine]

An Earl—the falcon peregrine [It is possible that the latter three are different sub-species of the peregrine, graded according to their performance and named differently to distinguish between them]

A Baron—the bastarde [possibly a cross-bred falcon or maybe a species hitherto unrecognized in the text]

A Knight—the saker and the sacret

A Squire—the lanner and the lanneret

A Lady—the merlin

A Youngman—the hobby

A Yeoman—the goshawk

A Priest—the sparrowhawk

A Holywater Clerk—the musket

A Knave—the kestrel

How rigidly this code was adhered to we do not know. However, it is an interesting and much quoted concept.

Hawks were very highly valued. Gyrfalcons in particular were greatly sought-after and often used by royalty as gifts, payment of dues or even as ransoms. During the Crusades, the knights obtained hawks to bring back with them, furthering the interest in different species. Many of the great rulers had large falconry establishments, including the Russian Czars, some of the Holy Roman Emperors, and Montezuma, the Aztec King in the early sixteenth century. One of the greatest royal falconers was Frederick II of Germany, who wrote a vast work on falconry which took him 30 years to complete. *De Arte Venandi cum Avibus* has been translated into English and German and enjoys the distinction of being the largest book ever written on the subject of falconry. Although some of it is obviously dated, the book is fascinating in its descriptions of the sport of falconry as it was pursued in the most lavish circumstances.

From Ethelbert II to George III, every British monarch enjoyed the sport of falconry; some were particularly dedicated, and various snippets of information can be found to illustrate this. James I hunted the Thames with cormorants and created the office of Master of the Royal Cormorants which was first held by John Wood.

History relates that Richard II founded the Royal Mews at Charing Cross where they remained until Henry VII turned the premises into stables for his horses.

Henry VIII fell into a dyke when his hawking pole snapped beneath him. He might well have drowned, but his fellow falconers pulled him out. Sir Ralph Sadler allowed Mary Queen of Scots to go hawking with her merlins in the countryside around Tutbury Castle where she was imprisoned. Elizabeth I was displeased by this, and the unfortunate Mary was deprived of further sorties. James II was responsible for conferring the honour of Hereditary Grand Falconer on the Duke of St Albans, a title held today by the present Duke.

In the nineteenth century, Holland was the main centre for European falconry. The celebrated Mollen family in Valkenswand made their living from trapping hawks, training them and selling them, and also from selling very fine equipment. The Dutch School of Falconry, as it was called, trained only passengers, while the Scottish School used eyasses. The Napoleonic wars had a damaging affect on falconry on the Continent, but at the end of the eighteenth century Colonel Thornton and Lord Orford made an effort to rekindle British interest in the sport, and introduced the Dutch schooling methods to England.

The Loo Hawking club was founded in 1838, with Alexander of the Netherlands as president. It held annual meetings at Loo, for crow, kite and heron hawking. The club was dissolved in 1853, when Royal Patronage was withdrawn. The Old Hawking Club was formed in Britain in 1853 and existed until 1927 when the British Falconers' Club was formed. This club is still active today.

The decline of falconry as a rich and glorious sport was due to a number of factors. The invention of guns decreased the apparent usefulness of hawks to provide food for the table. The enclosing of common land in Britain restricted the areas where people could hunt hawks, effectively limiting hawking to a sport for landowners only. The persecution of raptors as vermin greatly decreased the population, completely wiping out certain species from British shores, such as the White-tailed Sea Eagle. During the Second World War there was a bounty on peregrines lest they should kill British message-carrying pigeons. Visitors to the Natural History Museum in London can see drawerfuls of peregrine skins shot during this period. Since the 1954 Protection of Birds Act, the trapping of passage or haggard birds has been justly prohibited, but the loss of passage birds to the British falconer has inevitably lead to a decline in the standard of hawking

2 A modern-day hawking meet—members of the Northern England Falconry Club

activity. Falconers nowadays cannot hope to match the records achieved by the famous falconers of the past, who had almost unlimited supplies of freshly-taken passage peregrines, and the expert knowledge and facilities to put such birds to their best use. With the present difficulties of obtaining birds of prey in Britain due to the licensing laws (without which the remaining British raptors of certain species would disappear completely) the answer to the future of falconry is inevitably going to lie in captive breeding. The days of heron and kite hawking are gone. British falconers must fly eyasses rather than passagers at more lowly quarry. Thus falconry today is a different sport from that pursued by our forefathers. We cannot afford to bask in the reflected glory of the bygone era when falconry was practised under more royal and lavish circumstances. With new advances each year in the technical world of captive breeding, we must look to the future, taking with us, and furthering, the detailed knowledge imparted to us by generations of former devotees of the noble art of hawking.

2 General Husbandry

Accommodation for a hawk can take many forms, according to the circumstances of the falconer. You can either have a permanant outdoor weathering where the hawk will be tethered on a perch or 'blocked' day and night, or you can have a mews in the form of a shed or building for nighttime and a weathering or weathering ground for day-time. I distinguish between *a* weathering and *the* weathering ground because the former is generally accepted as meaning a three-sided and roofed section in which a bird is blocked, while the latter simply refers to a piece of ground on to which the bird is put during the day-time. To decide which arrangement is most suitable, you must first consider your individual circumstances. Do you (or your neighbours) keep other animals, such as cats? If so, your hawk must be kept in an enclosed weathering either for the safety of the cat (if you intend to keep a large hawk) or for the safety of the bird. Secondly, do you already have a building or shed where you can keep a hawk? If not, a shed can be quite expensive to buy or construct, so you might be better off to build a permanent outdoor weathering instead. Thirdly, if you rush to work five days a week to do a normal nine-to-five job, you might well find it easier to have your hawk in a permanent weathering to save you having to tear out at crack of dawn in your office suit to put your bird out. Fourthly, if you ever suffer any really ferocious weather conditions such as deep snow, your bird will undoubtedly need the protection of a shed rather than a permanent outdoor weathering. Having thus considered the practicalities involved, the choice is yours.

The Mews

A shed or building for a hawk should be light, airy and easily cleaned. It should contain a shelf for your scales and a perch for your hawk. The floor can be of earth, wood or concrete, but with earth floors beware of rats. I recommend the use of peat on the floor. A bed of peat four to six inches deep will absorb the mutes and all odours too. It needs only the castings lifted out and a rake over daily to look fresh again, and it will last without needing to be changed for months. It may be expensive to lay initially but it is a considerable saving of effort in the long term. For those who prefer to stick to the more traditional method of 'scrubbing out' a concrete or wooden based mews, a diluted disinfectant will have to be used twice weekly, and the floor well rinsed if the mews is to stay clean and fresh. A sheet of plastic or plastic fertilizer sacks can be used as a floor covering to make cleaning easier. Do not use newspaper on the floor as it very quickly becomes mucky and unpleasant, and it tends to blow about when a hawk flaps her wings; above all else, do *not* use straw or hay on the floor as these will cause aspergillosis or air-sacculitis. A dank or dusty mews is potentially highly damaging to a hawk's health, so do not experiment with ground covering such as shavings or sawdust which may create dust and eventually prove fatal.

12

3 Imperial Eagle in a weathering

A mews can also be adapted to turn a hawk loose, if necessary, through the moult, by removing the scales etc. and putting up suitable perches. Any windows should be slatted vertically with bamboo or similar.

The Weathering Ground
If you have a shed, generally enjoy good weather conditions, and do not suffer from an epidemic of local cats, dogs, children etc., you can have a straightforward day-time weathering ground for periods when your hawk is not being exercised. Here your hawk can be blocked on the grass in the open and left in peace with a bath and the natural elements until it is put into the mews for the night.

Weatherings
A weathering can be constructed most simply out of three sections of larch-lap or wicker panel fencing, or two sides of fencing backed on to a wall, and roofed with corrugated perspex roofing. It must be large enough to allow the hawk ample clearance for her outstretched wings in all directions when she bates and high enough to permit her to stand on her perch, and for you to be able to enter to take her up. It is best floored with pea-gravel which will not blow about as peat might outside, and which will stay looking relatively clean. This basic weathering can be adapted to become

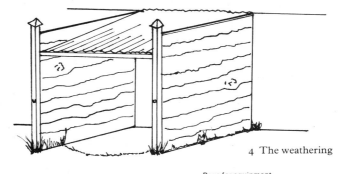

4 The weathering

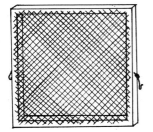

5 Optional mesh frame for the front of the weathering

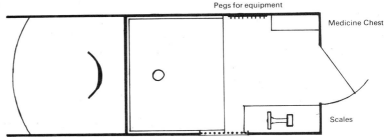

6 Ground plan for weathering and mews complex

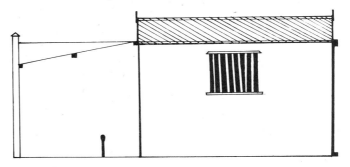

7 A simple design for a mews and weathering complex

a permanent outdoor weathering or simply an animal-proof weathering by two methods. Firstly a mesh frame can be placed on the fourth side, either on hinges or on a sliding or slotting fixture (see fig. 5). In this arrangement a hawk must be tethered so it cannot reach the mesh. Secondly, and preferably, a complete mesh surround can be constructed around the outside of the weathering of suitable height to keep out dogs and children or roofed like an aviary to keep out cats. Ideally, this complex can be backed on to a shed for bad weather accommodation and scales etc. (see figs 6 and 7), but if a shed is not available, a permanent weathering thus constructed will suffice.

Lastly, bear in mind that a bird is an intelligent, thinking being. It should not be shut up for days on end in the mews, seldom being put out to weather because its owner is too lazy or too busy. Nor will it appreciate being stuck away in some miserable little weathering, with nothing to see but the neighbour's fence opposite. Try to have some thought about the position of your weathering. Although it must be in a sheltered non-draughty spot, bear in mind that a hawk will be happiest if it can see some sort of activity from time to time, human or otherwise. This will both assist with its manning and keep it amused. Thus a weathering must not only be well designed but also well placed.

8 A Ferruginous Buzzard in moult, showing gaps where feathers are missing

MOULTING

Most birds of prey in Britain go into moult at the end of March or early April. The complete process takes about five or six months and so the moult will be completed in mid-September to early October. There are, however, various factors governing the moult which may alter the timing. Firstly, an imported hawk may not adjust to moulting during a British summer for a season or two. Secondly, certain species of hawk will not naturally go through a complete moult in this limited period of months. Many eagles, for example, will take two years and more to change all their major flight feathers. Thirdly, passage hawks tend to moult somewhat later than eyasses. Lastly, it is possible purposely to delay a hawk's moult by keeping its weight quite low through the summer. This means that the bird can be flown through the summer and put down to moult, having been fattened up during the winter months.

Wild raptors cannot afford to drop all their flight feathers in one go; they therefore drop them in matched pairs allowing the new feathers to come well down before the adjacent feathers are dropped. Captive hawks moult in the same way, unless their moult has been held over for a period when they will drop feathers very quickly, apparently to make up for lost time. There is a natural sequence for the dropping of the flight feathers which is different for falcons and hawks. Numbering the primaries from the outermost, as No 1, inwards, falcons usually drop the primary No 7 first, and thereafter the sequence goes Nos 8, 9, 10, 6, 5, 4, 3, 2, 1. In hawks the innermost primary is dropped first, in a natural sequence which works from the inside to the outermost primary. In falcons and hawks the two centre tail feathers are usually dropped first. Many books use the old names for the bird's feathers so I feel they are worth mentioning here. Correctly speaking, a hawk's breast feathering should be referred to as 'mails', the primaries as 'beams' or 'beam feathers', her secondaries as 'flags' and her centre tail feathers as 'decks'. The tail as a whole is called a 'train', and the wings are often referred to as 'sails'. A falcon's tail will become progressively shorter with each moult, the most marked reduction in length occurring during the first moult. An eyass will not, of course, moult during its first summer, but will go into moult when it is approximately 11 or 12 months old. Peregrines are described as being 'brown' or 'red' when they are in immature plumage, and 'blue' when they are adult. A 'sore hawk' is also a first-year hawk, and this term is most commonly applied to sparrowhawks.

There are several ways of taking a hawk through the moult. If the bird's old feathers are in reasonably good condition, if it can be flown 'high', or in other words in top condition and at a relatively high weight, and if it is not a nervous bird, it can be flown through the moult quite safely. This must not be attempted by an inexperienced falconer, for it requires fine judgement to fly a hawk with as high a food intake as possible without risk of losing it.

The reason that an active hawk must be fed more during the moult is because it will not only need the normal sufficiency of food to give it energy to fly, but will also need extra to grow new feathers. Thus, it is eating for two purposes and must be fed meat of a high nutritious value (see Chapter 5). Insufficient food intake during the moult will cause 'hunger traces' (see fig. 9). These take the form of a thin line across the webbing and shaft of a feather, rather as if a razor-blade had been drawn across to sever partially the feather structure. Such feathers are weakened and will snap off far more easily than healthy feathers.

A bird which is not to be flown through the moult can either be moulted out on the block, or it can be turned loose. Any well-manned bird which is not too scruffy can be moulted out cleanly on a block, with the advantage that daily handling and feeding off the fist will ensure that the hawk will be as well-manned and as manageable at the end of the moult as it was before the moult started. Very nervous hawks, however, and hawks whose old feathers are in very poor condition should be moulted loose. The reason for this is that when a hawk grows a new feather it will come down 'in blood'—meaning that before reaching full length and unfurling, the feather will be surrounded by a blood supply and encased in a sheath. Feathers which are knocked at this time will easily fall out, leaving an open wound which will bleed and must be disinfected with antibiotic powder. A nervous bird will be more likely to knock a new feather by bating, or catching its wings against the block. If something upsets a nervous hawk, it may throw out a partially grown feather. Such feathers are described as 'pinched' (see fig. 10). Both pinched feathers and feathers which have been knocked out while in the blood will usually grow again, but eventually rather than immediately. Lastly, nervous birds are also prone to 'fret marks', which are exactly the same as hunger traces except that they are caused by a shock or upset rather than by lack of food. It is worth noting that birds which travel to a new home during the moult will often produce fret marks as a result of the journey and change of environment. Some will even stop moulting altogether. Birds in bad feather should be moulted loose because new feathers need the support of the adjacent feathers while they grow. If the adjacent feathers are old ones which are broken off quite high up, the new feather is more likely to be knocked out if the bird is on a block, being handled and bating periodically. Therefore it is better to turn the hawk loose. It is worth noting that if a bird cannot be turned loose for this reason new tail feathers can, as a last resort, be strengthened individually by enclosing them in brown paper, as one would tape the whole tail (see fig. 116, Chapter 15).

Many falconers who have the necessary facilities prefer to turn their birds loose during the moult anyway, feeling that while it cannot be flown,

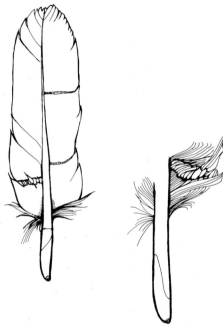

9 Hunger traces or fret marks showing damage to the webbing

10 A pinched feather

it is more pleasant for the bird to enjoy the gentle exercise which a loose mews can afford rather than to be subjected to a period of enforced inactivity.

A loose mews should be floored with a good layer of peat. It should be light and airy, with the windows slatted vertically rather than horizontally to prevent the hawk hanging on to the bars and breaking the tips off its tail. It should contain suitable perches, and a bath placed well clear of the perches. Two or more falcons of the same size can be moulted loose together, but an accipiter must enjoy exclusive accommodation. The food can be put in daily. It should be tied down to a food board if you wish to discourage your bird from getting into the habit of carrying. This will also prevent the bird from hiding pieces of food in dark corners—a habit which many loose birds adopt, probably to build up a reserve of emergency rations lest you should neglect to feed for a couple of days! It is not a harmful habit in itself, but such pieces of food will soon begin to smell in the summer if they are not found and removed. All scraps and leftovers should be removed daily to prevent flies and to maintain hygiene.

Birds to be put down to moult must be fattened up and must have their beak and talons well coped before being turned loose. A falcon which is turned loose to moult will not forget its training, nor will it lose much of its characteristic tameness, but it will lose condition rapidly. An accipiter, while miraculously maintaining much of its fit condition, will become wild very quickly when not handled. To avoid this, an accipiter can be hopped to and fed off the fist daily provided this treatment is started as soon as the bird is put down to moult. If it is continued every day right through the moult, the hawk will be ready to start immediately on a creance when the moult is completed. If, however, it is not handled at all, manning for an accipiter will have to start afresh at the end of the moult. Such birds are usually incredibly and irritatingly stupid, for, in the space of a few months, they manage to forget everything that you have taught them.

While your hawk is moulting by whichever method you have chosen to adopt as the most suitable, the unbroken flight feathers should be collected and saved for imping. Broken feathers are of no future use, but it is extremely satisfactory to see them being dropped out.

Falcons which are to be flown at game in Britain have to be taken up before the moult is completed to be ready for the season. Immature birds will not be subject to such problems and benefiting from the process of natural progression, will be able to be flown at quarry, which is itself slower due to the moult, and also at young quarry which is weak in flight, while the falcon is still inexperienced and looking for easy kills.

Some falconers, particularly in America, use drugs both to induce the start of the moult and to reduce its duration. For females, progesterone can be administered. Obtainable under the trade name of 'Norlutin', 10 mg a day can be administered initially, reduced to 5 mg when the moult is well under way. Thyroid tablets can be given to either sex at a dosage rate of two grains daily until the moult starts; then break for ten days, administer again for five to seven days, continuing the on and off process until the moult is completed. Thyroxene can also be fed in the form of beef thyroid. Vitamin B12 is thought to accelerate the moult as well. I can see little justification for accelerating the moult. Moulting is a natural process which must be endured patiently by falconers. The use of drugs will only succeed in reducing the duration of the moult to four months or so, and is therefore in my opinion unnecessary for all birds except perhaps for falcons which are to be flown at game, when such acceleration of the moult will prove useful.

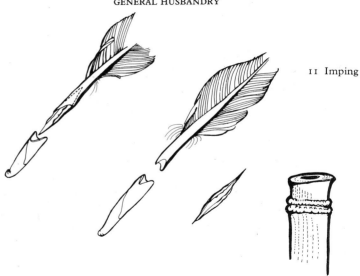

11 Imping

Imping

Imping is the process of mending a broken feather. It is an operation which is only necessary and suitable for the major flight and tail feathers which have had more than just the tip broken off.

A feather is hollow towards the end which goes into the bird's flesh. If a feather is broken it can be cut at the start of the webbing (not the fluffy webbing but the webbing proper) and another feather of corresponding size and shape can be cut in such a way that it will join end to end with the cut stub, being then of the right length in relation to the adjacent feathers. The two hollow ends can be joined by means of a plug running between them. The plug or 'imping needle' can be made of a variety of materials, the best of which is bamboo which is both strong and flexible like the natural shaft of the feather. Yew wood can be used too, and also sewing needles, if you wish to attempt a fine imp lower down the shaft. (This should only be performed if the feather is broken low down, and you do not have a replacement feather, so have to put the old tip back in.) The old imping needles were filed from soft iron wire to a triangular shape and dropped in a strong solution of brine, causing them to rust inside the feather, and thus to hold firm.

The shape of the inside of the feather-shaft is oval, so the bamboo needle must be filed or whittled to an oval shape which will exactly fit the inside of the two pieces of feather to be joined. This can only be done by trial and error. Having cast the bird, cut off the broken feather at a slant at the correct point (see fig. 11) and match up the broken feather by eye with one of your spare supply of old feathers from previous moults. The bird can then be taken out and the feather or feathers which are to be imped can be set up in readiness for the operation. When the plug has been cut and whittled to an oval shape half to one inch in length, depending on the size of the bird to be imped, with both ends pointed, the finer end can be tested for a friction-tight fit in the new feather which is to be put into the bird. Care must be taken not to split the shaft of the feather, nor the stub which is in the bird. Should this happen, the split must be bound around with waxed thread after the imp has been completed. When the bird is brought in for the second time, all the feathers to be inserted should be set up in readiness with one end of the imping needle protruding from the shaft of the new feather to be inserted into the old stub in the bird. The stub should be found among the coverts and adjacent feathers and a piece of card pushed under it (see fig. 12). The imping needle can now be gently tested

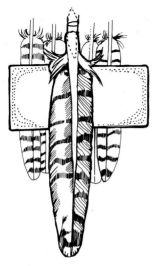

12 Card under feather to be imped

in the stub for a snug fit. When the two halves of feather will slot together over the imping needle tightly and without rotating, the needle can be taken out and coated with a thin layer of a strong glue such as clear Bostik, UHU or Super Epoxy. It is easiest to apply the glue to one half of the needle at a time so that it can be slotted into the new feather first, then the other half can be coated while holding the feather, to prevent sticky fingers. If, at this stage, the coverts are getting in the way, they can be damped down to prevent them from getting covered in glue. When the two halves are pushed together the surplus glue must be wiped off and care must be taken that the new feather is lying at the right angle in relation to those which are adjacent to it. When the imp is completed, the bird must be held for five to ten minutes until the glue has set.

Sewing in
This is another method of mending a feather. The broken feather is cut at the start of the webbing as for a normal imp. A corresponding feather is cut at the end to form a quill (see fig. 13). It is then inserted carefully inside the shaft of the old stub, but must *not* be pushed home beyond the flesh line, in other words the place where the stub goes inside the bird's flesh. The old method is to stitch it in place with waxed thread. To do this, a needle is threaded with double cotton, which is knotted at the end. The needle is pushed up through the shaft of the old stub, and also of the new feather, which is lying inside the stub. It is pulled up to the knot, whereupon the thread is cut at the needle, and the two ends are crossed over, bound around the shaft, and tied off on the top of the feather. This will hold the join firm.

Alternatively, the new feather, when cut to a quill, can be coated in one of the previously mentioned adhesives and 'glued in'. Both these methods are extremely effective if done properly, and are virtually undetectable. Imping, sewing in and gluing in can be practised effectively on old feathers. The choice of which method to adopt is a matter for the individual.

Bent, scruffy or dirty feathers
Bent or scruffy feathers can be straightened and tidied by dipping them in hot water. This process will greatly improve a scruffy tail, but must not be repeated too often, as frequent dipping will eventually make the feathers brittle. Dirty or soiled feathers can be damped and gently scrubbed in the direction of the grain of the webbing with a nailbrush (or for smaller birds, a toothbrush). A weak solution of soap, soapflakes or washing-up liquid in warm water can be used to bath a very grubby hawk, taking care to avoid the eyes. If it is a fine day, the bird can then be put outside in the sun to dry. If it is cold or wet, the hawk can be dried artificially with a hairdryer or blow heater on its lowest setting. However, this process will remove all the bird's natural oils and thus destroy its waterproofing for quite some time, as will repeated stroking with the finger. For this reason, hawks should never be stroked on their backs or heads with the bare hand.

COPING

Like human fingernails, a hawk's talons and beak will grow over a period of months. In the wild, birds of prey strop their beaks and wear down their feet on rocks or on the bones of their prey, but in captivity the beak and talons will often become overgrown. This extended growth must be removed, and the original shape restored with a file. This process is called 'coping'.

13 Sewing or gluing in

14 A Harris' Hawk preening its tail. Regular preening is important to maintain good feather condition

Coping should be performed whenever it appears necessary. Some birds maintain perfect shape of both beak and talons, while others suffer not only from overgrowth but also from small splits and cracks in their beaks. The latter usually occurs in birds which have not been coped when it was necessary and the thin overgrown sides of the beak have been fractured slightly by contact with a bone or similar object. The fracture impacts with stale meat and the split gradually extends in length, weakening the beak. Such instances can only be avoided by regular inspection. Experienced falconers who have several hawks will have no difficulty in spotting when a beak or talons become overgrown, but a novice with only one hawk cannot draw comparisons, and seeing his hawk every day may well not notice that the beak or feet have become overgrown. He must, therefore, be particularly on his guard and should cope his bird every six months or so as a precautionary measure.

The instruments necessary for coping are a pair of dog toenail clippers, available from any vet, or a pair of electrician's wire clippers, a varied set of needle or chain saw files, including a flat surfaced one, a thick round one, a thin round one and a triangular one, obtainable from hardware stores, and a silver nitrate 'shaving stick', obtainable from a vet or chemist. The latter is in case of accidents. Like human nails a hawk's beak and claws contain a living quick. If this is cut, it will hurt your hawk and it will bleed, indicating that you have taken too much growth off the tip. If a silver nitrate stick is applied, the blood at the surface will be cauterized and the bleeding will stop.

To cope a bird's beak thoroughly, you must do more than simply remove the tip. The inside will overgrow too, sometimes preventing the hawk from eating properly and even from closing its beak. Grey flaky scale will build up on the outside of the beak, giving it a rough appearance, and food will adhere to the sides of the beak around the crines and cere. Firstly the bird must be cast and held by an assistant. Then the tip of the beak can be removed with the aid of the clippers, if this is necessary. Sometimes the shape can be restored just by filing, but if the tip is very overgrown, it will be quicker to remove most of the excess growth with clippers first, and then file it back to a point. Next the beak must be opened and examined inside for overgrowth. A hawk's beak has a gentle curve to the lower edge of the upper mandible. This is called a 'festoon' (see fig. 15). A falcon's beak has a 'tooth' (see fig. 16). This must be gently filed to define the shape. The tooth is of great importance to a falcon, enabling it to break the neck of its prey, and thus must be carefully maintained with the aid of a triangular file. The lower mandible, if allowed to grow too long, will roll inwards. This must therefore be filed with a flat file evenly across both sides. Lastly the outside of the upper mandible must be gently filed with the flat file to remove excess scale. If there are any splits or cracks in the beak this is when you will notice them if you have not already seen them. I once bought a female Lugger Falcon whose beak was encased in a mass of loose grey scale. When this flaky matter was touched with a file, it disintegrated on one side of the beak revealing a layer of rotten meat and a deep crack running up the side of the upper mandible. When all the excess scale was carefully removed, a normal and fairly healthy beak became visible, but the crack took a year to grow out, having to be gently filed and cleaned at regular intervals. Care must be taken while filing the outside of the upper mandible not to damage the delicate waxy skin of the cere with the tip of the file. The edge of the beak around the line of the cere can be carefully cleaned with the point of a file, and when all the filing is finished, the beak can be polished with a little Vaseline on the fingertips to remove all traces of scale. Occasionally, the nostrils or nares of a bird may become partially blocked or obscured. These can be gently cleared with the aid of the blunt end of a needle. Any little pieces of food or egg yolk from the day-old chicks which are fed to hawks can be removed gently with the fingers or with a toothbrush and warm water.

The talons or claws (strictly a falcon has talons while a hawk has claws) can be clipped like the beak. They can then be filed to a point. Bear in mind that to be an effective killer a raptor must have sharp talons. They must not be blunted, neither must the beak. The back talon is of particular importance. It is longer than the rest and must retain a good point. Usually only the underside of a talon needs to be filed. Large hawks have a well defined groove in the underside of the claw, which will fill up with scale and rotten meat. It is this build-up of decaying matter which helps to cause foot infection, for if a bird snatches with its foot, it can pierce the sole with its talons and infect the wound. Kestrels and other very small birds will not need to have their talons filed. It is an operation which is fiddly and unnecessary, as such small talons sharpen up very quickly anyway when the tips are clipped. If you are uncertain whether your bird has overgrown talons or not, see if it can stand flat-footed comfortably; if it can it is probably all right, but if it looks unbalanced, or if the toes are pushed upwards to accommodate the curve of the talons, then they are overgrown and in need of attention.

Aviary birds must also be inspected for overgrowth from time to time. It is easy to neglect a hawk in an aviary in this respect, and it is a worthwhile precaution to include in the aviary interior a large stone or even a brick to enable the bird to strop its beak to keep it in shape. This is not a foolproof measure though, and the bird must still be checked at regular intervals. Should just the tip of beak or talons become overgrown the bird can be caught up in the aviary and the tip clipped there and then to save the

15 Beak showing festoon of the upper mandible of a hawk

16 Beak showing tooth of a falcon

trauma of being removed from the aviary. An aviary bird does not need such sharp talons and beak as a hunting bird. It is advisable to cope a hawk which is intended for an aviary really thoroughly immediately before it is put in.

Lastly, when a hawk is brought inside to be coped, it is well worth examining its jesses and leash for signs of wear, and spraying it with Johnson's Anti-mite to rid it of any unwelcome little visitors. Do not use anything but a pyrethrum-based spray or dusting powder. Many of the dog, cat and poultry insecticides are highly poisonous to raptors and should never be risked on hawks as they will often prove fatal within 48 hours.

Generally speaking coping is not a difficult operation and an inexperienced falconer need have no qualms at all about tackling his hawk's beak. Like most aspects of falconry, your expertise in this field will improve with practice.

HOW TO RECOGNIZE IF YOUR BIRD IS OFF COLOUR

There are various signs which enable you to tell if your hawk is enjoying good health. A healthy hawk will have bright, round eyes. It will sit with one foot tucked up as a sign of contentment, will preen regularly, and take a lively interest in the goings-on around it. Similarly there are various signs which enable a falconer to tell if his hawk is unwell, such as discoloured mutes, ill-formed castings and 'slitty' eyes. I do not intend to include in this work a detailed section on hawk diseases and their treatment. This subject is so vast that it now merits a book all of its own, and indeed, one has been written. *Veterinary Aspects of Captive Birds of Prey* by John Cooper MRCVS, is a must for every falconer. It is published by the Standfast Press and is the most advanced work on raptor medicine available at the time of writing, and includes detailed information about diagnosis and treatment. Should you have cause to take your bird to a vet, take John Cooper's book with you, as the majority of vets are not raptor specialists and will thus appreciate the expert guidance which this book can supply.

I am not a vet, and I will give only a layman's guide to the recognition of ill-health, with a few basic hints which I have found useful. If any of these danger signs are noticed, the hawk in question should be taken immediately to a qualified vet, who can, it is hoped, give it the professional attention that it needs. It is helpful for a vet if the falconer has kept a complete dossier on his bird ever since its arrival, as sometimes diagnosis can be made easier by location of a certain factor which might have accounted for the present condition of the hawk.

Mutes

A healthy mute has a black centre surrounded by a fairly thick white chalky liquid. Certain birds regularly pass brown mutes, and this is nothing to worry about provided that it is normal for the particular bird. Green mutes are an indication of a low food intake. This can occur over a period of a few days when the hawk's weight is being reduced for flying, but should it occur at any other time, the reason for it must be investigated. Loose mutes or diarrhoea are usually a sign of some sort of infection or possibly of lack of roughage. If they re-occur the following day a mute sample should be taken to a vet. Samples should be taken from the most dense part of the mute. In a healthy hawk this will be the black centre which can be scraped up with a piece of paper or card and taken to the vet for a precautionary check every few months or so. In a hawk with diarrhoea, the liquid mute must be scooped into a tube or bottle, and taken for testing. Mutes which contain blood should also be taken for testing immediately. This is often an indication of a heavy infestation of worms such as capillaria or coccidiosis. All hawks should be wormed every four months or so as a precautionary measure. A wormer should be obtained from your vet to ensure that it is suitable for birds of prey. The general rule to apply here is check your hawk's mutes daily, and if in doubt, take a mute sample to your vet to be checked straightaway.

Castings

A healthy casting is oval in shape, tapered at one end, firm to the touch, and covered in a thin layer of gleam. The colour will vary according to your hawk's diet. For example, a casting formed from day-old chicks will be yellow, while one formed from rabbit will be greyish. The size of the casting depends on the amount of roughage given, not on the size of the bird. Unhealthy castings do not hold together well, and may contain undigested food. Such castings can be taken to be checked by a vet but this may not reveal much. Regurgitation is also nearly always a sign of illness. The exception is when a hawk is being fed up from flying weight, perhaps to be put down to moult, and is given a lot of food which it eats too quickly. In such circumstances, regurgitation is only a natural response to gluttony, which affects hawks as it affects humans. Once again, check castings daily. If roughage has been fed, do not feed, fly or weigh a hawk the following day until it has produced a casting. If in doubt, always take a sample to your vet.

Feet

Hawks are particularly prone to foot troubles. These are normally manifested in the form of a swelling. The swelling can be caused by many things, including too tight jesses or ABCR rings, bad perches, overgrown talons puncturing the sole of the foot and causing infection, and more obscure causes such as arthritis and gout. The name given to the most common type of infected swelling is 'bumblefoot'. Bumblefoot can occur on the digits or under the sole of the foot. In its mildest form, described by vets as 'Type 1', it can be treated daily by the falconer, under guidance from a vet, with a suitable antibiotic. The scab, if one has formed, is removed, the yellow cheesy matter inside squeezed out, and the hole packed with antibiotic cream and dressed to keep out infection. The more serious Types 2 and 3 of this infection require more major attention, and probably surgery. I have a female European Eagle Owl who came to me suffering from chronic Type 3 bumblefoot. The whole of the bottoms of both feet were rotten and oozing pus from the edges of large scabs, and the toes were webbed with the infection. After months of varied treatment and six major operations performed by my vets, the infection still refused to clear up. The bird was saved by an American booklet on the care and rehabilitation of owls which recommends the use of plaster of paris. After the foot has had all the infection removed by surgery, the area is packed with antibiotics, and the whole foot, wrapped in paraffin gauze, is encased in plaster of paris for a period of four to six weeks, leaving the toes free. After six six-week periods of this treatment, the infection in my eagle owl had cleared completely and new healthy skin had grown back over the soles of both feet. Basically, the plaster of paris appears to keep the foot absolutely clean, preventing re-infection. I would recommend this method to anyone who is unfortunate enough to encounter a bird with such chronic bumblefoot. Longwings, and particularly small longwings such as merlins, are especially prone to bumblefoot, and should have their talons coped frequently.

17 Plaster cast on the toe of a Harris' Hawk. The hawk broke its toe whilst taking a rabbit

A hawk's feet should be checked regularly for swellings, and it must be taken to a vet immediately should one be noticed. Minor swellings are much easier to deal with than large ones, and thus early detection is essential, but above all, prevention is better than cure.

Head

One of the first signs which I have noticed with sick hawks is the variation in the shape of their eyes. The eyes of a healthy hawk are round, bright and quick to follow your movements. Those of a sick bird, particularly of falcons, take on a slitty appearance, elongated, and are not open quite as widely as usual. Such birds sit hunched, fluffed out and miserable, scarcely bothering to pay any attention to your movements, as if they were concentrating on their inner discomforts. If you know your hawk well enough you can recognize these subtle changes in expression very quickly. If you think that your hawk appears unwell, you are almost certainly right. Hawks do not usually assume an 'under the weather' appearance unless they are physically uncomfortable within themselves. They will also appear better than they actually are in your presence, tightening up their feathers and looking more alert. If you have any suspicions, put your hawk somewhere where you can observe it without it seeing you, so that you can get an accurate impression of how it is really feeling. If it now looks unwell, act immediately. Do not risk leaving it until the following day to see if it looks any better. Take it inside, put it in a darkened warm box and offer it something to eat. Warmth plays an essential part in the nursing of sick birds. It makes them dozy and encourages them to rest. Think back over the past few days to see if you can come up with any reason for your hawk's turn for the worse—any change of diet, or perhaps a good soaking from which it could have caught a chill. Ring your vet and fix an appointment for as soon as possible, and tell him anything which you think might be relevant. Bear in mind that you know your bird and also how to handle it better than your vet, who will need your help to cast and examine it.

Another area to watch on the head for signs of trouble is the mouth. Yellow cheesy lesions in the corners of the mouth, and yellow exudate on the tongue and throat are signs of the disease called frounce. Gaping and panting are possible signs of a number of illnesses including gapeworm, pneumonia and respiratory infections. Flicking of food is a possible indication of stomatitis, frounce or just generally low condition. Fluid from the mouth may be a sign of poisoning or capillariosis. Fluid from the nares usually occurs in response to food stimulus but may be something more serious.

Lastly, hawks occasionally get something in an eye which upsets them, or sometimes they pick up a slight eye infection, maybe from a chill. Every falconer should keep a small medicine chest for his hawk, in which a fresh bottle or tube of antibiotic eye ointment is present, such as chloromycetin ophthalmic ointment. Should an infection be noticed, this can be administered promptly by the falconer as directed by a vet.

Body

There are various feather disorders which can be attributed to more serious causes than moulting and breakages sustained through accidental causes. Feather mite or biting lice (*mallophaga*) will cause frayed or damaged feathers, trauma or upset may cause feathers to be thrown out, particularly during the moult, and new feathers to have fret marks. Nutritional deficiency will cause many defects, including hunger traces, frayed feathers, and non-replacement of moulted feathers. Mites, lice and fleas can be dealt with effectively by use of a pyrethrum-based insecticide or a solution of trichlorphon. Occasionally 'flat-flies' or hippoboseids are found on birds of prey, particularly hawks in low condition. In appearance they are similar to flattened house flies. Although these will not physically harm a bird, they are blood-sucking and unpleasant. They can be seen crawling sideways in and out of the depths of a bird's plumage, and can, if one is very quick, be removed by hand. Alternatively, they can be killed with Johnson's Anti-mite.

Swellings of the abdomen can be attributed mainly to two causes. Firstly a female bird carrying an egg will obviously have a distended abdomen. Secondly, it can be caused by a blockage, or impaction of the cloaca. Blockages occur in birds which have been recumbent for some reason, such as travelling, occasionally in eyasses, and for a variety of non-specific reasons. They can be treated by the falconer with the oral administration of liquid paraffin (another item for the medicine chest). If the hawk remains constipated two hours later, it must be taken promptly to a vet who can remove the blockage or 'calculus' by a stronger purgative or by digital exploration of the cloaca.

Fractures

Fractures are particularly distressing for the falconer should one occur in a trained hawk. Depending on where they occur, and how serious the break is, they do not necessarily mean the end of the bird's flying career. I have successfully flown birds which have suffered various fractures in the past, including a female peregrine who had previously suffered from a broken collar-bone, and a Changeable Hawk Eagle with an old fracture in one leg. More frequently, I have encountered fractures in birds of prey which have been handed in to me after undergoing some accident. The most common causes of such fractures have been impact with moving vehicles and gun-shot wounds. Fractures of limbs are most easily noticed if the bone has pierced the skin. Such wounds will soon become infected and often gangrenous if they are not dealt with quickly. Fractures over which the skin has not been broken can usually be located by a swelling which will form around the break. Often, though, a search for such signs to aid diagnosis will not be necessary. Broken wings will hang down, and broken

18 Female Hen Harrier with a broken wing. The fracture was pinned, then the wing was strapped to hold it firm

legs will trail, making diagnosis easy even for the most inexpert eyes. More difficult to locate are internal fractures, such as those of the collar-bone or pelvis. These can only be confirmed by X-ray.

A bird which has a fracture or suspected fracture (it may be only a dislocation or severe bruising) must obviously be taken immediately to a vet. Internal fractures cannot usually be mended surgically, and can only be left to heal spontaneously. However, considerable surgical assistance can be administered to broken limbs. If the break or fracture is situated in a straight length of a bone, it can be pinned. Pinning is undoubtedly a distinct improvement on the older method of strapping or plastering. Wiring and plating have also been applied successfully. Should your hawk suffer a broken limb, always ask your vet if the bone can be pinned in preference to being strapped, as the results are usually better. Breaks which occur at joints are more difficult to repair. Often such birds have to be strapped or splinted as there is no surgical alternative. If a wing is to be strapped, it should be closed to the bird's side in the correct position, with the primaries above the tail, and bound firmly but not tightly to the bird's body, around the chest and between the torso and the secondaries of the opposite wing, leaving the healthy wing completely free and unrestricted, avoiding the vent and allowing the bird free movement of the legs, enabling it to stand up. Normally a bird thus strapped will quickly learn to balance with one wing, and will be able to move about quite easily and happily during the next few weeks while it is strapped up. If the break is in the end bone of the wing, the wing can be closed up and strapped with three bands: one around the point of the wing, the next up and around the fold of the wing and the third around the top of the primaries. This saves strapping right around the torso. Thus the bird has free movement of the shoulder joint of the affected wing, and this will aid balance.

Occasionally a badly damaged or particularly a gangrenous limb will have to be amputated partially or completely. Birds which have undergone major amputations can often live for many years and be used for captive breeding where suitable.

3 Equipment

The equipment, or 'furniture' necessary for handling and training a bird of prey is a collection of accoutrements many of which are virtually unchanged in both form and function since the earliest days of falconry. Much of the equipment is crafted from leather, and can be made by the falconer to fit his bird. All falconers should be able to make jesses, traditional and aylmeri, to fit a hawk. However, there are some pieces of equipment which are extremely difficult or complicated to make in one way or another, and such items are best purchased from an equipment supplier, rather than attempted in very amateurish form by an inexperienced falconer (see appendix for list of equipment suppliers). I will list the equipment as individual items, explaining how to make and use each piece as appropriate.

SWIVELS

The swivel is made of metal and is attached between the bird's jesses and the leash to prevent them from becoming twisted. Normally, one end of a swivel is larger than the other—the leash is put through the small end and the jesses are attached to the larger end (see fig. 19). Swivels can be bought from equipment suppliers, or they can be purchased from a pet shop in the form of dog-lead swivels. Although these do not last as long as proper falconry swivels, they are so much cheaper that the falconer can afford to change them as soon as they become slightly worn. Occasionally, dog-lead swivels have a join in the small ring which should be soldered for safety. Very large swivels for eagles can sometimes be found on nylon leads or lunging reins used for horses. Fishing tackle shops are also a possible source for shark-fishing swivels, which are ideal, as are Sampo (ball bearing) swivels, but the best type are D swivels. To put the jesses on to a swivel you put the point of one jess through one ring of the swivel (the larger ring if appropriate) and split the lower slit up over the bottom of the swivel, sliding it up until it pulls tight at the top of the upper ring (see fig. 20). The second jess is put through from the opposite side of the upper ring and is then put on in the same manner.

LEASHES

Traditionally, the leash was made from leather. Nowadays, we tend to use braided nylon as this is stronger, and does not crack as leather sometimes does when it gets wet. Once again, leashes can be bought from equipment suppliers, but it is considerably cheaper to get a nylon dog leash and make a button on the end of it. If you buy a dog leash of suitable thickness for your bird you get with it a swivel of the right size and also a metal clip which can be put on to your belt, to which your glove can be clipped when you are not using it. Thus for the cost of one dog leash, you get three useful items at a bargain price.

19 Jesses and leash correctly attached to Swivel

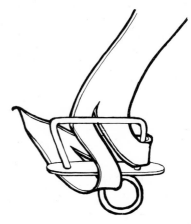

20 Putting the jess onto the swivel

21 Making a button

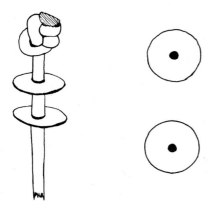

22 Leather washers can be put on a leash to enlarge the knot

The leash must be approximately four feet long for a middling sized bird. A kestrel can have a shorter leash—three feet should be more than adequate, and a large eagle will need slightly more length—perhaps four feet or so. Eagle leashes can be made from the nylon horse-lunging reins from which you get large swivels, as previously mentioned.

To make up the leash you must first cut a point at one end. This must be singed with a cigarette lighter or a match along the edges to stop it fraying. The other end must be made into a button. This is done by folding it over two or three times, then punching or burning a hole with a hot skewer or similar down through the middle of the folded section. The point of the other end of the leash is then threaded through the hole, and pulled tight, forming a button (see fig. 21).

Sometimes a thick round cord of suitable strength and substance can be used to make a leash. Such cord can be acquired from a ships' chandler. It must be singed at both ends and knotted securely at one end to form a knot which cannot be pulled through the ring of the swivel. Alternatively, a small knot can be tied and circular leather washers can be cut with a hole punched in the middle. These can then be slid down and used as stoppers against the knot (see fig. 22).

Kestrel, merlin or sparrowhawk leashes can be made from thinner braided nylon obtainable from ironmongers or DIY shops.

JESSES

These are the straps which are put around the bird's legs to retain it on the fist. There are two main types of jesses—traditional jesses and aylmeri jesses. The latter were an invention of the late Guy Aylmer. They should always be used in preference to traditional jesses for birds which have reached the stage of flying free. The reason for this will be explained in due course. All jesses, when made, must be well greased and stretched before being put on the bird.

Traditional jesses

These can be made quickly and easily to be put on a new arrival or indeed on any bird which is not being flown. They are cut out of a single piece of leather. Initially, two straps of the same length and thickness must be cut out of leather which is supple but strong enough to hold the bird without snapping as it bates. The length and thickness of the jess can be judged by common sense. The widest part of the jess which folds around the leg should be approximately twice the width of the strap section for a hawk. For a falcon, the thickness around the leg is only increased on the lower edge of the jess. They must be long enough to wrap around the bird's leg and run down from the legs into your gloved hand, under your thumb, and hang an inch below your little finger. For a kestrel they will need to be approximately 7 inches, for a buzzard or goshawk 12 inches, for a large falcon 11 inches, for an eagle 15 inches. The leather must then be cut to the correct shape according to whether they are for a longwing or a short-wing (see fig. 23). Traditional jesses must, unfortunately, be used in pre-ference to aylmeris for very large eagles at all times because aylmeris are more vulnerable to being severed just below the button, by the beak of such powerful birds.

The slits which are cut to fit the jess around the bird's leg must be long enough to pass the width of the jess through them. The first of these (A) can be cut in readiness in the pointed end just beyond, and extending slightly into, the widest part of the jess. The second slit (B) must not be cut until the jess has been measured around the bird's leg for size. The slit at

23 Jess patterns (a) Shortwings

(b) Longwings

the far end (C) must be long enough to pass over the swivel. To make a slit in the jess, first punch two small holes with a leather punch and cut carefully between them. This will stop the slit from tearing. When the slits have been marked out in the first jess, it can be laid on top of the second one to mark that out identically.

Putting on jesses (see fig. 24)
The bird must first be cast.

1 Put the jess around the bird's leg *below* anything else which is on the leg, such as an ABCR ring or a bewit. Jesses put on above a ring can damage the foot by causing the ring to cut in when the bird bates.
2 Pass point 1 through slit B.
3 Pass point 2 through slit A.

Make sure that the jess can move round the leg without pinching. The process is then repeated around the other leg. Some people prefer to pass point 2 through both slits B and A, to prevent the knot from slipping. This is essential for birds which pick their jesses.

AYLMERI JESSES

There are two types of aylmeris—true aylmeris and false aylmeris. I prefer the latter type as they are safer and easier to put on large birds, but I will describe both types. Either type is less inclined to become twisted than traditional jesses.

True aylmeris
These are made out of two pieces of leather—namely a leather anklet which passes round the bird's leg, and is secured by both a rivet and an eyelet, and a button strap which passes through the eyelet (see fig. 25, a and c). The anklet is cut to shape to fit around the bird's leg. The two halves of an appropriately sized eyelet (obtainable from ironmongers, haberdashery counters, DIY stores, and camping-equipment shops) are inserted in the holes in the anklet. If they are small eyelets (for kestrel, sparrowhawk or merlin), they can be joined by being pinched together with eyelet pliers, but if they are large eyelets, they must be punched together with a small anvil, a punch and a hammer. (I dislike having to go through this performance against a bird's leg.) The anklet is riveted, for if the eyelet alone were used to join the anklet, there would be a risk of the two halves parting, and the bird getting its leg out (see fig. 25b). A leather mews jess, consisting of a button at one end large enough to stop the strap pulling through the eyelet, and a swivel slit at the other, is put through the eyelet. The button is made in the same way as described for the making of a button on the end

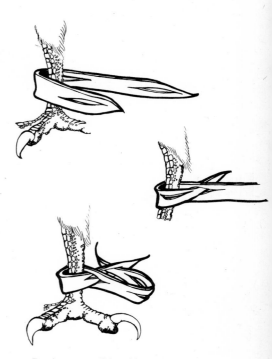

24 Putting on traditional jesses

25(a) True aylmeris: small hawk anklet

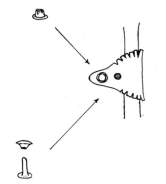

25(b) Fixing true aylmeris with rivets

25(c) Mews jess

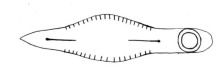

26 False aylmeris: anklet for a large hawk

of a leash. When the bird is to be flown free, the mews jess can be substituted for a field jess. These can take two forms. Firstly a button jess identical to the mews jess but without a swivel slit can be used. The omission of the swivel slit means that the jess cannot be caught up on a twig or on a barb of a fence, and this is why traditional jesses which contain a swivel slit should never be used on free-flying birds. Alternatively a piece of nylon cord can be looped around the little finger of the gloved hand, passed through the eyelet and held in between the second and third fingers. When the bird is cast from the fist, the cord is released by the second and third fingers and the eyelets pull free from the end, leaving the bird to fly with just the anklets around its legs. This latter sort of field jess is unsuitable for a bird which will not tolerate the falconer fiddling about putting the cord back through the eyelets while it is on quarry.

False aylmeris
These are cut and fitted around the bird's leg like traditional jesses, but they have an eyelet hole through which mews and field jesses (as already described) can be put instead of a continuous strap (see fig. 26). The advantage of this sort of aylmeri is that the eyelet can be secured in place before the jess is put around the leg, so with larger birds it is not necessary to use a hammer to close the eyelet while the jess is round the bird's leg.

False aylmeris are put on in exactly the same manner as traditional jesses. Sometimes it is very difficult to pass the eyelet through the jess slits. In such a case the slits must be cut slightly longer and a small pair of pliers can be used to help.

There is one disadvantage with false aylmeris—some birds manage to get their back talon hooked into the eyelet hole. In an attempt to avoid this, make sure that the eyelet lies as close to the bird's leg as possible when the anklet is in place.

BELLS

There are several types of bell which can be used for hawks. It is possible to make bells, but specialist equipment, such as suitable sheet metal, a doming block, and various other tools are necessary. Bells bought from equipment suppliers are usually inexpensive and considerably less trouble to procure. I will not, therefore, describe how to make bells, but I will explain the various types that can be bought.

Lahore bells
These are traditional bells which originated in Lahore in Pakistan. They are made out of a mixture of metals and are waisted in the middle (see fig. 27). Like all proper hawk bells, they do not have a clanger suspended in them, but have a loose metal chip. The pitch of different bells varies according to the thickness of the metal used. The choice of the two bells to make up a pair depends upon the ear of the individual. A pair which has a good tone as far as one falconer is concerned may well sound awful to another falconer.

Lahore bells tend to wear or even to be broken by some birds quite quickly. Poor bells are a false economy. The purpose of having bells on a hawk is to enable you to track it in cover. Bells with a poor tone obviously stand less chance of being heard. A damaged bell must therefore be replaced quickly. A bell which is tarnished may lose its tone because of this. It can be cleaned with Duraglit or with a drop of metal polish and a good rub.

27 Lahore bell

Acorn bells

These are made in America by Peter Asborno (see page 178 for address). They are excellent both in tone and in durability. The design is different from that of Lahore bells (see fig. 28). At the join they have a double thickness of metal which reinforces the structure of the bell at a vulnerable point. They are constructed in a variety of two-metal combinations to produce tones which cannot be achieved with one metal.

Two-tensile bells

These were the forerunners of the Acorn bell. They are rounded in shape and have a differing tensile in the upper and lower halves for improved tonal quality. They are also made by Peter Asborno.

28 Acorn bell

Other bells

Any bell of the right size is better than no bell at all. In desperation, even bells from pet and toy shops can be used, but they will not have a high degree of audibility, nor will they last very long. For those who wish to consider making their own bells, the best metals to use are silver, bronze, brass, monel and nickel. Some falconers place bells around hawks' necks on elasticated halsbands, so that the bell rings every time the hawk moves its head.

BEWITS

Bewits are the straps used to attach a bell to a hawk's leg. They are made out of leather and must be put on *above* the jesses but *below* the ABCR ring. There are two types of bewit.

Normal bewits

These are put on to the bird by means of threading a series of punched holes. They have a point at one end and an arrowhead, or nick in the leather, at the other which stops the bird from pulling the strap back through the hole.

Putting on normal bewits (see fig. 29)

1 The bewits are cut out of a strip of leather (small hawks can only manage a single bell). They should be as wide as possible for strength, but the width will be limited by the size of the metal loop at the top of the bell, through which the bewit must be passed. A hole is punched one-third of the way down the length from the arrowhead, and a slit is cut beside the arrowhead.
2 The bell is threaded onto the bewit in such a way that the metal will not be against the bird's leg.
3 The bewit is passed round the bird's leg, and the pointed end is pulled through the slit already cut just before the arrowhead or nick.
4 A second hole is now punched in the length of leather which has just been pulled through. The holes should lie as close to the bird's leg as possible.
5 The arrowhead is now pulled through the second hole.
6 The surplus is cut off. The bell should rotate freely around the leg, but should not be so loose that it hangs down and hinders the jesses.

Button bewits

These have a button in one end which is made in the same way as the button on the end of a leash. The button is pushed through a slit in the bewit. I do not like button bewits as they are always loose, and are easy for a bird to remove.

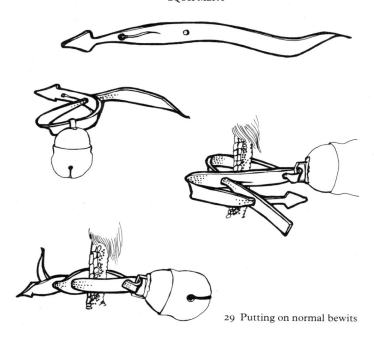

29 Putting on normal bewits

Putting on button bewits (see fig. 30)

1 The bewit is cut out and made up.
2 The bell is put on to the bewit.
3 The bewit is passed around the hawk's leg and the button is passed through the slit at the opposite end which must be cut as small as possible when the bewit has been tried around the leg for size.

An alternative method of putting on bewits

Some hawks are particularly adept at biting through arrowheads or nicks, and at pulling off buttons. Such birds should have bewits made out of straight strips of leather. The bells can be put on to the bewits in the manner previously described. The bewit can then be passed around the bird's leg, and pulled through the hole. The two ends can then be riveted together, and the surplus cut off.

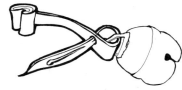

30 Putting on button bewit

TAIL BELLS

Short-winged hawks should have a tail bell attached before being flown free. The reason for this is that shortwings will shake their tails shortly after landing, and thus they can be heard in a tree when they cannot be seen. On quarry too, the tail will wag up and down as a hawk pulls at its kill. Tail bells are therefore invaluable for locating a hawk which has killed out of sight, and in this respect could be used to equal effect on falcons. Sparrowhawks and other small accipiters such as Sharp-shinned and Shik-ras normally wear only a tail bell, which should be very small with a clear, sharp tone. On the larger accipiters and buzzards, tail bells are usually used in conjunction with leg bells.

To attach a tail bell to a bird, you will need the bell, a guitar plectrum of suitable size (these are easily obtainable from music shops), or alternatively you can cut a plastic plectrum shape out of an old washing-up liquid bottle, and a strip of soft leather. There are several methods of attaching a tail bell. I will describe the two principal methods. For the first, you will also need a curved needle and waxed thread.

Method A (see fig. 31)

1 Punch two holes in a plectrum.
2 Thread the bell onto a strip of leather narrow enough to pass through the holes in the plectrum, in the same manner as described for a leg bewit.
3 Feed the two lengths of leather down through the holes in the plectrum.
4 Separate the two centre deck feathers from the rest of tail with the aid of a piece of card, and damp down the fluffy webbing at the top of the feather shafts and the surrounding coverts.
5 Coat the top of the shaft of the two deck feathers with a suitable glue such as Evostick or Super Epoxy.
6 Coat the underside of the two leather straps coming off the plectrum with glue.
7 Stick the glued leather straps to the glue-covered shafts.
8 Bind the strips of leather in place at two points with the aid of the curved needle and a single thickness of waxed thread, tying off firmly, but not tightly enough to damage the feather.

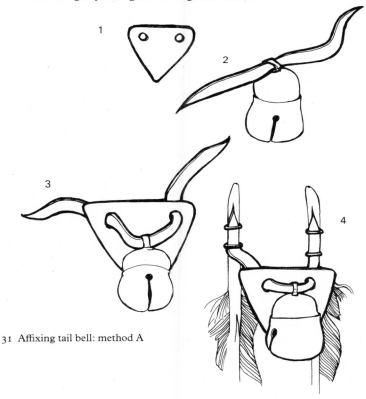

31 Affixing tail bell: method A

Method B (see fig. 32)

1 Punch three holes in a plectrum, the centre one slightly larger than the outer two, and cut a long strip of leather, pointed at both ends and narrow enough to pass through the holes.
2 Scratch the back of the plectrum with a knife or scalpel to roughen it (this will help to stick the plectrum to the shafts of the feathers when glue is applied), and punch a hole in the centre of the strip of leather.
3 Pass the pointed ends of the strip of leather downwards through the two outside holes in the plectrum, so that the hole in the leather lies directly above the hole in the plectrum.

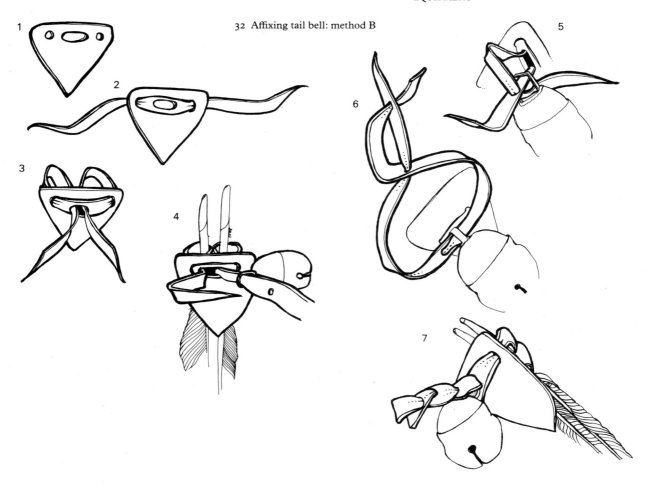

32 Affixing tail bell: method B

4 Fold the two pointed ends of the leather strip inwards and pass them together upwards through the central hole in the plectrum and the leather strip, leaving two loops at the back of the plectrum large enough to pass easily over the width of the hawk's deck feathers.

5 Apply glue to the roughened back of the plectrum and to the tops of the shafts of the deck feathers, prepared as for Method A, and slide the two loops up over the deck feathers up to where the glued back of the plectrum comes into contact with the glued tops of the shafts. Pull tight by pulling the pointed ends of the leather strips.

6 Punch a hole near the plectrum in one of the leather strips.

7 Slide the bell down this strip of leather until it lies just beyond the hole against the plectrum.

8 Feed the opposite pointed end out through the hole in the strip on which the bell is lying and then through the metal loop at the top of the bell. The bell should now lie at a right angle to the plectrum.

9 Take the two strips of leather above the bell and punch a hole close to the metal loop of the bell in one of them.

10 Pass the opposite strip through the hole and pull tight.

11 Punch another hole in the strip you have just pulled through and pass the opposite strip through it.

12 Cut off the surplus leather strips.

IDENTITY TAGS (See fig. 33)

These can take several forms, all of which are inexpensive to buy. Pet shops and key cutting shops sell various types of dog name tags which are designed to be attached to collars, but which can, just as easily, be put on bewits with the aid of a small split ring. Little metal discs can be engraved with your name and telephone number, or you can get tiny metal tubes which contain a slip of paper for the necessary details.

It is well worthwhile taking the time and trouble to put an identity tag on any bird which is flown free.

33 Indentity tag to attach to bewit

TELEMETRY

Telemetry is now being used more frequently on the more valuable birds of prey. It takes the form of a very small and lightweight radio transmitter, which is attached to the bird's tail, enabling it to be traced over a restricted range by a receiver. At the moment telemetry is expensive. The receiver is the most expensive part, but one can be used for any number of hawks which are fitted with transmitters. The longer the antenna of the transmitter the greater the range. Transmitters run off small, lightweight batteries which will usually last for the whole season. Although a transmitter does not guarantee safe recovery of a lost bird, as the receiver is subject to interference from other radio waves, and from hilly terrain, it is undoubtedly a great asset and one of the most significant advances in falconry in recent years. In the future, it is hoped, a supplier in Britain will market cheaper telemetry which will be more widely available, but at the moment the equipment has to be imported from the USA (See appendix for suppliers).

KNIVES

A good sharp knife is essential for a falconer, and should be carried in a pocket in the falconry bag. A penknife with lots of complicated blades is completely unsuitable—a lock knife is best. It should be kept clean and sharp. Avoid wearing an enormous sheath on your belt containing a very large and ostentatious knife. A large knife is quite unnecessary, and will evoke comment from those who see you wearing it while carrying your bird. A point to bear in mind is that you should be able to both open and to use your knife with one hand.

WHISTLES

People who cannot whistle their hawk loudly with their mouth will need a mechanical aid in the form of a metal whistle. Any type will do. A shepherd's whistle is quite good but it requires some practice to be able to use one of these. Once the art of blowing one has been perfected, however, the noise will carry quite a distance. Such a whistle can be carried in a pocket in the falconry bag, or a referee's whistle or similar can be carried around the neck. It is worthwhile having a spare whistle of the same sort as the one you use lest you should lose it. A hawk which becomes accustomed to one type of whistle may not respond to one with a different note.

GREASE

All the equipment which is made out of leather should be greased regularly to keep it supple and prevent it from cracking. Jesses particularly should be greased every week, because if one should snap, a hawk can break its leg when it bates, or if both snap, the bird is lost. Gloves, bewits and the braces of hoods will also need to be greased periodically.

It is possible to make jess grease, but I find it easier to use Kocholine, made by Burnaby and Chantrell Ltd of Liverpool. This can be bought in various sized pots from saddlers. Neatsfoot oil can also be used, but I find it messy.

CREANCE

This is a line which is attached to the bird during the early stages of training. A creance consists of light braided nylon line, obtainable from ironmongers and DIY shops, often in the form of curtain cord. The thickness should be in proportion to the weight of the bird that you are flying, and the length should be between 25 and 50 yards, again depending on the type of bird in question. Bear in mind that a bird on a creance can fly twice the length of the line. Thus a 25-yard creance will enable a bird to be called 50 yards to the fist. The ends of the creance must be singed to heat seal them and to stop them from fraying.

The creance stick should be brightly coloured so that it can be seen in the grass. The line is wound around the stick in a special way, enabling it to be wound and unwound very quickly. The method is best described as 'figure-of-eight winding'. The stick is turned slightly as the line is wound to prevent it from building up on one side. Initially the method must be learnt with the aid of both hands, but eventually it is possible by dint of much practice to wind up a creance with the ungloved hand only, by twisting the stick around the line, keeping the tension by running the creance through the fingers of your gloved hand. The same method can be used to wind up a lure line.

Never use fishing line or 'cat-gut' as a creance. It is difficult to see in grass, is easily tangled and will wrap itself around your hawk's legs and body.

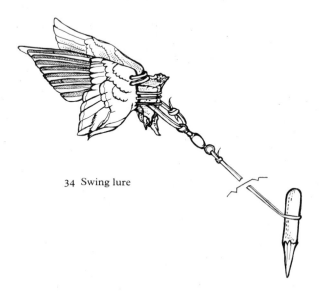

34 Swing lure

LURES

Lures are used by the falconer to exercise his hawk. They have food attached and resemble the prey which the bird is intended to hunt, and thus the bird eventually associates the appearance of quarry with the shape of the lure, and consequently will chase prey.

Swing lures (see fig. 34)

Swing lures resemble birds in flight and are used for falcons who take their quarry in mid-air. Ideally, a lure for a falcon should be a fresh dead bird of the type it is being trained to hunt, but usually it is not possible to have a daily supply of dead rooks, grouse, partridge etc., so an artificial substitute must be made up. To do this a pair of dried wings of the intended quarry must be obtained and tied or stitched firmly together, back to back. Strings are attached so that the lure can be garnished with a chunk of beef. This should make the lure just heavy enough to swing. A lure which is very heavy is dangerous because you might knock your falcon with it through inexpert swinging. A lure which has a solid chunk of wood or metal inside it to weight it would also be dangerous, as the falcon would injure her feet as she struck it. If a lure made out of wings is too light to swing, a small leather bag padded with a little sand can be attached between the wings. A swivel must be fastened securely to the top of the lure so that it will rotate. To the far end of this a braided cotton lure line is tied firmly. The line must be cotton rather than nylon as nylon will burn the fingers and cause blisters. The lure line should be 10–12 feet in length, and attached with small staples to an 8–10 inch lure stick. The cotton line must be checked daily for signs of wear, particularly if it should get wet for if it should snap the falcon may well carry the lure and be lost. The stick should be a piece of dowelling, grooved in the middle where the line is tied and stapled around it, and tapered at one end to enable it to be stuck in the ground while the bird is eating off the lure. Should any falcon show a tendency to carry a lure, more weight can be added to the stick, but never to the lure itself.

Rabbit lures (see fig. 35)

A shortwing can be flown to a rabbit lure. This is made from a dried skin which is stretched around a well padded piece of wood of about one inch in diameter. The padding can be of material or preferably foam which will

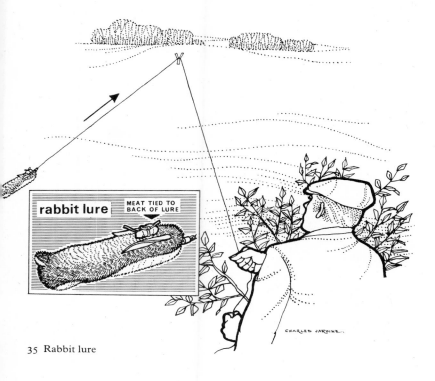

35 Rabbit lure

give under the hawk's feet. The wood is necessary to give the lure weight so that it can be dragged along the ground without bouncing too much, but the hawk's claws must never be able to hit the wood through the padding when it binds on to the lure. A swivel is stapled to one end of the wood and a length of line (in this instance nylon line is best) is tied securely to the far end of the swivel. The line should have a loop for the fingers at the far end, and can be as long as is necessary. Initially, I use approximately 15 feet of line. The lure must have strings attached at the swivel end to which the meat is tied. Eventually it will not be necessary to tie meat to the lure—the bird will associate the lure with food and the pick-up piece will suffice as reward. A lure stick is not necessary for a rabbit lure—the line can be wrapped around the body of the lure when it is not in use.

For the big eagles, a hare or fox-skin lure can be made up in the same way (according to the quarry at which you intend to fly your bird eventually).

GLOVES

Falconry gloves must be strong enough to withstand the bird's talons, yet supple enough to enable the fingers to bend easily and comfortably, and to feel the jesses. I am not going to describe how to make falconry gloves or give a pattern, as what is comfortable for one person's hand in terms of size is not always comfortable for another's. Those people who are skilled in leather work and who want to attempt to make their own glove are best advised to make up a pattern by studying an old glove, and adapting it to fit their own hand. Good gloves are available from the equipment suppliers listed in the appendix. A strong glove lasts me only one season because of the variety and quantity of birds which I work, but a well-made glove of the right thickness should last the average falconer, handling one or two birds only, a minimum of three seasons, However, once a bird goes through the glove and makes a hole it will invariably find the hole with a talon every time it is on the fist, so the hole must be repaired, which is difficult, or the glove replaced.

Gloves for handling eagles (and also eagle owls) are harder to come by. For birds with such strong feet, the leather must not only be thick enough to prevent the talons from piercing the hide, it must also be stiff enough to protect the hand from bruising. If you carry a large bird which grips hard on an unsuitable glove, your hand, when removed from the glove, will have painful reddish-blue indents where each of the talons have been. A glove made out of leather of sufficient thickness and stiffness will not usually be supple or comfortable in the fingers and thus the falconer will not be able to keep a good hold on the jesses (which is all important with a large bird prone to throwing its feet about). The glove must also extend right up to the elbow to accommodate the span of such a bird. The answer is to have a glove made up out of the thickest and most supple leather that you can find, or you can use two layers of leather to make a double thickness glove, grease it well, break it in, and then, if it is not thick enough, reinforce it with another layer which is stitched over all the glove except for the fingers, which would have their usefulness considerably lessened with the addition of another layer. The fact that the fingers are not as thick as the rest of the glove does not matter as large birds will sit with one foot over the back of the hand and one foot further up the arm. Ron Krupa, who manages the Philippine (Monkey-eating) Eagle breeding project, has a well padded metal plate in the back of his glove to protect his hand from the fearsome grip of these enormous birds!

All gloves should be fitted with a thong and tassel to enable them to be hung up when the glove is not in use. I also advise beginners to have another tassel under the wrist of the glove so that the leash can be tied through this as an extra security measure.

Overlay

An alternative to stitching another layer on a glove is to make up an overlay which can be removed when the glove is needed for a smaller bird. An overlay can be made out of stiff and fairly thick leather as it does not cover the fingers, and thus the substance of the leather overlay will not adversely affect the suppleness of the glove beneath it. An overlay should be made to fit over the glove snugly and also to cover the thumb, which is a vulnerable part. An overlay is also exceedingly useful for covering a damaged glove which would otherwise have to be discarded. All falconers hate breaking in a new glove and are thus loath to part with an old and comfortable favourite.

SLEEVES

Some of the larger eagles show a tendency to land higher up the arm, with one foot beyond the elbow. This is usually because their huge feet and wide span of the legs make it difficult for them to do otherwise. To accommodate such a bird without discomfort to the falconer, the upper arm must be covered by a leather sleeve. Some falconers have a jacket with one leather sleeve which they always wear when flying their bird, but I find it more convenient to have a separate sleeve which is loose enough to fit over a jumper or light jacket if the weather is cold or wet, but which can, in fine weather, be worn without a jacket. The sleeve should be fitted with a buckle and straps to tighten it around the upper arm near the shoulder, and it should be long enough to extend inside the cuff of the glove. If it is possible to find a large and elderly leather coat from which the relevant sleeve can be removed, this will be ideal. If such a sleeve is not thick enough, the opposite sleeve can be removed also, inverted, and stitched inside the other.

BAGS

There are many different designs of falconry bag, all of which must include certain points if they are to be functionally ideal. A bag must have at least two compartments, placed back to back so that there is one on each side, and must be large enough to accommodate the length of the creance stick, lure, etc. It must have a swivel at the top to facilitate easy turning from one side to another. This swivel must be stapled into a piece of thin dowelling at the top of the bag if it is to stay firm. The other end of the swivel must be clipped on to a shoulder strap. The compartments must be covered by flaps to prevent the bird from peering inside to see the meat. These are the basic necessities which must be incorporated in any bag. A falconry bag is hung on the opposite side to the gloved hand. Some falconers whose bird is at hunting standard wear a canvas game bag over the opposite shoulder.

There are various optional extras which can be included in the falconry bag. Firstly, a bag can have a separate compartment within a compartment, lined with heavy-duty polythene and used for meat. A knife sheath can be stitched inside one of the compartments, and a small separate pocket can be stitched on the outside of one of the flaps for the swivel. A leather square incorporating two eyelet holes can be stitched or riveted on to the bag to hold the flying jesses, or the mews jesses when the flying jesses are in use

36 Falconer's bag

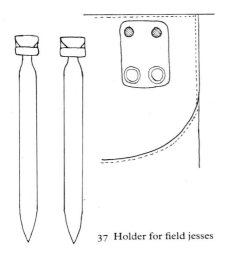

37 Holder for field jesses

(see fig. 37). The bag is best if made from canvas which can be washed and scrubbed when it gets really dirty. Bags can be obtained from equipment suppliers (see page 40), they can be custom made from scratch by the falconer, or they can be made cheaply from two canvas bags available from army surplus stores, and adapted accordingly by removing one from its shoulder strap and stitching it back to back with the other one. Provided equipment is functional that is all that is necessary, but some falconers would never consider using such an unorthodox and possibly rather shabby arrangement as this form of bag—indeed some falconers even have matching accessories such as glove, jesses, hood and shoulder strap all made from the same colour of leather. I have even seen fur-lined gloves and patent-leather bags with cowboy fringes and leopard-skin panels! However, good falconers are those whose hawks fly quarry well, not those who dress themselves and their hawks to catch the eye. I am always highly suspicious of anyone claiming to be a falconer who sports an immaculate bag and brand new glove. True falconers are more often those whose gloves are stained with meat and worn with age, and whose game bags give off a pungent smell of former triumphs.

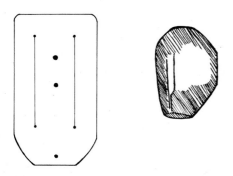

38 The design for a hood block

BELTS

The shoulder strap of a falconry bag must be held against the body with a belt to stop it from bouncing around when you run. A belt can incorporate certain useful features such as a clip on which you can hang a glove which is not in use. The leash can be looped around the belt by doubling it up, poking the loop down through the belt, and pulling the ends through the loop. A hood block for Dutch hoods can be carved out of wood, varnished and screwed on to a leather pad, which is then slotted on to the belt (see fig. 38). This will prevent a hood from becoming crushed in the bag. Anglo-Indian hoods are also awkward in a bag—they tend to bounce out when you run, and they will also lose much of their shape if they are crushed frequently. To accommodate this you can put a split ring around the outermost brace of the hood. This does not hinder the function of the braces, and can be snapped onto a clip on the belt when the hood is not in use (see fig. 39).

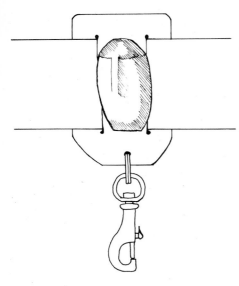

39 Hood block on belt

ARM BRACE (see fig. 40)

This is a device to aid a falconer in the carrying of a large eagle. It supports the gloved hand and thus takes much of the weight off the arm. It can be made up out of an adapted and adjustable leather shoulder strap and a metal rod which must be bent outwards from the body and onto the top of which a shallow V-shaped piece of metal must be welded. This must be padded and covered in leather, and the end of the metal rod is sunk into a pocket at the base of the shoulder strap, which rests in the fold of the thigh. Support straps to hold the rod steady must be stitched around the rod and fastened one on to each side of the shoulder strap. The shoulder strap must be held against the body by a belt. When the strap has been adjusted to position, with the arm brace at the correct height for the falconer's arm, the base of the gloved hand is placed in the rest, pushing slightly outwards. To the best of my knowledge, no equipment supplier makes such arm braces, and thus they must be constructed by the falconer himself.

BLOCKS AND PERCHES

There are three main types of perches, the block, the bow and the ring. There is a fourth variety still unfortunately used by some falconers, called the screen perch. Screen perches should never be used for reasons which are described later. The other three are designed to be best suited to a particular species of bird, and it is advisable to use the correct type accordingly.

Block perches (see fig. 42)

Block perches should be used for falcons, because in their wild state falcons usually perch on a flat surface. The diameter of the wood can be altered to suit the size of the falcon, but care must be taken that neither the falcon's jesses are too long nor the diameter of the block so small that the jesses can slip separately over the diameter of the block and down the sides, thus imprisoning the bird by the swivel against the stem of the block. The ring on the stem of the block through which the leash is tied must be able to rotate easily. Some falconers have block perches which have the ring positioned around a waist in the block itself. I find these rings do not rotate as easily, particularly if the ring should rust slightly in wet weather. The metal stem of the block must have a cross section welded to it at the ground line to prevent it from sinking in too far. There should be ten inches of spike sunk into the ground beyond the cross section, and the top of the block itself need not be more than 14 inches above ground level. Some falconers like to top their block perches with carpet, cork or Astroturf.

Block perches inside a mews with a concrete floor under the layer of peat must have a hole drilled out for them and be sunk securely into the concrete. Various types of bases for block perches inside have been tried, but generally they have proved impractical, as the bird gets hooked up on them and breaks its feathers. A heavy metal plate is perhaps the best.

Bow perches (see fig. 43)

Bow perches are designed for shortwings, because in their wild state they usually perch in trees and thus are accustomed to gripping around a branch. Bow perches are also designed to accommodate the length of a hawk's train. Bows can be made out of laminated wood, out of a naturally curved branch (if one can be found) or out of metal piping. The last is most commonly used as it is the easiest to obtain. Natural wood bows must be fitted into adjustable metal frames. Metal bow perches must be well padded with foam or material and bound with leather, or covered with pipe lagging or hose pipe. The ring must be large enough to pass over the padding without catching. Bow perches can be designed for use indoors by welding metal feet, made out of scaffolding filled with cement for weight, onto the ends of the bow, instead of having a ground line and metal spikes to stick into the ground (see fig. 44).

Strictly speaking, eagles should be put on bow perches, but it is difficult to make bows heavy enough for large eagles, so I usually put them on enormous block perches of traditional shape.

Ring perches (see fig. 45)

Ring perches can be used for shortwings as a substitute for bow perches. They must have leather straps stretched across the ring to discourage the bird from bating through the circle, and they must be well padded like a bow perch. Indoor ring perches must have a concrete base heavy enough

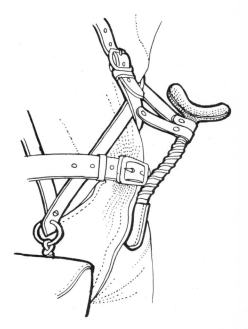

40 Arm brace for carrying large eagles

41 The arm brace in use as Stephen Ford carries a Golden Eagle

41

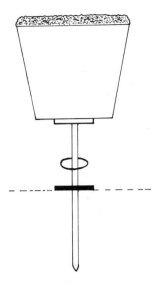

42 The block perch

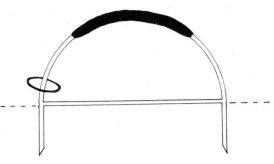

43 The outdoor bow perch

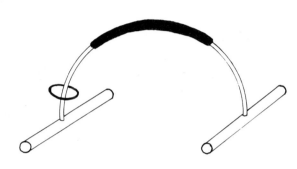

44 The indoor bow perch

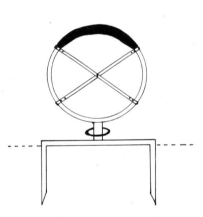

45 The outdoor ring perch

to hold them steady (see fig. 46). I have found that circular garage signs, such as Castrol GTX signs, make ideal ring perches for indoor use for large shortwings. The rotating middle can either be secured at both edges, or it can be removed and replaced with leather straps. These perches already have a cast-iron base of adequate proportions. The problem with a ready-made perch of this sort has always been the necessity to saw through the stem to put on a ring, and then to weld it back together again, but I have solved this difficulty by the use of bull rings (obtainable from agricultural suppliers, and used to pierce a bull's nose). These can be clipped around the stem and the metal screw sheared off, as described in the instructions on the packet. These rings (provided that they are large enough) can be used on any of the aforementioned perches.

Screen perches

Screen perches are condemned as dangerous by all sensible falconers. They are a straight beam of wood below which hessian is hung. The bird is tied up against the swivel, and thus can only move within the length of the jesses. If the bird should bate, it can climb back up by using the hessian. The dangerous features of this arrangement are that if a hawk feels unwell and wants to lie down on the ground it cannot as it cannot reach the ground, but will hang upside down and die. Secondly the tail feathers are easily broken and damaged by the wooden beam and the jesses if the bird should turn sideways on the perch. Thirdly, I feel that it is most unfair to restrict a bird's movements to the few inches of jess length. Should the jesses become twisted, the bird cannot even scratch.

I can only hope that in the future these perches will be less widely used.

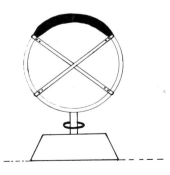

46 The indoor ring perch

HOODS

The use of the hood

The function of a hood is to cover a hawk's eyes and exclude all light so that the bird is, in effect, blindfolded. When a hawk cannot see, it will sit quietly and stay relatively still. There are many reasons arising from different circumstances for wishing to achieve this effect. For example, it is useful to be able to hood a bird which will not sit still when it is to be transported on a cadge in a car, and when it is necessary to perform some duty which requires a nervous or difficult hawk to be cast, such as imping or the fitting of new jesses, and when the bird is sick and must undergo close examination by a vet.

When a falcon is taken into the hunting field it is often hooded after each flight and carried with the braces of the hood 'struck', or open, so that the hood can be taken off quickly when suitable quarry is sighted, but meanwhile the falcon does not waste her energy bating at quarry which would be too distant for her to catch. This is called 'flying out of hood'. When more than one large falcon is taken out at one time, hoods are used similarly to prevent waste of energy while bating at quarry intended for the other falcon.

Finally, some falconers use a hood initially to get a hawk to sit on the fist, gradually unhooding it for short periods of time to accustom the bird firstly to the sight of its handler in a given place, and subsequently to different environments and things hitherto unencountered, such as strange people, dogs, and cars. This method works very well with longwings. It is unnecessary and indeed inadvisable to use the hood a great deal in the early stages, for it is very difficult to man a new arrival which spends the majority of its time hooded, and is thus ignorant of the strange sights and circumstances to which the very act of manning requires her to grow accustomed.

Many species of bird used for falconry purposes do not need to be made to the hood. Small falcons, for example, will quickly become tame and behave well in any given set of circumstances, and thus it is not common practice to hood them. Some shortwings intensely dislike being hooded, so while it is useful to be able to hood an accipiter on occasion, if the bird is obviously unhappy about your attempts to make it to the hood, there is usually no real justification for pressing the point. Various other birds such as buzzards are, like the small falcons, so quickly and thoroughly manned that the use of a hood would be superfluous. Large falcons should always be made to the hood so that they can be flown out of the hood, and so should large eagles, for the sheer size of the latter renders it advisable to be able to hood them in certain awkward circumstances where a smaller hawk in a similar situation would present no particular problem. For example, if a kestrel was travelling on a cadge in the back of a vehicle and bated, the driver would not be at risk, whereas to suffer an eagle bating thus would be a menace and possibly dangerous.

Making a bird to the hood

If a previously unmanned bird is to be made to the hood, the process should be started as soon as possible after its arrival as it is easier to hood a bird while it is more nervous of you than of the hood. It is more difficult to hood-train a bird which has already been well manned by someone else, but has never been hooded before, as such a bird will often concentrate its energy into avoiding the hood. Even more difficult, and usually impossible, is the act of attempting to make a bird to the hood which has already undergone similar unsuccessful attempts by a previous owner. Such a bird will have become 'hood-shy', a process which is usually irreversible, and

47 Hooding: Robert Boucher hoods his female peregrine   (a)   (b)

(c)   (d)

(e)

it will know all the tricks of the trade, including dodging, bating and tucking its neck between its shoulders. Ill-fitting hoods too often cause a hawk to become hood-shy, as the bird associates any hood with discomfort.

To hood a bird requires a skilful hand. It also requires co-ordination of hand and eye, for the art of hooding is based largely on accurate timing. Firstly it must be explained that most hoods have braces in the back used to open and close the hood. The button ends of the braces must be pulled simultaneously to open the hood, and the longer knotted ends will close the hood. While the bird is held on the gloved hand, the plume or topknot of the hood is held between the fingers and thumb of your ungloved hand. The braces of the hood must be as wide open as possible. The bird should be held facing the body with the fist slightly raised. If the bird is at all restless, or shows signs of bating, you must wait until it has settled and is sitting relaxed. Slowly raise the hood until the opening rests lightly against the bird's upper breast, and stroke the chest gently with the edge of the hood which is nearest to the beak hole. If the bird remains relaxed, the hood can be slipped over the beak and into place without hesitation. Make sure that the hood is correctly positioned with the beak well through the opening before closing the braces by pulling the furthest brace with the ungloved hand and the nearest one between the teeth simultaneously. A hood should never be crammed on to a bird's head with a forceful motion induced by irritation. One such incident is sufficient to render a bird hood-shy. If patience and perseverance cannot triumph, brute force certainly will not.

The removal of a hood should be divided into two distinct movements— the 'striking' or opening of the braces by pulling the button ends, and the tipping of the hood off the head by holding the plume. The bird should not be allowed to develop the habit of flicking the hood off as soon as the braces are struck, for to hunt a bird out of the hood it must be carried on the fist with the braces of the hood struck, as previously described.

Some falconers like to feed their bird while it is hooded. While feeding through the hood may encourage a bird's willingness to take a hood well, it is a messy practice, and it encourages a particularly irritating vice. A bird fed in this manner will constantly bend down and bite the glove, even when there is no food present. In the hunting field a falcon thus inclined is more than likely to be concentrating on locating some non-existent piece of food at the crucial moment, rather than sitting upright, eager for the moment when the hood is to be removed.

Some falcons develop a habit when hooded of moving their heads back and forth in a manner best described as similar to that adopted by somebody reading a newspaper. The reason for this I have never determined, but it could well be because the hood is not sitting comfortably on the head. Indeed, the action of loosening the braces and slightly adjusting the position of the hood often causes the bird to cease this peculiar motion.

Never leave a hawk untethered when it is hooded for some birds will take off with a hood on and will fly a considerable distance before crash-landing.

TYPES OF HOOD

Before describing the various types of hood, I would like to make a couple of important points. Firstly, it is of the utmost importance to have a hood made to fit the individual for which it is intended. There can be considerable variation in the size of head between two birds of the same species and sex, and thus a hood made from a pattern labelled to fit a female lanner might well be too large or too small for the lanner in question. For this reason, I have not included ready-made hood patterns in this book, but I have included a pattern for an Anglo-Indian hood which can be made up from a single accurate measurement of an individual hawk's head. Secondly, hoods should be kept clean and free from dust inside. Always check and if necessary blow the inside of a hood before putting it on a bird in order to protect its eyes from particles of dust. When a hood is not in use, the braces should be left open.

48 Dutch hood

Dutch hoods ('The hood proper') (see fig. 48)
To make a Dutch hood is by no means easy. It is made out of three pieces of leather which are stitched together edge on edge, soaked, and domed over a hood block, where it is allowed to shrink and dry to fit the shape of the block, and once removed, remains firm. The three pieces of leather which constitute the hood are a central body piece and two eye patches which are covered with baize, felt or thin suede. The last is the longest lasting, for a falcon which scratches her hood will eventually tear baize or felt. The colour of the side panels traditionally indicates the type of quarry which the falcon was trained to hunt—green for a rook hawk, red for a game hawk, and purple for a falcon which had taken a heron. Dutch hoods also have a coloured wool plume topped with feathers which are usually game-bird breast or flank feathers, or cockerel hackles. Dutch hoods have a tendency to be comparatively heavy, and thus the leather from which they are made has to be carefully selected to be light but firm. These hoods, which are undoubtedly the most visually attractive of all hoods, are usually used for falcons. As proper hood blocks are virtually unobtainable nowadays, it is pointless for me to describe the making of Dutch hoods in detail.

Further to this, a badly made and ill-fitting Dutch hood will cause considerable damage. I therefore feel that the best way to learn how to make this type of hood is to be taught by a skilled and experienced hood maker. Equipment suppliers (see page 178) sell Dutch hoods very reasonably considering the amount of work and craftsmanship involved (my husband who makes Dutch hoods for our falcons reckons that they take an average of six to eight hours each to complete), and should the hood not prove to be a good fit most suppliers will exchange it, if necessary several times, until one is found which fits perfectly.

Rufter hoods
These were originally used by hawk trappers. They are simple, adaptable hoods which were put on freshly trapped hawks to keep them quiet. Some falconers used to use them on a new arrival to accustom the bird to a hood and until a proper hood of a better fit could be made.

Bahraini or Arabic hoods (see fig. 49)
These hoods are generally made from soft leather, as they have a system of braces which thread in and out of the back of the hood, causing it to concertina when opening and closing. Bahraini hoods are mostly used in Arabia on sakers and peregrines.

Indian hoods
These are lightweight hoods made out of one piece of leather. They do not open or shut but stay on the bird's head by being as friction tight as is reasonably possible. They are therefore relatively easy for a determined bird to remove. Since their origin in India they have been modified to include a pair of European braces of the type used on a Dutch hood, and have thus been christened 'Anglo-Indian' hoods.

Anglo-Indian hoods (see fig. 50)
These embody all the advantages of the Indian hood in that they are lightweight, and do not need to be blocked in the manner of a Dutch hood. They can be used on any hawk which is suitable for hooding. Some falcons prefer them to the heavier Dutch hoods. Other species, particularly eagles, show a tendency to hang their heads in a hood, even in a very light Anglo-Indian hood, and there is no way of avoiding this. The majority of the time, however, if they are well made, they appear to be comfortable for birds. My Changeable Hawk Eagle would go to sleep with her Anglo-Indian hood on, tucking her head, hood and all, under one wing in the normal manner. There can be no better indication that a bird finds its hood comfortable.

Anglo-Indian hoods have a wide beak hole (which is essential for a bird which needs to cast, as it may do when travelling hooded), unlike the Dutch hoods which traditionally have a 'slot' beak hole, but which are now more frequently being made with a wider beak hole. Anglo-Indian hoods also usually have a leather topknot rather than a plume of wool and feathers.

Making an Anglo-Indian hood
The bird for which the hood is intended must be cast, and the top of the head measured across the widest part directly behind the eyes. The measurement thus attained is used to build up the geometrical pattern which must be drawn accurately (see fig. 51).

When the paper pattern has been cut out, it is laid on the leather. The leather should be of good quality, lightweight and non-stretchable, but thick enough to give it substance, so that the hood will hold its shape when

49 Bahraini or Arabic hood

50 Anglo-Indian hood

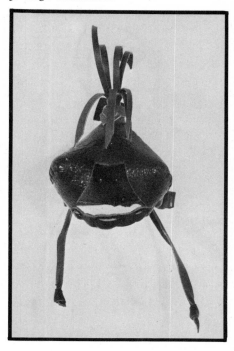

51 PATTERN FOR ANGLO-INDIAN HOOD, MODIFIED FROM AN ORIGINAL DESIGN BY H. J. SLIJPER.

1 Measure across the top of hawk's head at widest part directly behind the eyes. Using BC as this measured width of x mm, draw equilateral triangles ABC and BDC with BC as common side.

2 Join AD to cross BC at Y and extend all lines from B and C.

3 Draw EG and FH parallel to and the same length as AD and join EF and GH. Extend BC to I and J.

4 Mark off points K and L, x mm from E and F.

5 Extend AY by the same length to form AM.

6 Draw MN and MO to cut points B and C to meet GH. Label intersections with line KL, P and Q respectively.

7 Draw BR and CS, parallel to IG and JH.

8 Join DP and DQ and extend to EI and FJ respectively, to form points T and U.

9 a) With radius IG and compass point on I draw arc from G to meet line IJ, and with compass point on J and same radius draw arc from H to meet line IJ.

b) Where arcs cut BR and CS label W and W_1 and join. Where WW_1 cuts YD label V.

10 With compass point on V and radius VN, draw arcs NP and OQ.

11 Extend lines GE and HF. With compass point on K, and radius KA, draw arcs cutting GE extended at X and MN at X_1. Extend slightly beyond X. With compass point on L and same radius draw arc cutting HF at Z and MO at Z_1. Extend on slightly beyond Z.

12 a) Draw curves TP, UQ, NO and WW by hand.

b) Join E to the extended arc AX and F to the extended arc AZ by hand.

c) Join X_1 and Z_1 to meet MA at the same level as XZ.

d) Where arc from G and arc from H join IJ, draw lines to meet the intersection of KL and AD.

13 Cut out completed pattern.

14 Mark out stitches, cut slits for top knot and braces, and punch holes for throat lash.

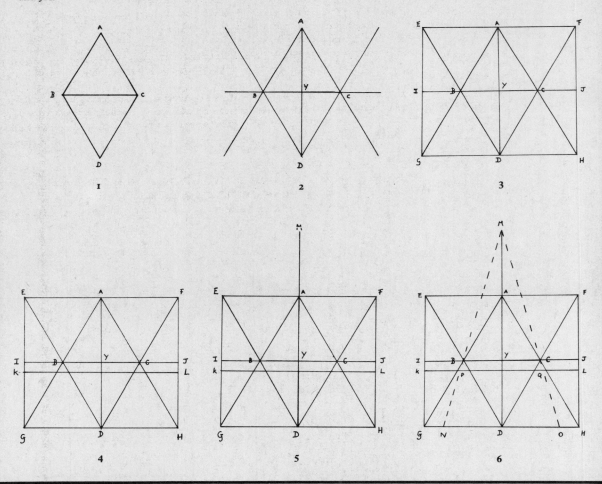

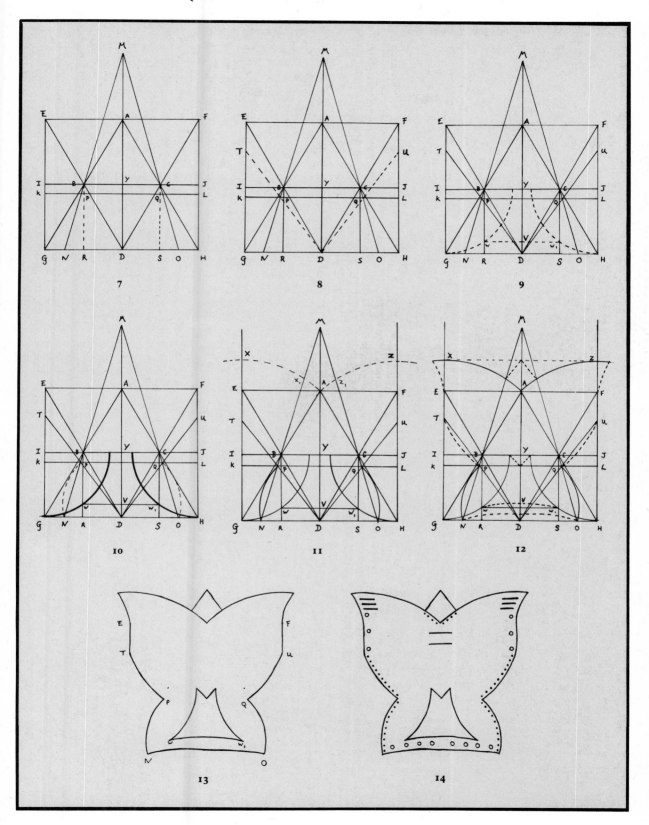

completed. The pattern must be cut out of the leather carefully with a sharp knife or scalpel. It is better to cut the beak hole slightly too small than slightly too large, for the former can be altered, while the latter is irreversible. When cut out, the beak hole must be chamfered, or in other words the thickness of the leather must be slightly shaved around the inside edge. Two slits for the topknot and three each side for the braces must be cut, the holes for the stitches, of equal number on both sides to ensure symmetry, marked out with a stitch marker or bradawl, and the holes must be punched for the throat lash. The hood is then ready to be stitched in an over-and-over manner with waxed linen thread knotted at one end. Start stitching outwards from points P and Q. Each stitch must be pulled tight after the succeeding one has been completed, to ensure that the seams meet perfectly edge on edge. The final hole should be double-stitched and tied off. When the stitches down both sides and the four at the back have been completed, place a suitable object (such as a broom handle) inside the hood against the seam and hit the outside of the seam with a hammer, or preferably with a small wooden mallet, to dome and shape the seam of the hood to a tightly closed and well defined curve. The hood can be held up to a light to check that the seams prevent all light from entering.

Next the braces must be made. Cut two strips of soft leather of equal length, and thin enough to lie flat when threaded through the brace slits. Grease the strips thoroughly, stretch them, and ensure that they are not going to snap when you pull them. Make a button at one end (see fig. 21) and cut a long point at the other. Punch a hole in each brace about three-quarters of an inch away from the button and increase it to a slit of approximately one inch in length. With one brace on each side thread the back of both sides of the hood. Cross one brace through the other (it does not matter which) and complete the threading (see fig. 52). The diagram shows the threading for one side only, but the process is identical on both sides. Open the braces fully and cut the long ends of the braces off to a point about one-and-a-half inches beyond the button ends. Knot the pointed ends with a single knot. Cut a strip of leather thin enough to be passed through the holes already punched for the throat lash and thread it in and out, starting by going from the inside outwards at a hole on one side nearest to the braces. Cut off the surplus when threading is completed, leaving a small flap which can be stuck flat on the inside of the hood.

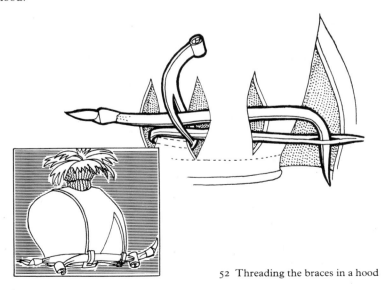

52 Threading the braces in a hood

Finally, cut a strip of leather for the topknot, pointed at both ends, and feed it down through one slit and up through the other. Punch a hole in one side and thread the opposite end through it and then repeat the process. This is the simplest form of topknot. The more complicated but equally more attractive turk's head knot is too difficult to be depicted in either words or diagrams and must consequently be learnt from another falconer who is familiar with it. Anglo-Indian hoods can be decorated with subtle gold embossing, and the general appearance of the hood is enhanced if the topknot, throat lash and braces are of the same colour, perhaps contrasting with the overall colour of the hood. The edges of the beak hole can be lined with thin suede if desired. This is a useful tip if the beak hole has been cut a fraction too large. When the completed hood is put on the bird it should fit snugly but without pinching when the braces are closed, and above all else, the bird must not be able to see out of the beak hole. If it does not fit the original pattern must be checked and redrawn. To achieve a perfect fit several attempts may be necessary.

4 Lure Swinging

The art of swinging a lure expertly can only be perfected by a great deal of practice. Ideally, a beginner wanting to fly falcons should learn with a kestrel. Kestrels are much slower than some of the other falcons, such as merlins, luggars, lanners and peregrines, and are therefore less likely to catch you out while you are learning. A young falcon, particularly, is an advantage, as it will learn and improve as you do.

Firstly, though, lure swinging must be practised without the bird in the form of individual passes, each of which can be learned separately and then strung together to form a variable pass sequence. Primarily it is important to learn how to hold the lure correctly. The lure line should be fully unwound off the stick, which is held in the gloved hand. The line passes between the middle fingers and is looped onto the little finger. From here it is looped again and held between the thumb and the forefinger. It then runs across to the other hand, where it is again held between the thumb and forefinger, and the lure hangs below the arm on a length of line whereby, when your arm is horizontal to the ground, it is level with your ankle. From this position, the lure is swung backwards in a full circle. This swinging is the first move which requires practice as it is the basic linking movement between the passes. The swing should be slow and even, fast enough only to keep the lure turning. The movement of the swing comes mainly from the wrist—not from the whole arm. You should practice walking in a circle and turning, keeping the lure swinging in a vertical plane.

When you have perfected this stage, and can turn easily without wondering if the lure is going to hit you over the head or wrap itself around your neck, you can progress to the first pass. Pass No 1 is the basic under-arm pass—you swing the lure as you have been, until your imaginary bird flies towards you, when you put the lure out towards it and pull it away by passing it through under your swinging arm. This movement is performed when the lure has just been swung under your arm which then straightens in front of your body, pointing towards the imaginary bird. Your gloved hand comes close to your swinging hand and the line between them slips through the fingers and is pulled taut by the weight of the lure. To bring the lure back under your arm, the line is pulled back slightly by the gloved hand and you turn in one movement through 180° by pivoting on your feet and turning in the direction the lure is travelling as it passes beside you, and resume your swing facing in the opposite direction. When you have mastered the basic movement, you must practice this pass until it is fluent.

Pass No 2 is the same pass but performed across the body rather than under your swinging arm. The movement is thus to put the lure out to your gloved side, so that the lure is like a straight extension of your swinging arm which will come across your body. Your hands will again come almost together, putting the line out at its fullest extent; then as you turn to follow through, your gloved hand will pull the line downwards to shorten it, facilitating the follow through and turn. So, assuming that you normally carry your bird on your left hand, and that you are therefore swinging with your right hand and holding the stick in your gloved left hand, during pass No 1 you are turning to your right, taking the lure under your arm, while for pass No 2 you are taking the lure across your body and turning to the left. Both turns should pivot you through 180°. When you have mastered pass No 2, you can try alternating passes 1 and 2 swinging the lure maybe three or four times in between each and walking around as though following your bird's flight path with your eyes. Remember that it is the falcon who decides when to stoop, so you must be ready to perform a pass at any given time.

Pass No 3 is the overhead pass. The lure is swung up to the falcon as though she was to take it above your head. The hands both go upwards for this pass, but they stay apart, with the line between them taut. When the falcon is almost on to the lure, it is pulled sharply downwards by spreading the arms further apart, and continuing the swinging path of the lure.

Pass No 4 is relatively simple. The lure is thrown out on to the ground in front of you, both hands maintaining their hold on the line but coming together as it lands in the path of the falcon. Before she can reach it, it is jerked out of her way towards your feet. When this pass is performed there are two things to be wary of. Firstly, you must keep the line as low to the ground as possible, crouching down if necessary to prevent your falcon from becoming caught in it as you jerk the lure away. Secondly, a falcon will grow cunning if this pass is used too frequently, and will start to cut in to where the lure normally ends up. If she shows a tendency to do this you can try to fool her (if you are very confident) by throwing the lure out and leaving it still, while she cuts in to where she thought it was going.

Pass No 5 is the last movement of any lure-swinging sequence. It is the act of throwing the lure up for the bird to catch in the air, releasing your hold on the line. To do this, the lure must be swung much faster than usual—then released at the top of the swing with a fast upward thrust which will send it spinning up into the air for the bird to catch. It requires some nicety of timing to give the falcon the best chance of catching it as the lure reaches its highest point. Too early and the lure will hit the ground before the falcon can reach it—too late and your bird will fly above you before the lure reaches her height. Sometimes a particularly lazy falcon (especially kestrels) will just follow the lure down to the ground and take it there. Some will slice it with their feet as they would their prey, and then follow it down instead of binding to it in the air.

This need not be used as the movement to finish each flying time—you should vary it occasionally by letting the bird take the lure on the ground. You can also pretend to let your falcon catch you out on a normal pass. If she takes it thus at a time when she thinks you did not intend her to have it she will redouble her efforts to catch you out again next time. This is the psychology behind lure swinging—your falcon should always feel that if she was just to fly that little bit harder, she would get it next time. Thus your aim should be to place the lure a few inches in front of your bird on every pass. You will know that you have executed a good pass if you see your falcon's feet extending towards the lure in anticipation of a catch. Conversely, if your swinging is not good enough to make your falcon believe she stands a chance, she will soon become bored.

When you can string the five passes together interspersed with regular even swinging, and when you can vary the speed and the height of passes 1 and 2 to suit your imaginary bird, and can throw out the lure for pass 4— getting it to land on the exact spot on the ground that you were aiming for—then you can introduce your falcon to the proceedings. Initially she will probably catch you out occasionally, but do not despair, as you will gradually improve. Above all else, try to avoid hitting your bird with the lure. There is nothing like a good klonk on the head with a heavy lure to put your bird off chasing lures completely. Good lure swinging is a pleasure to watch. It is an art which involves fluency, timing and co-ordination of mind with movement. Some people are naturally more adept with a lure than others, but with practice and determination, anyone can produce a performance with a falcon which is pleasing to the eye of the beholder, enjoyable and interesting for the bird, and tremendously satisfying for the falconer.

5 The Hawk's Larder

Birds of prey in captivity eat only raw meat, as they do in their wild state. The number of people who are ignorant of this fact never ceases to amaze me. As they feed monkeys in a zoo with peanuts, people will throw pieces of jam sandwich, crisps and boiled sweets to hawks. Often I have travelled to collect an injured hawk from someone who has found one a day or so previously and who has, in the meantime, forced bread and milk, cooked meat or even (on one memorable occasion) cornflakes down its throat. The result of such ignorance may well prove fatal.

However, assuming that those who are reading this chapter are aware of such basics as the necessity of feeding only raw meat, let us look at the various types of meat and discuss their relative merits.

The first point to mention is that to maintain good health, a hawk must be given roughage, in the form of fur or feather, on a regular basis. The reason for this is that when swallowed, a hawk's food goes down into its crop. Once here the digestion starts and the crop is 'put over'. When roughage is fed, the fur or feather is formed into a pellet or 'casting' which is then regurgitated or 'cast' up from the crop and out through the mouth 12–18 hours after the hawk has eaten, cleaning out the crop.

I have heard of people who have run out of roughage for their hawk and have combed a domestic cat or dog to get hair to stick on the meat. Someone even fed cotton wool regularly instead of natural roughage, and this was cast up in the normal manner covered with the gleam from the crop.

In their wild state, hawks will eat some of the vital organs, such as the heart and liver, from their kills. In captivity, falconers tend to feed just the flesh of the animal, such as the hind leg of a rabbit or shin of beef. Thus hawks are deprived of many of the trace elements or vitamins found in the organs of their natural food. These can therefore be given in another form, such as a vitamin supplement powder. SA 37 is perhaps the best of these. It can be obtained from most veterinary surgeries, and should be sprinkled on the meat as one would sprinkle salt on food, two or three times a week. It may be particularly important for birds during the breeding season and the moult, and is essential for young hawks, when it is used in conjunction with sterilized bone flour for added calcium. Although extra vitamins may not be strictly essential for adult birds, any aid to the general health of a hawk is worth using. Hawks do not need to be given water. They seldom drink, obtaining necessary moisture from their food, although they may occasionally sip their bath water.

BEEF

Beef is a handy and nutritious meat to feed to hawks. For flying birds it is easy to cut into pieces of the right size, and it is not at all messy. Only very lean pieces should be fed. Shin of beef is relatively cheap and, provided all the fat is trimmed off, it is ideal. Horsemeat, if it can be obtained, is very similar to beef, having a slightly coarser grain. Both beef and horsemeat are of middling nutritious value, and can be supplemented with SA 37.

CHICKS

Day-old chicks are extremely valuable as a form of food for hawks. They can usually be obtained relatively cheaply and easily from a hatchery where the hens are reared for egg-laying while the cockerels are gassed with carbon dioxide shortly after hatching. They can be fed in their entirety, and thus provide roughage which is regurgitated in the form of a yellow casting. Day-old chicks also have the yolk sac still intact inside them. The colour of the yolk will eventually affect the colour of the cere and feet of a hawk which is fed regularly on chicks, causing them to become a healthy orangey-yellow colour. The substance which causes this colouring is called carotine, and it is also found in the fat and livers of birds. It may also deepen the eye colour of certain accipiters such as goshawks.

Nutritiously, chicks contain roughly the same food value as equivalent amounts of beef, so that when supplemented with SA 37 they can be interchanged with beef to form a good quality diet providing roughage and variation. They can, if necessary, be fed exclusively for extended periods, particularly to eyasses and to birds in aviaries.

RABBIT AND HARE

Rabbit is a natural food for many species of raptor, but it has a very low nutritional value. The flesh of rabbit is very pale, rather like that of chicken. A hawk which is accustomed to eating beef or chicks will need a much larger amount of rabbit flesh to keep it at the same weight.

Hare is much more nourishing than rabbit, and should be fed very fresh. Both meats can be fed occasionally to hawks which would eat off it in their natural state, but rabbit should not be fed exclusively for any period of time as it is not possible to maintain high condition on this meat. Like beef and chicks, both can be supplemented with SA 37.

RATS AND MICE

These are most easily and cheaply obtained from laboratories. The ones for which you should ask are the control rodents, or, in other words, those which have not been treated in any way. They can also be obtained from pet shops, but this is a rather expensive way of feeding your hawk.

Both rat and mouse are highly nutritious, and can be fed in their entirety. Thus the hawk will get natural trace elements from the intestines of the rodent, and a vitamin supplement will not be necessary. Although this is an excellent source of food, unfortunately some birds do not find them palatable and therefore cannot be persuaded to eat them on a regular basis. For hawks which like them, though, they can be fed every so often as a change of diet.

FISH

Fish such as whiting and sprats can be fed whole to fish eagles and other fish-eating hawks. All my fish-eaters are given fresh fish at least once a week.

MOORHEN

Moorhen is a very rich meat and consequently has a very high food value. If fed its normal weight of food in moorhen flesh instead of beef or chicks, a bird will put on weight very quickly, so moorhen should only be fed for two reasons—firstly if a hawk is too low and needs to put on weight, or if it is sick and needs to be fed up rapidly, when moorhen is excellent, if available. Secondly, if your hawk kills a moorhen, it should be allowed to eat a small amount of the warm breast meat. Some hawks dislike the skin of moorhen as it is very greasy.

PHEASANT, PARTRIDGE AND QUAIL

All three are excellent food for hawks and all birds seem to eat them with relish. Although it is difficult and extremely costly to procure pheasant, partridge or quail on a regular basis, if you are not flying a hawk at any of these birds, never let an opportunity to feed this game to your hawk pass you by. If you have the facilities to breed quail, they make an excellent regular food source, particularly for large falcons.

GROUSE

Grouse is a very rich meat and should be fed with discretion. Falcons which fly game are usually rewarded with only the head and neck of a grouse.

ROOK

Rook is similar in food value to beef. It can be fed to rook hawks in the full confidence that it will not upset their weight for the following day. One word of warning—rooks are usually heavily infested with lice, and falcons which are flown at rook should be sprayed regularly with Johnson's Antimite to prevent them becoming infested as well.

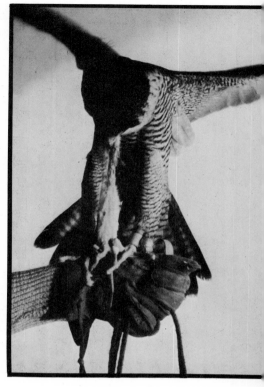

53 Female peregrine feeding up on a mouse

PIGEON

Pigeon is a very rich meat. Wild pigeon should not be fed as they carry the frouce protozoan. House or domestic pigeon should also be checked carefully for disease. A young pigeon can be split open and the liver and lungs examined for lesions. If it is clear, the breast meat can be fed cold to put weight on a sick hawk, to a moulting hawk, or, in very small quantities, as a change of diet to a flying hawk. Old pigeon tends to make a working hawk obstreperous, and also appears to be somewhat indigestible, so this should be avoided.

SQUIRREL

Squirrel is a very good meat for a hawk. It is tough and provides good exercise. It has middling nutritious value and will not upset a balanced diet.

VENISON

Venison is a very rich dark meat, and should therefore be fed sparingly. Eagles particularly are excessively fond of venison, but they must be exercised hard to burn it off. Like all game fed to hawks it should be fed fresh rather than hung. Unfortunately, venison is extremely hard to come by and expensive nowadays.

DUCK

Duck is a very fatty meat and should not be fed to hawks unless it has been taken by a bird, when just a few mouthfuls can be permitted.

MUTTON AND PORK

In Arabia, mutton is widely used as a falcon's staple diet. It is lighter in colour than beef and of middling nutritious value. It should only be fed very lean. Personally, I do not use it.

Pork should never be fed to hawks. It has a low nutritious value and is also extremely fatty.

BLACKBIRD, THRUSH ETC. (NB These are protected by the 1954 Protection of Birds Act, so a licence is required.)

Small birds are particularly good for small hawks, such as sparrowhawks and kestrels as they are a natural food providing excellent casting and plenty of vitamins and minerals. They are also very easily digested. As with all wild birds the intestines should be removed before feeding in case the bird has been eating poisoned or insecticidally infected food. Although this is not foolproof, it may help.

OFFAL

Liver is high in iron and other minerals, and is therefore useful for sick hawks, to which it can be fed in small, easily swallowed slivers. It can be fed occasionally to trained hawks as a valuable variation to a diet of beef and chicks.

Heart has a low food value, and should therefore be fed only in conjunction with more nutritious meats. For small hawks, it is the equivalent of washed meat and should thus be avoided except as a washed meat substitute.

None of the other vital organs such as kidney should ever be fed to hawks.

WASHED MEAT

When you wish to reduce your hawk's condition without starving it of all food, you can feed it washed meat for a few days. Strips of beef are soaked in water and put in a refrigerator overnight. They are then squeezed out in warm water and dried, whereupon they will be very pale, almost white in colour. Washed meat is not very palatable to hawks, and some persuasion may be necessary before they will recognise it as food. Such a diet should not be maintained for more than three or four days, after which the hawk should be fed a good red meat again.

This is a diet which is most often used if a bird is taken up from the moult to get rid of surplus fat. The process is called 'enseaming'.

RANGLE

Rangle are seldom used nowadays. They are smooth round stones or pebbles, a little larger than a pea. When pushed down a hawk's throat into the crop they mingle with the grease and slime around the edges of the crop, and are then cast up coated with gleam. The mutes of the hawk will be greasy for the next few days showing that some of the accumulation of fat in the crop has been broken up. They are given in the place of casting, normally when a hawk is taken up from the moult, and are used in conjunction with washed meat. Although they are not widely administered today, rangle can be left beside a hawk's perch so that if she wishes she can pick them up and swallow them to aid her digestion. I have seen a hawk taking rangle in this manner on several occasions.

TIRINGS

Tirings are tough pieces of bone and sinew with only a thin covering of meat on them. They exercise and build up the muscles on the back of the necks of hawks as they pull at the bones to strip off the meat. They also help to keep a hawk's beak in shape.

The best forms of tiring are the wings of quarry, from which the feathers can be lightly plucked, and chicken necks. They can be given in the morning after the hawk has cast. Care must be taken that the pieces are not small enough to permit the bird to swallow them whole. Such paltry amounts of meat will not affect her performance in the afternoon, but they will keep her entertained while also serving a useful purpose. Although it is not strictly necessary to give tirings on a regular basis, it is particularly helpful to give them after the moult to assist with the process of regaining fitness.

ROAD CASUALTIES

These should be avoided at all times for a variety of reasons. Firstly, although the cause of death may appear to be obvious, the creature may also have been suffering from some other affliction such as poisoning. Secondly, a road casualty is not necessarily fresh (unless it is still warm). Thirdly, they may well be covered in exhaust fumes and possibly grease or oil from the undersides of vehicles. I have never fed any road casualties except those which I have accidentally knocked over cleanly myself as I feel it is only sensible to take all reasonable precautions when feeding a hawk.

FRESHNESS

Although in their wild state hawks are often seen picking at elderly and even maggoty carcasses, they should not be fed anything but the freshest of meat in captivity. Once again, there is no point in taking any risks with your hawk, and stale or stinking fly-blown meat might well harbour salmonella and other such harmful organisms. Clean hands, clean feed dishes, frequently scrubbed hawking bags and gloves, and, above all, fresh meat, are essential aids to basic hygiene.

All falconers should have access to a deep-freeze, as those who can always lay hand to freshly killed meat nowadays are certainly in the minority. Blocks of day-old chicks, beef, the occasional rabbit, and a bag of mice or rats will form the basis of a substantial deep-freeze larder. Food should be taken out of the deep-freeze the night before it is to be fed, and allowed to defrost thoroughly on a clean platter and, in the summer, under a fly-proof mesh. If hawk food is to be kept in the same deep-freeze as food for human consumption, it should, out of deference to other members of the household, be properly bagged and sealed. If one stale bag of food is introduced to a deep-freeze at the same time as fresh food, it will turn the rest. Chicks particularly, will 'sweat' in hot weather and should be frozen within eight hours of being gassed. If large quantities of food are to be frozen in the same day, the bags should be put into the deep-freeze at staggered intervals, allowing the first layer to freeze slightly before the next is put in. This prevents the middle layers from going off while the outer layers freeze first. No deep-freeze should be packed too tightly, or the bags of food will, when frozen, prove extremely difficult to remove. Should this happen, the deep-freeze must be switched off and allowed to defrost for a couple of hours with the lid open until the bags can be moved. Remember always: if in doubt about a particular meat, do not feed it. It is better always to err on the side of caution.

6 The Choice of a Hawk

54 A longwing: the Lanner Falcon

Choosing the right bird to suit your individual circumstances is undoubtedly a very important step. Beginners are usually expected to start with a kestrel, but, as I have explained further on in the relevant chapters, I dispute this advice and strongly recommend a Common Buzzard. Thereafter the choice is fairly wide and the decisions are more difficult. First and foremost, you must consider your individual circumstances and decide whether the facilities and flying area that you have available for a bird are best suited to a longwing or a shortwing. These two terms are used to denote the difference between the two major groups of birds of prey. Longwings are the true falcons. They have pointed wings, comparatively short tails, and dark eyes. They generally take their quarry in the air. Strictly speaking, a shortwing is a hawk, but the word shortwing is also used to cover a very large category including everything which is not a falcon, such as eagles, owls and vultures. Correctly, this category should be subdivided into shortwings and broadwings. Broadwing is a term used to denote the eagles, vultures and buzzards. Shortwings appear in flight to have rounded ends to their wings. They have comparatively long tails and they usually take their prey on the ground. Longwings need to be flown in very open areas where the falconer can see his falcon chasing winged quarry for at least a couple of miles, without losing sight of his bird behind trees. Longwings cannot be flown successfully at quarry in enclosed areas. Shortwings can be flown in enclosed or wooded country, for it is in this type of countryside that their quarry is found. Their tails are long to aid manoeuvrability in enclosed areas, and their wings are rounded to facilitate soaring. Eagles cannot be flown in countryside which is too enclosed. They work best in hill country where they can use the thermals.

In this way the area in which you live will largely dictate the type of bird you can fly. Those who live near open downland, marshland or moorland will be able to fly falcons, whereas those who live in more enclosed countryside will be restricted to flying shortwings. Those who live in the centre of a large town or city should not consider getting a hawk unless they can travel out of town to fly it on a regular basis. Some people who live in cities exercise their hawks daily in parks or on commons in the town centre and travel into the countryside every weekend to hunt their bird. Anyone who considers doing this must first check with the local authority that they will be permitted to fly a hawk in a public place. There are also those people who want to keep a bird of prey as a 'pet', or, still worse, as a status symbol. They have no intention of ever training and flying their bird, but wish to keep it only to satisfy their personal gratification. Such a practice is despicable. Hawks are not suited to being pets. They are not domestic animals. If one must draw comparisons they can, perhaps be best compared to a gun dog, which must also be trained and worked on a regular basis, and

55 A shortwing: Mac Cook with his male Harris' Hawk

which establishes with its owner a relationship based on a working partnership. But, unlike a dog, a hawk will not give its owner devotion and loyalty. Although a bond can be formed between a man and a hawk it is based upon familiarity and the provision of food. A hawk does not return to your fist because it is fond of you, it does so purely for food. You may become extremely attached to your bird, but if it appears to prefer your fist to that of a stranger, it is only because it is more used to you.

Other considerations to bear in mind when choosing a bird are the amount of time, income and space that you have available. For example, if you know that you are not going to have time to work your hawk every day, you should not get a goshawk, which needs constant handling to stay well manned. Similarly, if you have limited means you will not be able to get a peregrine and take four or five months of the year off work to fly your falcon at game. The question of housing has already been discussed in detail under accommodation in the chapter on General Husbandry, but if you only have a small garden with dogs, cats, children and close neighbours, you should not consider getting a large eagle which will take over the garden, petrify the children and terrify the neighbours.

Initially, it is best for most beginners to train a Common Buzzard, and then to decide whether they should specialize in flying longwings or shortwings. At a later stage, and with some experience behind you, you can, if you wish, change your mind and fly the opposite type, circumstances permitting, but generally speaking it is better to decide on one or other type at the beginning, unless you have the time and the facilities to work both. Overleaf is a list of suggested priority for each group of birds:

Common Buzzard

Kestrel	Red-tailed Buzzard	Ferruginous Buzzard
Lanner, Lugger or Prairie Falcon	Harris' Hawk	Tawny or Steppes Eagle
Merlin	Goshawk	
Peregrine Falcon	Sparrowhawk	Golden Eagle etc.

People reading this list may be surprised to see how far down a sparrow-hawk is positioned. In my opinion, sparrowhawks are very tricky to fly and maintain over long periods, and thus they should not be attempted by anyone who has not had a fair amount of experience with other shortwings.

There are obviously many more species which I have not mentioned. Most countries have their native equivalents of many of the birds which I have included in the list and should thus substitute these in their relevant places. All kinds of more unusual birds are sometimes available, and provided that you feel you have sufficient experience, there is no reason why you should not attempt to train anything which is offered to you, even if it is not a recognized falconry species as such. I have discussed this point in more depth in Chapter 13.

Another interesting point to consider when acquiring a bird of prey is longevity. Some raptors can live to incredible ages, and on the whole, birds of prey in captivity seem to live longer than those in the wild. This is probably because captive birds do not face the natural hazards encountered by wild birds. For example, although they may fly or breed, as they would in their wild state, they do not have to protect a large aerial territory against intruders, or to hunt for food for a family of downy young. Usually the potential life span of a bird depends upon its reproductive capabilities. For example, a condor which only lays one egg at a time and does not lay every year can live up to 50 or 60 years, whereas a kestrel which normally lays four to six eggs a year, every year, will only live up to 10 or 15 years. Generally, large birds live longer than small ones. Buzzards can live up to 25 years, and the larger eagles up to 40 or 50 years. London Zoo, which has a remarkable record for longevity, has a pair of Caracaras which are over 45 years old. They also have records of two Bateleur Eagles living to 45 and 55 years respectively. This certainly seems to show that proper daily care even in an unnatural environment will achieve good results. However, falconers should not automatically assume that their hawks will live to a tremendous age. Quite apart from the fact that falconers' birds possibly have the unfortunate but, it is hoped, unlikely element of serious human error to contend with, they are, like any living creature, subject to disease and infection. The falconer who keeps his bird from an eyass until it dies of old age can consider himself not only a good manager of hawks but also extremely fortunate. I choose the words 'good manager' with care. There are those who can keep a hawk in excellent body and feather condition on a perch without ever giving it any exercise whatsoever. I have seen many such birds. They sit, fat and immaculate, shining examples of good health, but their owners cannot be described as good falconers if the bird is never flown.

If you are offered a type of bird about which you know very little, it is often a valuable exercise to consult an authoritative book, such as *Eagles, Hawks and Falcons of the World*, by Brown and Amadon (Hamlyn, 1968), not only to get an idea of what the bird looks like and its vital statistics, but also to find out the type of quarry it takes in its wild state. This will give you an indication of the natural ability of the species in question, and thus

56 Shortwings use trees as vantage points

of its potential for falconry. A bird which is described as feeding largely on carrion, for example, is going to be pretty useless as a hunting bird.

The basic guidelines to apply when choosing a hawk are as follows. Do not be prematurely ambitious, or in other words, do not take on a hawk which you are not experienced enough to handle. You will not be able to put it to its best use and it will not appreciate your ignorant mismanagement. Do not allow yourself to become over-hawked, and take on more hawks than you can do justice to. Be prepared to part with a hawk if you find that you have not got the time to fly it regularly and cannot put it up with a mate for breeding.

Finally, a note for parents of keen, falconry-orientated children. Do not let them get a hawk too young as they may well lose interest in it within a few months. Falconry is a demanding sport, and it involves a living creature which cannot be left as one would leave a dog or cat in the care of a neighbour for the duration of the family holiday. Such things must be considered before getting a hawk. My husband and I teach falconry, but will not teach any youngster under the age of twelve as, on the whole, children under this age have neither the time nor the perseverance and enthusiasm necessary to complete the training of a hawk. Anyone taking on a bird of prey must realize that they are taking on a dependant which will need regular daily attention if it is to maintain good health and work to the best of its ability.

7 The Early Stages

THE INITIAL PREPARATIONS

Let us assume that you have decided to get a hawk, and that it will be arriving within a couple of weeks. It is therefore of primary importance that you have the necessary accommodation, equipment and food-supply ready for its imminent arrival. You will need accommodation as described in the section about housing in Chapter 2. You will need a deep-freeze well stocked with chicks, beef or whatever else you intend to feed (see Chapter 5). You must also ensure that you have a regular supply of food for the future. You must buy a pot of SA 37, a suitable general worming powder, a can of Johnson's Anti-mite, a silver nitrate stick, some sulphanilamide powder, and some eye-drops (chloramycetin or similar) from your local vet. This will form the basis of your hawk's medicine chest. You can add to it later, if necessary. You must also ensure that you have a set of needle files for coping, a good supply of leather and tools, such as knives, a hole punch, eyelets of the right size for aylmeris and other instruments described in Chapter 3. By way of your personal 'falconry furniture' you will need a glove of suitable length and thickness, and a bag complete with shoulder strap and belt. For your hawk you will need perches, jesses (made up completely except for the final slit, to be judged from the thickness of the leg (see Chapter 3), a leash and swivel, plus a spare of each in case one is lost in the field, bells on semi-completed bewits, a creance, and a pair of scales, accurate to a quarter ounce. The latter are an item of great importance, often neglected during the pre-arrival preparations, but they are of course essential if you hope to fly your bird. They are also often difficult to obtain, for they must be of the right variety. They should be a pair of balance scales, with one side for the weights—you will need $\frac{1}{4}$ oz, $\frac{1}{2}$ oz, 1 oz, 2 oz, 4 oz, 8 oz, 1 lb and upwards according to the size of bird that you are getting—and the other side adapted for the bird to sit on, by means of attaching a piece of wood where the bowl usually goes (see fig. 57). Scales of this sort can often be obtained second-hand from scales manufacturers, as can the weights, but occasionally you will find a suitable pair in an antique or junk shop. Do not, under any circumstances use spring balance scales, like the ones often used in a kitchen. These tend to be inaccurate, and are also extremely hard to read if your bird is not sitting absolutely still. Finally, a bath of suitable proportions, such as an upturned dustbin lid or Eltex pigeon bath for a falcon or a washing up bowl for a buzzard, must be obtained and positioned in readiness in the weathering or weathering ground.

A brancher will require different accommodation. A shed must be prepared, such as the one described under accommodation in Chapter 3 for moulting a hawk in a loose mews. Food for a brancher can be tied on to a food board at night, again as it should be for a moulting hawk. This will serve the dual purpose of firstly helping to prevent imprinting, for the eyass will not see you if you feed in the dark, and secondly, discouraging a brancher from developing the habit of carrying food. An eyass should not

57 Scales suitable for weighing hawks

be taken up for training until it is hard penned, unless you intend to imprint it deliberately—sparrowhawks intended both for flying and breeding lend themselves particularly well to this practice (see Chapter 14). Under such circumstances you can start close contact as soon as you get your brancher by way of feeding off the fist, which, together with manning, is the first stage of training.

EXAMINING A BIRD BEFORE PURCHASE

In America it is illegal to buy birds of prey, but in Britain ABCR birds can be legally sold. If the bird that you are getting is already hard-penned or adult, you would be well advised to collect it on a day when you will be able to devote some time to its welfare during the next few days. Thus it is best for the majority of people to collect a bird over the early part of a weekend. Before you buy a hawk you should give it a thorough checking over. Even the most inexperienced falconer can perform a few simple checks to ensure that he is not buying a hawk which has some serious defect. Firstly, check the wing movement. If the hawk is loose in an aviary or shed this is simple enough—you have only to encourage it to fly across to a different perch to see if both wings are functioning properly. If it is on jesses, take it on to the fist and encourage it to bate off to see if both wings flap strongly and evenly. Look into its eyes for any signs of lesions or opacity and around the surrounding feathers for signs of liquid discharge. Next, ask the owner of the hawk to help you cast it so that you can examine its feet and legs. Check the feet for swellings and scabs, and feel the length of the legs for swellings or deformities. Flex the leg to check the joints and test the toes for grip around a gloved finger, and the talons for splits and cracks. Inspect the cere for scabs and cuts. Open the bird's beak to check that the inside of the mouth is a clean healthy-looking pink colour. Examine the beak itself for cracks. Finally check the feather condition. Most falconers will warn you in advance if the hawk you are travelling to see is in poor feather condition, but occasionally you will be told that a hawk has 'a few broken tips' and will arrive to find that it has primaries of about two inches in length and no tail whatsoever. Such a hawk cannot be flown until it has gone through a moult.

If you decide that the hawk is worth the asking price, buy it without further ado. If it is not, point out its defects and either ask for a reduction in price or leave it well alone—according to the circumstances. Some people do not appreciate your giving their hawk a thorough once-over, maintaining that you should take their word for it. However, once you have taken the hawk and left the premises, you have no come-back as you have accepted the bird in the condition in which you saw it. If you were buying a car, you would first check that it was in good working order, and thus it is sensible to do likewise with a bird. Lastly, do not believe everything you are told about the prowess of the bird which you are buying. Rather like anglers and their tales about 'the one that got away', some falconers tend to exaggerate their hawk's former triumphs in the field. Take anything you are told about its previous training and ability with a large pinch of salt. You will find out soon enough if the bird has really taken hare or grouse or roe deer before from its attitude. Nine times out of ten, it will not even hop to the fist when you get it, either because its previous owner has been exercising his rights of salesmanship, or because it has not been flown since he decided to part with it and is consequently fat and lazy. The only way to ensure that the bird has really been flown before is to see it flying. I mention all this only in an attempt to avert disappointment. If the owner tells you the bird's flying weight bear in mind that his scales may be different to yours. However, most people want to train their hawk themselves from scratch so previous training should not be an important consideration when purchasing a bird. Ideally, you are better-off in the long run with an eyass which has never been trained before, for then you will know where you stand. Before you leave with the bird, ask what it has been accustomed to eating—if it has been fed exclusively on day-old chicks it may not be willing to eat beef to begin with.

58 'Casting' a Harris' Hawk

CASTING A HAWK (see fig. 58)

When you arrive home with your hawk, you will need someone to help you if the bird is to have jesses put on. Often it is a worthwhile precaution to replace old jesses too, if the hawk is already wearing some, in case they are worn. It is virtually a physical impossibility to jess a hawk by yourself unless it will sit completely still with a hood on, which is highly unlikely. You must therefore cast the bird and get the other person to hold it while you put on or change the jesses. Casting a hawk is sometimes difficult, and requires practice. There are basically two ways of doing it. Firstly, if the bird is in a box, you must reach in and grasp it firmly about both wings, holding the legs back, flat to the tail, with your fingers to prevent the hawk from footing you. Alternatively, you can take the box into the mews and allow the hawk to hop out in its own time on to a perch. Never tow a bird out of the box by one leg or wing, as you might damage it. When you cast a hawk, you can use a silk scarf around its shoulders and back to protect the bloom on its plumage from your fingers. If the hawk is on someone else's fist you can, if you are very quick, and if the other person can divert its attention, grab it from behind and lift it off the fist. Hawks tend to get wise to this method after a while, and will open their wings at the crucial moment and spoil it. With such birds, you must encourage them to bate off the fist, take hold of the legs and scoop up the wings to the closed position as best you can. This can be done by yourself but again it requires practice. When the bird has been cast, you can put on the jesses, bells, swivel and leash as explained in Chapter 3.

THE FALCONER'S KNOT

It is essential to learn how to tie a falconer's knot properly. Birds are extremely adept at untying careless knots—such as a couple of half-hitches. It is also necessary to tie up and to untie hawks quickly and easily with one hand. The knot is basically a quick-release knot with the end pulled through to prevent the bird from releasing itself. As a precaution I always tie two falconers' knots one after the other. I will explain the knot point by point (see fig. 59).

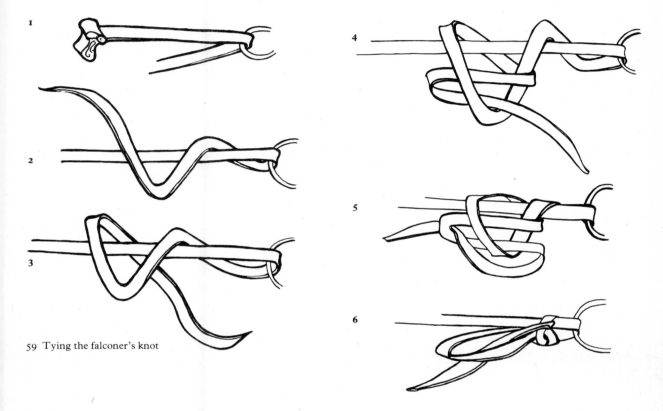

59 Tying the falconer's knot

1 With the bird held on your gloved hand, pass the free end of the leash down through the ring of the perch and back towards you. Hold it about half leash length up from the loose end with your first finger on top and your second finger underneath the line.
2 Put your thumb over the top of the leash which runs upwards from the ring across the palm of your hand to the bird and hook a loop beyond your fingers in the lower length of leash.
3 Pull the loop up and backwards and twist your thumb away from you.
4 Turn your hand up the other way and bring the line which is between your fingers up to meet the point of your thumb.
5 Pull a second loop through the first loop, and tighten it by pulling on the side of the loop which does *not* run through to the loose end.
6 Slide the loop down to the ring by pulling the end connected to the bird with your free hand, and pull tight before putting the loose end through the loop.
7 For extra security repeat the knot with the remainder of the loose end.
8 To release, pull out the free end, pull it sharply and the knot will undo.

This knot should be practised before you get a bird by holding the end which will be attached to the bird's swivel in your gloved hand. Do not use both hands at this stage to help you—you will not be able to do so when you have a bird sitting on the other one. Before you get your bird you should be able to tie this knot confidently with your eyes shut. Do not pull your knots too tight as you will have trouble undoing them.

I once had a kestrel which could undo two falconer's knots and a half hitch. I called him Houdini. Fortunately most hawks are not quite as clever as this, but such a bird must have a strong spring clip on the ring of its block and a small ring on the end of its leash. It can then be clipped on.

It is always worth taking the time and trouble to check a knot if you are at all in doubt. The loss of a bird with jesses, swivel and leash is usually fatal, as it can easily get caught up in a tree where it will hang upside down and die.

SETTLING IN THE NEW ARRIVAL

Once the bird has been jessed, put it in a semi-darkened mews or room to settle down after its journey. Some falconers like to start getting a new arrival sitting on the fist immediately, but if a bird has just been travelling, I feel it is better to leave it alone to recover from the journey. Later it will be more amenable and consequently progress will be quicker. When left alone in a quiet place it will soon relax and concentrate its attention on pulling at its new jesses. Leave it in peace for an hour or so and then throw it some food. It might well ignore it, but if it does eat it this shows that the bird is beginning to settle in. At this stage you should not be concerned about feeding it off the fist. Primarily it is important that it should enjoy a good feed in its new surroundings. If it refuses to eat even after you have left it alone with food, do not worry. It is obviously not hungry now, but it will probably eat the next day. Later on in the day, you can start getting

60 The Changeable Hawk Eagle enjoying a shower on a hot day

(a)

(b)

it to sit on the fist, and if it makes progress you can put it outside after an hour or so and offer it a bath. Some birds love bathing and will dive straight in and start splashing about. Others will only bath in very hot weather, and some will not bath at all. If such a bird gets very soiled feathers, it can be sprinkled lightly with a hose pipe on a hot day (see fig. 60) if it is well manned. Some birds enjoy this very much and will open their wings and turn this way and that to absorb the flow of water, while others loathe it and must just be given a quick soak and left to preen themselves clean. Birds which like to bathe must be offered a bath every morning before flying, leaving them time to dry out thoroughly. Most falcons particularly like regular baths, and will not fly as well without one. Desert falcons prefer dust baths. No bird should be allowed to get soaking wet in the late afternoon, as it will not be dry before nightfall and consequently it will not sleep if it is really wet on the body and under the wings, and it may also catch a chill. In cases of extreme emergency, a wet bird can be dried off with a hairdryer on a low setting.

During the days which follow you must occupy yourself with the business of manning your hawk. Obviously a bird which has already been handled and flown by another falconer will only need a little manning to grow used to you and the area in which you live. Such a bird can then be taken through the early stages of feeding from the fist and jumping fairly rapidly. A hawk which has never been handled before will need much more attention. You must start in easy stages—first sitting still, encouraging it to stand upright on the fist, and replacing it gently with your ungloved hand every time it bates. Some hawks will climb back on to the fist after a bate from the outset, but the majority take more time to master this and will hang suspended by their ankles until you pick them up.

A bird can be picked up in one of two ways—with the hand placed on the chest, just above the legs, or on the back just above the tail. This will largely depend which way round the bird is hanging after the bate. Some birds, particularly falcons and eagles, will try to bite your hand as you pick them up. Although you may be sorely tempted to let them hang after they have sunk their beak into your rescuing hand umpteen times, you should not leave any bird to hang for more than a few moments before you replace it gently and patiently on the fist. If necessary, you can always wear a thin right-hand glove to protect your long-suffering hand. Should you at any time receive a cut which is deeper than just a scratch, always wash it and put some antiseptic cream on it. Bird's beaks and feet are not always spotlessly clean, and a cut may well become infected. This is not only extremely painful, but if it is on a finger, it will also hinder you during the day-to-day processes of tying and untying your bird.

There is a right way and a wrong way to pick a bird up off its block. The wrong way is to march in and untie the bird and then scoop it up on to the fist. If it bates while you are untying it you are more than likely to lose it. The right way is to make in slowly, pick up the leash in your ungloved hand and use it to transfer the jesses into your gloved hand. Take the bird up onto the fist. Correctly, a hawk should step backwards on to the fist after the back of its legs have been touched with the glove, but in practice it may hop up forwards as soon as the fist is presented. At this early stage, many birds will bate away, in which case they must be scooped up as quickly and efficiently as possible. Next, wrap a turn of the leash around your little gloved finger. This acts as a security lock while you are untying the bird. You can then untie the bird and wrap the leash around your fingers in the correct manner. Some people split their leash in half and then wrap it around their lower gloved fingers. I can see little advantage in splitting the leash in this way—if you pull the wrong end accidentally

61 Golden Eagle during early stages of training

when you want to tie your bird up, you will pull the leash right out of the swivel.

Similarly, when you tie your hawk up, unwind the leash from your fingers; leave the lock around your little finger and keep the bird on the fist while you tie the knots. Keep your fist above the block to discourage the bird from bating towards the perch. Do *not* let your bird hop onto the block and then tie it up. If it bates you might lose it, or alternatively it might foot you while you are trying to tie it down. Footing, incidentally, is something with which most falconers become painfully familiar in the early stages. It is the action of throwing out one or both feet and latching on firmly or snatching with the talons—employing the same action as a hawk uses when grabbing its quarry. This use of the feet is used by a hawk as an alternative to biting when directed towards a human being. It is usually aimed at the ungloved hand, which is probably performing some irritating form of motion, such as attempting to stroke the bird's chest, scratching your nose, or, indeed, tying a knot. The resulting wounds, should the hawk have quicker reactions than you, will be exceedingly painful, and often quite deep.

HELPFUL HINTS

There are a couple of choice hints which I will mention here to help during the early stages with the more stubborn individuals which you may encounter. Firstly, a time saver. With a bird which will eat on its block but refuses to eat on the fist, put it back on its block and let it settle. Then make in slowly with the food in your outstretched fist and rest your fist, at arm's length, on the block. The bird should eventually bend its head to pull at the meat, and, after a few mouthfuls, you can raise your fist as it pulls and it will step up.

Secondly, a note to help you to get an awkward bird to jump. Put the bird, still tethered, on the ground beside its block, and put your fist on the block. When the bird hops up on its block to sit, as it will do quickly for birds do not generally like to sit on the ground, it will land on your fist and see the food. After a couple of goes at this it will connect the food with the act of jumping, and it should be a simple step to get it to jump from the block to the fist. If this does not work, you can reverse the process by throwing the bird a little bit of meat onto the ground. After it has hopped down to get it, you can repeat the process by laying your fist on the ground with the food, and the bird will then hop down to the ground and come on to the fist to get the food. Such methods, which incidentally rely on the fact that the bird is, at least, keen for its food, may sound somewhat far-fetched and unnecessary, but they have worked for me in the past when I have despaired of ever getting a certain bird to take the plunge and jump the few inches down from block to fist.

Thirdly, a useful hint which I discovered quite by accident when I was flying a hawk, very late in the evening. This particular bird was a female kestrel which I had been flying for three days. She had been very slow off the mark previously, and was not progressing as fast as I would have liked. However, that evening I took her out and, despite the fact that it was beginning to get dark, she flew like a rocket, coming to the lure the full length of the creance when on the previous day she had refused to come further than about 20 feet. I was delighted, but puzzled by this sudden change of spirit. The next day I took her out late again and she was again much improved. Later it occurred to me that the reason for the sudden improvement at dusk was probably because in its wild state, if a hawk has not made a kill as dusk approaches, it must redouble its efforts to do so before it gets dark, or else it will go hungry. Since then, I have tested this theory with a number of difficult hawks, and have enjoyed a similar degree of success in most cases. I feel, therefore, that it is certainly worth a try with a stubborn bird, but only when it is still on a creance. If you fly a bird loose at this time of night and lose it, it will be dark before you can retrieve it.

WEIGHING

When your hawk will sit on the fist while you are stationary, you can start taking it for walks, accustoming it to all manner of different things. It must be weighed daily, and a record kept of its weight. Teaching a bird to sit on the scales often requires much patience. If it will not sit still you cannot get an accurate weight. Until it will sit properly on the scales you must not start reducing its weight as it is important to have a note of its top weight before you start cutting it down for flying. Do not weigh a bird in the morning until it has cast, or once again, you will not get an accurate weight. It is best always to weigh your bird at the same time every day, which should be just before flying. I will give a rough guide as to the amount of food various birds eat daily when at flying weight. I must stress, though, that this is only intended as a very approximate guide. Each species and every individual varies and thus I cannot be more specific:

Kestrel, merlin and sparrowhawks	1–2 oz
Buzzard	3–4 oz
Large falcons	2–4 oz
Large hawks	4–5 oz
Small eagles	4–6 oz
Large eagles	6–9 oz

(a) 'Oh, you want me, do you?'

(b) 'I'll have to think about it'

(c) 'I must just scratch this itch'

(d) 'Oh, all right, if you insist'

Through weighing both your bird and the amount which you feed it daily, and keeping a record of food given, weight and daily achievement, you will be able to establish how much food is necessary for it to put on a little weight, to lose a little weight, and to hold it steady. Each bird is different in this respect, and the appropriate amounts will vary again when the bird starts doing some work, whereupon it will burn the food up and will consequently need slightly more to hold it steady. Experienced falconers can judge a hawk's condition by feeling its breastbone, but this should not be attempted by a beginner.

Once you consider your bird is reasonably steady on the fist you can start feeding it off the fist and getting it jumping. The training from here onwards is described in the next part of the book. I have divided it up into chapters on the various families and groups, including notes on the individual species. Although the basic training is very much the same for any hawk, the different groups have their own idiosyncrasies and abilities and it is these that I wish to discuss in as much depth as possible.

62 Female Peregrine Falcon on a creance

8 The Kestrel

The European Kestrel (*falco tinnunculus*) is one of the most common of all falcons. Originally a bird of the countryside, it is now extending its range and breeding habitat into urban areas, and nesting pairs can now be found in the centres of large cities.

It is the easiest to recognize of all birds of prey. Its characteristic hovering motion, which earned it the country name of 'windhover', is a familiar sight near motorways. To watch a kestrel hovering is to be privileged to see one of the most astonishing performances in the world of nature. On pointed wings, with piercing eyes scanning the ground below, the kestrel is able to maintain its poise with head motionless in the face of the strongest blustering winds, with a precision and ease that is scarcely believable when you consider the physical difficulties involved.

63 The author with two eyass kestrels

Measuring only 12 to 14 inches, the kestrel is not a large bird, but its wing span of about 24 inches makes it appear much bigger in flight. The sexes are easily distinguishable in adult plumage (as immatures they are virtually identical) for although they are both brown above with flecked creamy underparts, the adult male has a blue-grey head and tail with a spotted chestnut back, and the female is brown all over with black bars on her back and tail. They often lay in an old crow's or magpie's nest, but also in holes in trees, on ledges, and even in window boxes. The eggs, between four and seven, are laid from April on, and are brown-marbled in appearance. The male brings the food to the female and then incubates while she feeds. The incubation period is 28 days and the young normally leave the nest after a further 28–32 days. Persecuted by gamekeepers and poisoned by pesticides in the late 1950s, their recovery has been impressive and their status in Britain and Europe is now reasonably secure.

In falconry circles, the kestrel is widely recommended as the beginner's bird, being commonly bred in captivity, comparatively inexpensive, and relatively easy to handle. I do not agree, however, that a kestrel should be a first bird because it takes experience to judge its correct flying weight. A kestrel weighs between 6 and 9 ounces and usually only needs to lose half to one ounce to be at its flying weight. If the weight is dropped even a quarter of an ounce too low, the effects can be disastrous. Thus it is not uncommon for a male kestrel to refuse to fly at $6\frac{1}{4}$ ounces, fly well at 6 ounces, and be dead at $5\frac{3}{4}$ ounces. The beginner is far better advised to start with a larger bird, such as a buzzard, which will give him a greater safety margin. Once accustomed to recording a bird's daily weight, and judging its performance accordingly, the beginner can try keeping a kestrel with some confidence.

In my experience, kestrels fall into two categories; those which are so responsive that it is quite easy to get them stooping to a lure within a week; and those which look as though they would rather sit and starve to death than budge an inch. Unfortunately, the majority seem to be of the latter type. There is no way of telling when purchasing your bird which category it belongs to; it is just a question of luck. I do, however, recommend a first-year kestrel rather than one that has had someone else attempting to fly it. In fact, this is a good rule to apply to the purchase of most birds of prey. An apparently trained bird will frequently have learned nothing from its previous owner except some rather bad habits.

Kestrels can often be tricky to get feeding from the fist, and much patience is required to overcome this reluctance. I have found it a good idea to take the bird and its food indoors on the fist, and then to ignore it unless it bates. I sit and watch television or read a book, while the bird makes up its own mind that I am not going to hurt it as soon as it turns its attention away from me. Sooner or later, it will start to pull at the meat, but if it is really stubborn, leave it with its food on its block and watch from a discreet distance until it starts to eat—which it invariably will as soon as you are out of sight—and then, after it has consumed a few mouthfuls, go and pick it up with the meat. Usually it will continue to eat almost immediately, for having got the taste of the meat it will be unable to resist the temptation. As soon as the bird is feeding readily from the fist, you should start weighing it daily, keeping a record of both the weight of the bird and the weight of its food. Kestrels normally need three-quarters to one ounce of meat each day, to keep them at a steady weight, and slightly less to drop them to flying-weight, but these amounts are only approximate since each bird is different.

Once your bird is feeding from the fist with confidence, the next step is to get it jumping. Initially, this may be done while it is still tethered to its

64 The correct position for the gloved hand
when calling a hawk to the fist

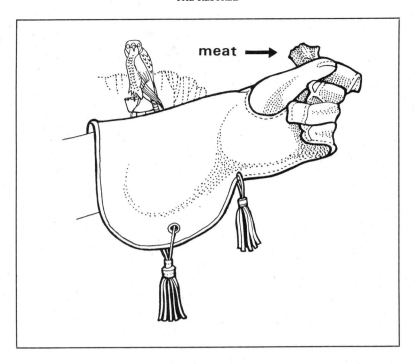

block. The aim is to get it to jump a couple of inches to take a piece of meat from your fist. The best method is to crouch on the ground with your side towards the bird, and your gloved hand outstretched a few inches above the height of the block. Hold the meat firmly between your thumb and forefinger and encourage the kestrel to jump towards you (see fig. 64). It may be necessary to attract the bird's attention by wiggling the meat, tapping your fist with a finger of your other hand, and whistling softly. Do not allow your fist to stray close enough to the kestrel to let it snatch the meat or it will spend the next ten minutes leaning precariously off the block while trying to grab the meat without jumping. It is advisable to cut a kestrel's meat into long slivers so that they can be swallowed in one, or easily pulled to pieces. Kestrels are fussy eaters, and if the pieces are too large or too tough they will spend ages, however keen they are, picking delicately at their meat in an infuriating manner.

Keep a hold on the meat when the bird lands and pick up the jesses immediately to stop it grabbing the meat and taking off again. When it is jumping the length of its leash, a light creance can be attached to the swivel with a falconer's knot, and—with one foot on the line at all times—you can start to increase the distance, and to move the daily training sessions to your chosen flying site. As the length of the flight is increased, make sure that the grass is cut very short in the area where you are flying the bird, as the effort of pulling even a light line through long grass will soon prove too much.

Once a kestrel will come approximately six feet instantly to the fist, it can be introduced to the lure, which should be made up for a kestrel as described under the section on lures in Chapter 3. The meat tied onto the lure may either be a large enough chunk to allow the bird to pull off mouthfuls each time it catches the lure, or a series of small pieces that can be consumed immediately and then replaced for the next flight. The first step in this new stage of the training is to get the kestrel to associate the lure with food. Introduce the lure while your kestrel is on its block on the weathering ground. Drop the lure, with the meat firmly attached, onto the

65 Male kestrel
mantling over lure

ground next to the block. By twitching the lure to draw attention to the meat, encourage the bird to hop down and eat from the lure. Repeat the process until the kestrel bates at the lure as soon as it is produced. When it is thus showing instant recognition of the lure, move the training session back to the flying ground again. Hold the lure stick in your gloved hand and the lure line in the other, then drop the lure on the ground a few feet from the flying post. If the kestrel ignores it, either pick it up and drop it again, or jerk the lure to attract the bird's attention, being careful to ensure that the meat is easily visible. When the kestrel lands on the lure, keep hold of the lure line, keep your foot on the creance, and 'make in'—meaning crouch down on the ground and edge slowly towards the bird, so as not to frighten it. If it does take fright, it may try to fly off, with or without the lure. If it flies away with the lure, this can become a vice later on known as 'carrying', when the bird, flying free, catches the lure and attempts to fly off with it to eat it in a more secluded place—a particularly irritating habit which can be avoided by correct management in the early stages. As you reach the kestrel, you should have ready in your fist a piece of meat which serves as a pick-up piece. Place your fist over the lure and encourage the bird to step up, taking the jesses and putting the lure in your bag. Replace the bird on its post and gradually increase the distance until it is coming quickly from about 15 yards. Now try hanging the lure about eight inches above the ground; if the kestrel lands on the ground below the meat, rather than taking it in flight, lower the meat so that it can reach up to it. As it does this, drop the lure onto the ground so that it can take the food, and make in. Eventually, or you may have been lucky first time, the kestrel will hit the lure as it hangs in mid-air. Again, drop the line immediately so that it can take the meat. Once it is coming quickly from 50 yards and taking the lure in the air, you can start swinging the lure (see Chapter 4) and trying to get your bird to make a pass. You begin this next stage in training by pulling the lure out of the bird's flight path as it approaches. Try to avoid having trees behind you, since a kestrel will often head straight for a tree as soon as the lure is removed from its path. In open ground a kestrel will either come to land somewhere beyond you, or, and this is what you are hoping for, fly on a short distance and turn back towards the lure. On the second approach, it should be allowed to take the lure on the ground. When the bird is turning back to the lure it is ready to be flown free. When flying a bird free for the first time it is advisable to have someone else present to help keep the bird in sight should something go wrong. Take off the creance, the swivel and the mews jesses, and insert flying jesses in the aylmeri holes (see Chapter 3). Never fly your kestrel free for the first time on its initial flight of the day; always give it a flight to the lure on the creance first. Call it off a slightly shorter distance for the first free flight, and make in slowly as usual when it is on the lure.

From now on it is simply a matter of working the bird to increase the number of stoops to the lure, but take things gently and allow the bird to catch the lure—on the ground or, preferably, in the air—as soon as it shows signs of tiring. When you intend the kestrel to take the lure in the air, swing the lure faster and throw it upwards to encourage the bird to climb to take it. It may miss the lure and follow it down to the ground, but this is only an error in timing on the bird's part, and it will improve with practice. Most falconers use a call to indicate to the bird that it can take the lure the next time it comes in. The traditional call is 'Ho!' However, do not use the call every time you are going to let the bird catch the lure or it will soon get the habit of not coming unless it hears the call.

European kestrels cannot generally speaking be used for hunting and are, therefore, not strictly falconry birds. I have known one person who had a kestrel that took a pigeon, and I myself have taken sparrows with a good kestrel, but these experiences are the exception rather than the rule. Most falconers, however, though they may not like to admit it, have flown a kestrel at some time, with a great deal of enjoyment. In my opinion, the beginner who has already flown a buzzard can then learn a lot from these little birds, which will be of particular value if you hope eventually to train a larger longwing or a merlin. Do not, therefore, miss out on training a kestrel as your second bird.

Before concluding this chapter, I would like to point out that there are some 13 different species of kestrel, 14 if you include the Red-footed Falcon (*Falco vespertinus*), and many subspecies. When trained for falconry, many of these would probably perform much as our European kestrel does. I have only heard reports of two other species being trained. One is the American Kestrel (*Falco sparverius*) which is the smallest of the kestrel race. Apparently these little birds put up a good performance to the lure, and can, in some cases, be persuaded to take sparrows, starlings and even doves. The other is the Nankeen Kestrel (*Falco cenchroides*) of Australia, which is apparently far more ambitious than our native kestrel. An Australian falconer, Egon Russell, told me that he regularly took quail with his Nankeen. Unfortunately I know of only one Nankeen Kestrel in Britain, and he is, at the time of writing, 18 years old and resides in the Zoological Gardens of Regents Park, London.

9 The Buzzards

66 Common or European Buzzard: the ideal beginner's bird

The Common or European Buzzard was once one of the commonest hawks to be found in Britain, and was universally distributed throughout the country. However, the buzzard not only suffered as other British raptors from the use of pesticides and vicious attacks by game-keepers in the 1950s and 1960s, it also had to contend with myxomatosis, which came to Britain in 1952. This hit the buzzards very hard as rabbit formed the mainstay of their diet. Unfortunately the reduction of the rabbit population was not the only ill-effect of this dreadful disease. Some pairs ceased to breed at all, while others laid smaller clutches, among which there was a higher proportion of addled eggs. Fortunately the buzzard survived the onslaught and is now steadily increasing in numbers. The population seems secure in Wales and Scotland, but in England buzzards are found mainly in the West Country, although they are creeping back into the south-east in certain areas, and there is no ecological reason why the population should not spread further if allowed to do so.

In flight, buzzards can be easily recognized, wheeling in large circles on rounded wings. Measuring 19–22 inches, the buzzard is usually dark brown on the back, with varying proportions of white and brown on the chest, although many different colour phases have been observed. The sexes are distinguished by size, the larger female weighing up to one pound more than the male. They eat a varied diet which includes rabbit, small birds, rodents, a few reptiles and occasionally even carrion.

The breeding cycle is controlled by the photo-period (daylength). Buzzards add annually to their original nests, which are normally in trees, although in many areas of Scotland, they nest on cliffs. The nests themselves are substantial structures, liberally decorated with greenery or heather. The two to four eggs are laid in April and are incubated by both sexes, with the female taking the major share. The incubation period takes 34 days, and the young remain in the nest for 50–55 days.

The *Buteo* family, as a whole, is useful to falconers. There is great variation in size and colour between the different subspecies, and similarly tremendous variation in the performance of different types when trained for falconry, but if all the buzzards have one thing in common it is their steadiness in the hands of the most inexperienced handler. For this reason, they are ideally suited as beginners' birds. Different countries have different native subspecies, some of which, like the Red-tailed Buzzard of North America, make better falconry birds than others.

Britain's Common Buzzard (*Buteo buteo*) is not as ambitious in terms of performance as its larger American cousin. However, it is undoubtedly the best of the British raptors for beginners. Buzzards have several points in their favour; firstly, they are reasonably tough, and can withstand a certain amount of mismanagement, in terms of finding their flying weight, and will often respond to initial efforts to fly them while still well above their correct flying weight. Similarly, if their weight is dropped too low, the warning signs of lethargy and sitting 'fluffed up' will be quickly apparent, whereas a kestrel undergoing proportionately the same drop in weight would be dead. Secondly, buzzards are blessed with relatively even temperaments, and the work put into manning a buzzard is quickly rewarded. Additional points in their favour are that they are not easy to lose, being larger than a kestrel and working reasonably close to the falconer, and you do also stand a chance of eventually being able to hunt a buzzard.

At our Centre, students on falconry courses are taught how to train Common Buzzards. I have in the past, therefore, worked approximately 30 buzzards up to the stage of flying free, and I have never encountered one which has not responded reasonably quickly to training. As these birds were a variety of ages, some imprinted and some non-imprinted, and from varying backgrounds, I am of the opinion that an 'untrainable' buzzard is indeed a rare occurrence. I sympathize with people who have in the past come across a totally unresponsive kestrel or eagle, or some other variety of raptor, but I am sure that if a buzzard refuses to progress, it is normally due to a mistake on the part of the falconer rather than to stubbornness on the part of the bird.

A first year ABCR buzzard, if available, is ideal for the average beginner, although a buzzard of any age can be trained fairly easily. Here though, I must point out the relative merits of imprinted and non-imprinted buzzards—a non-imprinted buzzard will not scream incessantly, a distinct advantage if you have close neighbours or sensitive ear-drums, but with an imprinted bird you stand a much better chance of eventually being able to hunt with it. This has been proven many times, and imprinted buzzards have taken rabbit, moorhen, squirrel, rat and even woodpigeon. I am not saying that non-imprinted buzzards will never hunt, but that I have in the past seen and heard of more success with imprints.

Buzzards can usually be manned quite quickly, depending on how much time you are able to devote to them. They are frequently described as lazy, but this is normally because the correct flying weight has not been obtained. A fat male bird will weigh approximately 2 lb–2 lb 4 oz, and will normally fly at 1 lb 8 oz–1 lb 12 oz depending on the size of the individual. The average female will weigh 2 lb 4 oz–2 lb 12 oz when at top weight, and will fly at 1 lb 14 oz–2 lb 2 oz. Do bear in mind, though, that there are always exceptions. I have known a male buzzard which flew at 1 lb 4¾ oz, and I have heard of a fat female which weighed in at 3 lb 2 oz! When you first get a buzzard, if it is at an in-between weight, and you are not sure of its sex, it is worth taking the time to feed it up to see how heavy it will go, to try to determine the sex.

The initial process of gradual reduction in weight, jumping to the fist, and flying on a creance are exactly the same as described in the chapter on the training of the kestrel. But, unlike a kestrel which is put onto a lure when it will come six feet or so to the fist, a buzzard must be flown free to the fist before it is put on to a rabbit lure, and so the distance flown on a creance to the fist must be increased. Do not push a buzzard too far too quickly. If you increase the distance of each flight too rapidly, you may find that the bird will veer off as it comes towards you and settle on the ground or in a tree. The latter is particularly irritating as the business of untangling the creance and pulling the buzzard out of the tree will undoubtedly destroy the confidence of both the bird and the falconer for the rest of that particular training session. When your buzzard will come to you immediately at the sight of your raised fist from a distance of 50 yards or so, it is ready to be flown free. Once your buzzard is flying free to the fist, you must start casting it from the fist into trees. Buzzards are short-winged hawks or 'birds of the fist', and they hunt directly from the fist or out of a tree. It is harder to get a shortwing fit than a longwing, as a longwing can be stooped to a lure, with the number of stoops increased every day, while a shortwing can only be flown from point A to point B. Trees are therefore essential to serve as point B while the falconer's fist serves as point A. To cast a bird properly from the fist takes practice in order to achieve accuracy and good timing, rather like timing a golf swing. Take a good hold on the jesses and bring your gloved fist out to the side of your body. Propel the bird gently through a 45-degree angle, opening your fist to release the jesses when your arm is nearly at full stretch. Buzzards are notoriously 'sticky-footed', meaning that they grip tightly to the glove with clenched feet even if they want to let go. If this happens, gently twisting the fist back and forth will often loosen the feet, but occasionally the talons must be individually prised open with the ungloved hand, before the bird can be sufficiently loose-footed and balanced for casting. I have a male buzzard which is so sticky-footed that he will try to fly out of a tree while still holding firmly to the branches with one or both feet. Before you cast your bird, you must know which branch of the tree you want it to land on, as this will help you to aim the bird correctly. Check too that you are casting it into the wind, as aerodynamically it is extremely difficult for a bird to take off or land with the wind behind it.

When your buzzard lands in a tree, it will undoubtedly take longer to return to the fist than it did when flying from a post. You must be persistent, and in a few days it should fly to a tree, land and come straight out to the fist again as soon as you call. If it does not, then drop a further half ounce or so off its weight. Once you can cast your buzzard successfully into trees and call it out quickly at a distance of 100 yards, it is ready to be introduced to the lure. The process of flying to a lure should be condensed into as short a time as possible, as otherwise a buzzard will quickly become lure-bound, and will never show any interest in live quarry. You should, therefore, only fly your bird to the lure for two or three flights a day, and the whole process of training a bird to fly to the lure should only take about one week, depending on the species of buzzard and the individual bird. If the bird is keen, the progression through the stages of lure flying should be remarkably quick.

A rabbit lure should be used for a buzzard (see fig. 35), with the meat tied firmly to the head end. It is advisable to put your buzzard back on the creance for this new stage, and return to your original flying post. Keeping hold of the lure line, drop the lure a few feet in front of the post, ensuring that the meat is clearly visible. If necessary, twitch the line to attract the bird's attention. Eventually, the bird will fly down to take the meat. If it lands on the ground, twitch the line again to encourage the buzzard to foot it, and allow it to eat. Make in slowly, crouching down and keeping hold of both the creance and the lure line. Offer the bird a pick-up piece, held firmly in your gloved hand, and encourage it to step up. Remove the lure and place it in your bag. The distance can now be increased to maybe four feet or further, depending on how quickly the buzzard came the first time. When the bird will fly quickly to the lure as soon as it is thrown out on to the ground, at a distance of 20 feet, you can start to move the lure by pulling the lure line as the bird flies towards it, first at walking pace, and then, as the bird's timing improves, start running with the lure. The second the bird touches the lure, stop dead, because if you tow your bird along on the lure it will lead to broken tail feathers and loss of confidence. Admittedly, a real rabbit might well tow a buzzard latched on its back a short distance, but this is not something to simulate with the lure at this stage.

When the bird is responding well, the creance can be removed, and within a day or two, the buzzard should be flown to the lure from trees. This is as far as some people ever have any hopes of going with a Common Buzzard; however, for those who wish to try to get a buzzard fit for hunting, or for those who hope to progress to a Red-tailed Buzzard or some other more promising sub-species, I will explain how to get a *Buteo* fit for entering.

Assuming that your buzzard is now flying free to the fist and to the lure, and is coming readily out of trees, you must give thought to the fact that it requires a great deal more effort to catch a wild rabbit than it does to catch a rabbit lure dragged by a person. It also requires sharper reflexes, and indeed, a better idea of what a real rabbit looks like. You must remember that from your buzzard's point of view, all it has had to do up to this stage is watch you to see where you are going to throw out the lure, so if you were to take your buzzard out into the hunting field at this point, it would be more than likely to ignore a live rabbit simply because it would not have meat tied round its neck, with a length of line attached and a human pulling it.

To overcome these difficulties, there are several things that you must do. Firstly, stop using a rabbit lure with meat tied to it, and start, whenever possible, using a dead rabbit on a long length of creance. Secondly, to get your bird fit, try putting it into a tree and going for a long walk, encouraging it to follow you from tree to tree by whistling, and calling it down to the fist periodically. If your bird will not do this, it will be much harder to get it fit, as you will only be able to increase the distance and number of the flights that you give it daily. While your bird is getting fit and learning to recognize a dead rabbit, you must also concentrate on sharpening its reflexes. The best way that I have found to do this is to introduce the element of surprise. Persuade a friend or relation to hide the lure and themselves, and to pull the rabbit out of some bushes or some grass by a long lure line while you are walking with the bird on the fist. This will teach the bird that it will not necessarily be flying from a tree or a perch to your fist or you pulling the line, but will in fact be flying from your fist to the rabbit. In the wild, buzzards will also 'still-hunt'—they will sit in trees and wait for a rabbit to come out below. Although this is rather boring for a falconer to watch, a shortwing must still be taught to look for quarry while it is in a tree. This is best done by arranging the lure so that the line runs off the rabbit and round a peg which is placed in the ground about 20 yards further on. You can then put your bird in a tree and pull the line round the peg so that you and the rabbit are going in opposite directions (see fig. 35). This is a useful method to use if you have no one to help you with the lure, as it removes the connection in the bird's mind of you running with the lure following you. When your bird is flying strongly on the wing without getting too out of breath after half a dozen flights at the lure and fist and is spotting the lure quickly from the fist and from trees, in a variety of different places and circumstances, it is then as ready as it will ever be to be entered at quarry.

Make sure that you have permission to hunt over land as hunting a hawk over someone's land without permission can lead to a prosecution for poaching. A few days before you want to enter your hawk, it is advisable to ask the landowner to walk over the fields with you to show you where you can go and also where the rabbits are usually found. If you can find an area where the rabbits are suffering from myxomatosis, it is very advantageous. The disease itself will not harm your hawk, and afflicted rabbits make easy first kills for a hawk, building its confidence and enthusiasm. There are few things more disappointing than going out day after day with a hawk, missing kill after kill and becoming disillusioned.

The day before you intend to enter your hawk, only give it a couple of flights, and reduce the usual amount of food by half. It is worth waiting for a fine day as rabbits will not usually appear in the wet. Do not expect too much. If your hawk puts up a decent chase on the first quarry sighted, then you are extremely lucky. Remember that the chase is more important than the kill, and that success need not necessarily be measured in the number of kills. It will depend not just on your hawk, but on your area, the number of rabbits around, the time of year, and the amount of cover. If, however, you do not have a kill in the first three or four hunting trips, it is best to call a halt for a few days so that your hawk does not get bored and spend longer in trees, flying only half-heartedly.

THE RED-TAILED BUZZARD (*Buteo jamaicensis*)

The Red-tail has a very high potential as a general-purpose hawk, which can be used successfully at varied quarry. They are mainly successful at ground quarries, particularly rabbit, and females are quite capable of taking and holding a brown hare. Occasionally, and without any encouragement from the falconer, they will fly pheasant. They will start from the fist as though after a rabbit, and attempt to take a pheasant just as it gets up off the ground. Usually, the pheasant will pull away fairly quickly in flight, but if it should decide to put into cover again, the Red-tail will pitch above and wait for the falconer to re-flush the quarry. With the advantages of height and expectation, the hawk will usually manage to take the pheasant on the second attempt.

A male Red-tail will fly at approximately 1 lb 14 oz–2 lb 5 oz, and a female at 2 lb 6 oz–3 lb 3 oz, although there are, according to Frank L. Beebe, 14 different sub-species among which there is considerable variation in size. The largest female I have heard of tipped the scales at 4 lb 12 oz. In America, the Red-tail is referred to as the Red-tailed Hawk, which is both incorrect and confusing.

67 Red-tailed Buzzard

I think very highly of Red-tails, as, in contrast to the goshawk, they are amiable and they remain tame through the period while they are put down to moult. They can, in fact, be flown through the moult if so desired but will take considerably longer to complete it.

THE FERRUGINOUS BUZZARD (*Buteo regalis*)

These buzzards from western North America are slightly larger than the Red-tail, males flying at 2 lb 3 oz–3 lb 2 oz, and females at 3 lb 4 oz–4 lb 12 oz. A fat female can weigh over 5 lb. Once again some Americans refer to the Ferruginous incorrectly as a hawk. Some American naturalists feel that the Ferruginous should be re-classified as a true eagle (*aquila*) because it resembles an eagle both in habits and structure including its feet which are feathered right down to the toes. The Ferruginous which I have flown have, without exception, proved excellent after quarry. Initially they were more difficult to man than a typical *Buteo*, but once flying free they were easy to enter. They have a surprising turn of speed off the fist. Imprinted females can be particularly aggressive. Both sexes have proportionately small feet, but they are very powerful. Rabbit and moorhen are the quarries most easily taken. In their wild state they take pheasant, partridge and chukar, but trained birds need a close slip to take game. Ferruginous seldom perch in trees, preferring the ground as a natural perch. Consequently they have tremendous acceleration from the fist, pushing off with their long legs which are designed to give them spring to help them off the ground. My Ferruginous will often go off of her own accord to soar over the terrain in search of quarry, returning instantly to the fist on a whistle.

68 Ferruginous Buzzard

Although they are worthwhile hawks for any falconer, I would particularly recommend that anyone who wishes to train an eagle should attempt to train a female Ferruginous first, to experience something of the size and temperament which are similar to those of a Tawny or Steppe Eagle.

HARRIS' HAWK (*Parabuteo unicinctus*)

Sometimes referred to as the Bay-winged Hawk, the Harris' Hawk is extremely responsive when used for falconry. It is often described as the ideal 'weekend falconer's' bird, for a variety of reasons. Firstly, once trained it does not need a great deal of exercise to stay fit. Secondly, its steadiness of temperament enables the falconer to pick it up, having not worked it at all during the week, take it straight out and enjoy two days of hunting. Obviously, though, if a Harris' Hawk can be hunted five or six days a week, the quality of the flights will be greatly improved for, like most hawks, the harder they are flown the better they perform. Harris' are very good-tempered and tame, and the females are particularly demonstrative, often developing little affectionate idiosyncrasies such as preening your hair or gently nibbling up and down the length of your fingers.

69 Harris' Hawk

They love bathing, and, like all birds of prey, should always be offered a bath in the mornings before flying. I once knew a falconer who did not offer his Harris' a bath prior to an afternoon's hunting. When cast off at a rabbit for the first flight of the day, his hawk sailed past the fortunate rabbit and headed with great deliberation for a little brook which flowed down the side of the field. It promptly had a good bath, after which it could not be flown but had to be carried on the fist for the rest of the afternoon's hawking.

Harris' Hawks are usually easy to enter, but may need a little encouragement to chase quarry initially. They will often soar and make a series of shallow stoops at flying game. Males fly at 1 lb 2 oz–1 lb 8 oz, and females at 1 lb 12 oz–2 lb 8 oz. Any doubts about the sex of a Harris' can be resolved by measuring the tail which is eight inches long in a male and ten inches long in a female. Males will take birds as small as sparrows (which should not be encouraged if you ever hope for your hawk to aspire to greater things) and they will also take quail, duck, pheasant, rabbit and squirrel. The females will also take such quarry and, according to the American falconers who fly large females, the occasional hare. In flight the sexes are very different; the males are much quicker on the turn by virtue of their size. They have astonishing powers of acceleration and they can also wait above cover in a motion best described as hovering. Often they will kill prey which they have followed right into cover. The females fly in a more deliberate manner in accordance with their size and power, but they too are capable of dramatic acceleration when in hot pursuit. On the whole they will not enter cover but will wait for the game to be reflushed. Generally speaking, the males are more stylish and versatile, whereas the females are steadier and more reliable. An interesting point is that when flown in a cast with a female, a male is often more ambitious than usual in the size of the quarry he will chase. This phenomenon can probably be attributed to their gregarious behaviour in the wild state.

According to the American falconers, Harris' are notorious for being screamers. If taken as an eyass or a brancher, a Harris will certainly scream. More disconcertingly, they will also be screamers if taken as passagers up to one month after leaving the nest. A healthy Harris' can safely be flown through the moult, and if kept on a high quality diet and flown as fat as is reasonably possible, it will moult out cleanly. A Harris' in poor feather should be put down to moult to ensure perfect results, as should all hawks.

70 Honey Buzzard

71 Broad-winged Hawk

72 Long-legged Buzzard   (a) Sighting a rabbit   (b) In hot pursuit

(c) Smack!   (d) 'Blast, missed it!'

When taken up after the moult they will retrain quickly, often at a slightly heavier weight than previously, and they will have lost none of their characteristic tameness. They breed relatively easily in captivity, but the greatest care must be taken if you hope to avoid imprinting.

Harris' Hawks are often compared to goshawks. My opinion is that someone who can work a hawk every day will get better results from the faster goshawk than from a Harris', but for those who can only hunt a hawk at weekends, a Harris' is infinitely preferable. They are undoubtedly one of the best shortwings used for falconry, combining the hunting ability of an accipiter with the temperament of a *Buteo*.

This covers the majority of the species of *Buteo* which are commonly flown. However, many other species have been flown. I have flown a Honey Buzzard and a Broadwinged Hawk (*Buteo platypterus*) to the fist only, and my husband Steve and I have also flown two female Long-legged Buzzards which would hunt at 2 lb 12 oz, and with which we have taken rabbit, moorhen and one pigeon (which I must admit was heavily in moult and missing many of its flight feathers!). These birds have also flown squirrel, blackbird and pheasant. Steve has flown two Upland Buzzards as well which took rabbit. I am reasonably confident that most species of buzzard from the size of the European upwards could be persuaded to hunt by a persevering falconer.

10 Sparrowhawks and Goshawks

73 Female sparrowhawk

Although the number of wild sparrowhawks in Britain declined considerably until the end of the 1960s, a relatively stable population now exists. Like the buzzard, it suffered from the effects of pesticides and from illegal persecution, but it has made a rapid and reassuring recovery in the last few years.

Wild Sparrowhawks (*Accipiter nisus*) tend to be elusive, due to their preference for woodland and particularly for conifer plantations. They are difficult to observe in their wild state because their method of hunting is very fast and precise, and even the keenest of ornithologists is lucky to catch more than a glimpse of a spar flitting along a hedgerow in pursuit of quarry. They prey on small birds such as finches, sparrows, blackbirds and chaffinches, but females can take prey up to the size of woodpigeon.

74 A female European Goshawk in mature plumage

There is a marked variation in both size and plumage between the male and female sparrowhawk; the males are considerably smaller, weighing 5–7oz, while the females weigh 10–11oz. Mature males have blue-grey backs with reddish cheeks and rufous underparts, heavily barred with dark brown, and long slate-grey tails barred with brown and tipped with white. The females have brown backs and buff cheeks and underparts, barred with brown. Both sexes have yellow eyes, becoming progressively more orange as the bird ages. The same breeding site is used every year, but a new nest is built annually by the female. As the breeding season approaches, soaring displays can be observed. The eggs are laid in a deep cup, lined with fresh twigs or chips of bark. Three to seven eggs are laid on alternate days. The female incubates for the entire 30 days, and is fed during this time by the male. The eggs hatch early to mid-June and the young will start feeding themselves when 18–21 days old. They are fully fledged and branching 28 days after hatching.

We can only hope that in the future the wild population of sparrowhawks will increase rather than decrease. The common belief that they present a threat to the rearing of gamebirds is, to a large extent, unfounded, as once poults are over four weeks of age, they are too large to be killed by a female sparrowhawk. Therefore, if young gamebirds are properly protected in their early weeks, gamekeepers should have nothing to fear from wild sparrowhawks.

There is only one other accipiter indigenous to the British Isles, namely, the European Goshawk (*Accipiter gentilis*). It is impossible to estimate the number of breeding pairs of goshawks in Britain. Like the osprey, the goshawk probably became virtually extinct in Britain in the early twentieth century, and is now struggling to re-establish itself in a very small way. Leslie Brown estimated in his book *British Birds of Prey* in 1976 that there are probably no more than ten pairs in the wild, and possibly none of these were regular breeders. Nowadays there are more pairs on record. Many of the total number of goshawks in Britain today can be attributed to losses from falconers, and to corroborate this, I have heard evidence that there is a pair on the Isle of Wight, the female of which still wears one bell and is consequently more often heard than seen.

The differences in coloration between the sexes are less marked than with the sparrowhawk, but the females are still considerably larger than the males, with up to one pound difference in weight between them. In mature plumage, the females are often more heavily barred than the males, and are generally browner in appearance.

Although goshawks are notable for their ability to kill large animals and birds, up to the size of hare and capercaillie, they will normally feed mainly on the commonest prey in their area, which in Britain is usually rabbit or the larger passerines. They always pluck their prey carefully before eating it, usually on the ground, whereas a sparrowhawk prefers a 'plucking post'.

Goshawks nest in woodland, and, like sparrowhawks, prefer coniferous plantations. The birds indulge in displays of soaring, slow wing flapping, and undulating flight, similar to the antics performed by sparrowhawks before nest-building. The nests themselves are broad flattish structures, lined with greenery and bark chips. Normally three to five eggs are laid, and they are incubated for 34 days by the female alone, who uses this time to undergo part of her annual moult, while the male feeds her. The eggs hatch in the beginning of June, and the young are fully feathered at 38 days.

The future of the British goshawk does not look particularly bright. It can only be re-established by a determined and prolonged effort, together with a more tolerant and law-abiding attitude on the part of gamekeepers

75 'Biggles'—a typical musket

and their employers. From the small nucleus which survives in Britain, we can only hope that the numbers will gradually increase, but at the moment it is not possible to assess accurately the goshawk's chances.

As falconry birds, sparrowhawks and goshawks are fairly easily obtainable. Neither of them are suitable for beginners, and, despite its larger size, I feel that the goshawk is easier to train than the sparrowhawk. Having said this, I must point out that although like most accipiters these birds will, when trained, make excellent hunting birds, neither of these species can strictly be described as easy in any stage of their early training. Before attempting to fly a gos or a spar, you should have had a variety of experience with other shortwings, certainly with a Common Buzzard, and preferably with a Red-Tail or similar.

Manning a spar or gos is extremely difficult, though normally the latter tends to be a shade more responsive. Both species are highly strung and are consequently prone to throwing fits, particularly as they are nearing the completion of the moult. The reason for this could be because they are very active birds, and when fattened up for the moult, they are not burning off their excess energy by flying, so they do it by throwing fits. If this theory is accurate, the answer would obviously be always to moult them loose in the mews. Fits at other times can generally be attributed to temperament. Sparrowhawks are exceptionally tricky, requiring a high degree of expertise to maintain. Many times I have warned a falconer who has insufficient experience for an accipiter not to take on a sparrowhawk. My warnings usually fall unheeded, and the result is usually the same. The falconer spends long tedious hours manning his hawk, gets it to the stage when it is nearly ready to enter, and then, unaccountably, finds it dead in the mews one morning. As with kestrels, the size of the sparrowhawk greatly decreases the margin for error in finding the correct flying weight, particularly with the muskets or male sparrowhawks, which are extremely delicate.

With any bird other than an accipiter, you can reasonably expect to have it sitting on the fist for short periods within the first couple of days, and reasonably well-manned after a couple of weeks. With spars and gosses you can be sure that each stage will take considerably longer. With most birds, reward is in proportion to effort, or, in other words, the amount of time spent manning your bird will be directly related to the degree of daily improvement. This is not so with spars and gosses. More than any other species of raptor they appear to loathe the sight of humans in the early days, and, this being the case, if they are forced to endure the human presence apparently needlessly for many hours each day, they will show no sign of preference for the fist over the perch. However, if they can come to associate the fist with food, they will quickly become far more amenable to the action of sitting up and behaving properly, as they will soon learn that they cannot eat while suspended by their ankles. Obviously initially you cannot drop the bird's weight sharply to get it sufficiently hungry to want to eat from the fist. You must first spend an hour or so morning and evening going through the motions of endlessly picking your hawk up and placing it gently on the fist while it tirelessly bates off again as soon as its feet touch the leather of your glove. I have found it best to take the hawk indoors, preferably into a semi-darkened room to begin with. The time that it takes to get a hawk to sit up on the fist for the first time can be greatly reduced as you get the knack of balancing your hawk correctly with the aid of your ungloved hand. As you lift your hawk onto your gloved hand, its feet are often tightly clenched, thereby making it impossible for it to hold the glove. I have found it best to balance such a hawk in a crouching position on the gloved hand, then carefully to remove the ungloved hand. Allow the hawk to rest, if it will, in this position for a few moments, and then very gently twist your gloved hand a fraction to encourage the hawk to stand up and take a grip. To begin with it will bate again, but repeat the process and eventually it will stand upright, glaring into your eyes with the accusing yellow fury that only an accipiter can so successfully convey. As your hawk begins to stand on the fist you dare not even breathe too heavily, let alone scratch your nose or shift your position a little, as the slightest movement on your part will cause your hawk to bate furiously once more, and you will be back to square one.

As soon as your hawk will sit relaxed on your fist indoors for half an hour or so at a stretch, only bating occasionally while you accustom it to slight movements of your hands or body, it is then ready to be taken outside on the fist. To begin with try sitting or leaning on a suitable object, restricting your movements as much as possible until your hawk grows accustomed to sitting on the fist in the open air. Gradually, if she behaves, you can start walking for short intervals of perhaps 15 minutes morning and evening for the first day. A really difficult hawk will respond better if it is walked late in the evening when it is nearly dark, as it will be less inclined to bate. By this stage it is advisable to have leg and tail bells on your bird so that it becomes accustomed to them while the manning progresses. Now is the time to start reducing your hawk's weight. A fat female sparrowhawk will weigh approximately 11 oz. If you can reduce the weight of a spar by half an ounce or so at this stage, you should stand a reasonable chance of encouraging your partially manned hawk to start feeding off the fist. Goshawks are less predictable weight-wise; a female will weigh anything from 2 lb to 3 lb 8 oz, and a male from 1 lb 4 oz to 1 lb 15 oz. Generally a 1½-oz drop in the weight of a fat goshawk will be sufficient to induce it to eat off the fist at this stage. Twenty-four hours without food will normally result in such a weight loss in both cases. For your first attempt to persuade your hawk to eat from the fist, try as far as is humanly possible to choose a place where you stand a reasonable chance of having 30 or so consecutive minutes of total and uninterrupted peace. There are few things more annoying than to stand stock still for 20 minutes while your hawk eyes the proffered food suspiciously, eventually lowers her head to take a first hesitant pull at the meat, and then bates frantically because something or someone has sought you out in your quiet retreat and appeared boisterously round the corner. For the first attempt select some suitably tempting freshly killed morsel from your hawk's larder and break open the flesh a little so that it can see the meat. At this stage I must note that some hawks are surprisingly quick to start feeding from the fist. Some do not even need their weight reduced at all and will consume a good meal from the fist during the first day, but I will not dwell on the delights of such unexpectedly amiable behaviour. It is best always to be prepared for any difficulties which an unduly nervous hawk may present, and to know how to cope with such contingencies.

When your hawk will eat with gusto from the fist when you are standing or sitting, you can start to walk with her. In easy stages, introduce her to other people, different places, animals, even cars and other such horrors. Use a tougher bit of meat which will last her longer, and only take her up when you intend to feed her. In this manner, your presence will become more acceptable as the sight of you arriving in the mews or the weathering ground will mean food. When she will no longer bate at your approach, but step up calmly on to the fist, and when she will eat happily and without fuss under a variety of conditions not necessarily conducive to peace of mind, then you may start encouraging her to jump to the fist, secure in the knowledge that any problems that lie ahead of you cannot be attributed to insufficient manning.

The initial stages up to and including the point of flying free are, for both spars and gosses, exactly the same as described in Chapter 9 on the training of the buzzard. Thereafter, the training varies because you should be aiming shortly to enter your spar or your gos at quarry, and therefore you must use the type of lure appropriate for the species. Sparrowhawks should be flown to a swing lure, preferably a freshly killed bird of suitable size with a length of line tied securely around its neck. Failing this, use a compact little swing lure, garnished with the wings of the quarry you consider to be most suitable according to availability in your area. Fix a chunk of meat firmly onto the lure and feed your hawk up from the lure on the fist. Then carefully remove the lure and drop it out for her on the ground. She will soon recognize the lure and hop onto it. Stay close to her while she feeds on the ground, and make in from different angles, offering her juicy little pieces from your fingers. She should be back on the creance at this stage until you are confident that she recognizes the lure instantly. The lure should be swung and dropped on to the ground, never held in the air, as you do not intend to stoop your hawk to the lure. You should be able to increase the distance of the flights to the lure reasonably quickly, removing the creance once more when she is responding instantly. Correctly speaking, the sparrowhawk is a bird of the fist, and introduction of the lure at an early stage will quickly result in her ignoring the fist in preference for the lure. This is why I feel that the lure should not be introduced until your hawk is coming quickly to the fist up to the point of flying free. If, however, your spar even now switches her loyalties completely and refuses the fist, do not worry unduly for you can either swing the lure up into the fist and let her take it there, or you can try not to worry about this preference and just be sure always to take the lure with you. Do not, as I have once witnessed with a falconer, delay entering your hawk and attempt to retrain her to the fist for this will bore and irritate both you and the hawk and will in the end achieve nothing. Above all else, sparrowhawks and goshawks must be entered as soon as possible.

Sparrowhawks can be flown at a variety of quarry. Undoubtedly, one of the best is blackbird, but a licence must be obtained before you can take them. Starlings must be flown from a close slip because they are very fast when at full stretch. Moorhen are relatively easy quarry, and useful to give an eyass the experience of dealing with larger game. Partridge, when flown early in the season, are excellent sport. Pheasant, when fully grown, are too large, and pheasant poults, although extremely catchable, are not legitimate quarry. Woodpigeon can be taken occasionally under ideal conditions. Sparrowhawks are, it must be admitted, extremely fond of flying little owls, which are, of course, protected. Flights at little owl are, therefore, not to be encouraged, but occasionally an owl will pop up in the flight path of a spar in hot pursuit of a different quarry, and if she should catch the owl instead it is normally possible, if you make in quickly, to rescue the owl, dust it off, and release it hastily. Sparrows should be avoided because a spar flown frequently at such small fry will tend to shy-off larger quarry, and will develop a tendency to carry.

When you feel that you are ready to enter your spar, you must choose a day which is fine and not too breezy, because sparrowhawks have the advantage on windy days only if the quarry breaks downwind, and continues downwind, which does not happen very often. Although there are various methods of entering a sparrowhawk, the most straightforward and therefore the best for the early slips is simply to keep the hawk on the fist and your grip on the jesses, casting gently forward as the quarry is sighted. There will always be the problem of timing associated with flying a hawk at quarry from the fist. If the hawk bates before you release the jesses, she will have lessened her chances by the time she comes back up on the fist, and she will also become sticky-footed, which will complicate matters still further. However, co-ordination with your hawk will improve with practice. An alternative method of slipping a spar can be taken from the eastern method of slipping shikras. The ungloved hand (which should be covered by a cloth or light glove) is inverted and is used to pick the hawk up off the fist with the wings held to the sides of the body (see fig. 76). The hawk is then thrown like a dart at the quarry. This method requires practice to perfect, but is worth persevering with as it is particularly useful on windy days, to give the hawk a better start against quarry flying upwind. It also eliminates the risk of bad timing as you are totally in control of the slip.

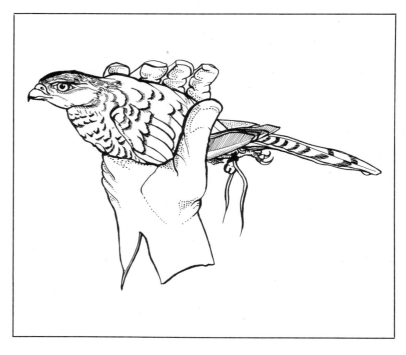

76 Throwing a sparrowhawk

77 A male European Goshawk in immature plumage

The other method of flying a sparrowhawk at quarry is to put your hawk into a tree, and flush quarry out beneath her. With the advantages which height can give her, her chances at quarry are considerably improved. However, I have found that hawks that are flown regularly in this method grow to despise certainly the fist and often the lure too. They remain superciliously in their tree until live quarry appears. Such scorn for the falconer is most unsatisfactory, even if the incident does eventually result in a good flight. For this reason I do not advise encouraging deliberate flights from trees. Some will occur incidentally through the course of an afternoon's sport, and these will be sufficient.

A goshawk in yarak will need but little persuasion to be induced to chase quarry. A day or so of flying to a dead rabbit in the manner described in Chapter 9, will usually be all that is necessary. Above all else, spars and gosses must not be allowed to become bored, and must therefore be entered as quickly as possible. One of the few things I have noticed which will put an inexperienced goshawk off its stride is fear of beaters. A gos should therefore be acclimatized to strangers and sticks and indeed dogs if required, at an early stage. Rabbits present no problems to female goshawks and eyass males, but will rarely be attempted by passage males, most of which prefer feathered quarry. Only female goshawks can hold a hare. Although an exceptional male may take a half-grown hare, I consider it inadvisable to fly a male at hare as if he does not get a good hold, a kick from the hare's hind legs will cave in his rib cage. Pheasant, partridge and duck are ideal game for a fast goshawk. Moorhen are poor sport as they present no challenge to an experienced gos. Squirrel are quite frequently taken both on the ground and in trees. Various vermin and smaller birds including crows are sometimes taken. One of the problems encountered when flying goshawks at quarry on a regular basis is the variation in the mood of the hawk. This problem with temperament occasionally shows itself as a lack of enthusiasm at quarry, resulting in ill-humour all round, but it more often results in the hawk's refusal to come quickly out of trees. You can try to avoid this by educating your hawk in the early days to expect particularly juicy tit-bits whenever it returns to the fist from a tree.

However, if you do experience difficulty in persuading a goshawk to come out of a tree, firstly get any strangers you might have out hawking with you to move away. Secondly, if your hawk has already made a kill, or if you are using a dead rabbit as a lure, then throw it out near to the tree, and retire to a discreet distance, if necessary attaching a creance to pull or jerk the object. Goshawks, of all trained hawks, seem particularly prone to stubbornness on coming out of trees, and it is very irritating and often embarrassing for the falconer. However, if such minor irritations can be considered insignificant, the goshawk can surely be regarded as one of the best, if not the ultimate in short-winged hawks used for the sport of falconry.

THE SHARP-SHINNED HAWK (*Accipiter striatus*)

This little hawk is found in various parts of America, Mexico and Canada. It is even smaller than Britain's native sparrowhawk, western females flying at about $5\frac{1}{4}$ oz and males at $3\frac{1}{4}$ oz although there is much variation between the different sub-species. Their size obviously makes them extremely vulnerable to the slightest error on the part of the falconer. Beebe describes them as 'easily injured, difficult to handle, fearful and touchy'. However, the more experienced and persevering of the American falconers have apparently had a great deal of success with them. They are normally entered at sparrows, and can be persuaded to fly a variety of small birds including meadowlarks, quail, pheasant poults and occasionally snipe. They can be very persistent and will sometimes chase for maybe a hundred feet, culminating in a dive into cover, where, aided by their small size, they can take sparrows while actually in the midst of relatively dense ground cover.

THE SHIKRA (*Accipiter badius*)

Commonly described as a miniature goshawk, opinions about the capabilities of this hawk seem to vary. They are about the same size as the European sparrowhawk, females flying at approximately 5–8 oz and males at 4–5 oz. The Indian falconers fly them at small game birds, especially quail, and obviously find them worth bothering with. Those that have ever been in Britain seem to have performed tolerably well if a great deal of time was devoted to them. The general concensus of opinion is that although they are hardier than the British spar, they are slightly slower off the mark at quarry.

COOPER'S HAWK (*Accipiter cooperii*)

In America these hawks are very easily obtained, and consequently are treated, according to Beebe, fairly casually, not always having the reputation that they deserve. There are, however, only a few individuals in Britain, and they are prized not only for their rarity in Britain but also for their ability. Like the majority of small accipiters, they are normally flown at small birds, but they can also take young rabbits, and are exceptionally skilful at small birds, but they can also take young rabbits, and are exceptionally skilful at flying tree-living quarries, especially squirrel. Their special qualities are their calculating attacks on clearly visible quarry, and their eagerness to follow quarry, particularly quail, into dense cover. Females weigh 15 oz–1 lb 2 oz, and males 10 oz–12 oz, at flying weight.

Red-tailed Buzzard

Bateleur Eagle

Changeable Hawk Eagle

Goshawk

Philippine Eagle

Lanner Falcon

Lugger Falcon

Pallas's Sea Eagle

Prairie Falcon

Peregrine Falcon

Merlin

Sparrowhawk

THE OTHER ACCIPITERS

In most countries where falconers train birds, there appears to be a near equivalent to the sparrowhawk and the goshawk. These are worked accordingly but are seldom seen outside their native countries. If a few of a certain species are exported to another country, and perform reasonably well, the ensuing demand usually results in further individuals being imported into that country in the near future. At the moment the few Black Sparrowhawks (*Accipiter melanoleucus*) that are in Britain are gaining a small following among British falconers, and I feel sure that they will prove popular in the future if more can be imported.

11 The Falcons

Four species of falcon breed in Britain, namely the kestrel, the merlin, the hobby and the peregrine. I have already dedicated an entire chapter to the kestrel; here I shall only describe the habits and habitat of the other three. The celebrated peregrine appears to be gaining a foothold in Britain once more. It suffered a drastic decline in population from 1950–65, but it now appears to be recovering fast. From the figures which are available, it appears that there are at least 500 breeding pairs in the British Isles, and probably considerably more. The majority are found in Scotland but they are also found in varying numbers in Wales and Ireland, with occasional pairs being sighted in the West Country and the south of England.

The peregrine, like all the British falcons, is easily recognizable in the wild state because of its distinctive wing silhouette, which in flight assumes the shape of a half-drawn bow. They are relatively large, with dark heads and black moustachial streaks, blue-grey above and white barred with black below. Their eyes are dark and the voice is loud and hacking.

Nearly all the peregrine's prey is taken in flight. With their spectacular flying skills, they take mainly gamebirds, pigeon, waders and passerines of medium size. The speed at which a peregrine can travel on a vertical stoop is an extremely controversial subject, and one on which I am not prepared to express an opinion. Claims for its prowess have ranged from no more than 75 mph to 275 mph.

Peregrines nest mainly on cliff ledges, but occasionally they will breed on buildings, quarry faces or trees. They make scrapes in soft earth or vegetation on their chosen ledge, and in some sites a shallow indent can be seen in a rocky ledge where peregrines have scraped away at the surface of the rock for generations. The three to four eggs are laid in late March or early April at two to three day intervals. The incubation period is 30–32 days and the young leave the nest after 35–42 days.

The issue of protection of the peregrine is one which has a very wide appeal. In Britain and in America the public interest in the survival of this species is probably more intense than in any other native raptor, and justifiably so, for there are few birds which can match either its powers of flight or its compact but streamlined beauty.

The merlin frequents mainly Yorkshire and Derbyshire, although it breeds thinly throughout most of Wales and on the moors of Scotland. It is not a common raptor, as it declined in the mid-twentieth century like the majority of British raptors, but failed to recover in the same manner.

It is an attractive, agile little falcon, slightly smaller than the kestrel. The upper parts are blue-grey on the male and brown in the female, both having buff underparts streaked with brown.

Merlins feed predominantly on small birds taken on the wing. However, they will take small mammals and insects on the ground. They seldom

78 A mature female peregrine

stoop in pursuit of prey, preferring to skim low over the ground in search of quarry, which when sighted, is pursued in a series of twists and turns of astonishing rapidity. As the breeding season approaches, they leave the low-lying moors that are their hunting grounds and return to the upland moors to breed. They nest in trees in Wales and on the ground in the north, usually in deep heather, which is hollowed out for the female to sit while the male supplies her with food. The eggs are laid from early May to early June, usually 4 or 5 in number. The female sits very tight, and only the closest of approaches will dislodge her. The eggs hatch after 28–32 days of incubation and the young fly 25–30 days after hatching.

This small and dashing falcon has not been as extensively studied as some of the consequently better known British raptors. Its habitat is being threatened by the afforestation of moorland and the burning of heather on the moors, so it is uncertain whether the number of merlins will increase in the future.

The hobby is a relatively rare bird in Britain. It is mainly found in Hampshire, Wiltshire, Dorset, Berkshire, Surrey and Sussex, with a few pairs in the area of the Welsh border. There are probably no more than 100 pairs in Britain, but as there is not a great deal of data available, accurate assessment is difficult. The hobby looks very much like a small peregrine, being slate-grey above with a white underside streaked with dark, and a heavy moustachial stripe, but the distinctive feature enabling instant recognition when seen close-to is the beautiful rufous colour of the legs and undertail coverts. It is roughly the same size as the European Kestrel, males weighing approximately 6½ oz and females 8 oz. In flight they are recognizable by their long wings. Hobbies are migratory and they winter on the eastern side of Africa, returning to their breeding grounds in Britain during May. They perform spectacular aerial courtship displays, soaring, diving and climbing in the late evening. The robin, as the male is called, hunts for small birds and often passes them to the female in mid-air. They are exceptionally late breeders, selecting their nest site, which is usually in light woodland, preferably pine, in late May. No nest is built, and the pair choose an old crow's nest or similar, usually at a height of more than 30 feet. Two or three eggs are laid during the second week of June at two or three day intervals. The female incubates alone for the 28-day period, and is fed during this time by the male. The young hatch during the second week of July, and leave the nest after 28–32 days.

The hobby is certainly one of Britain's least known raptors. It is a graceful and colourful little falcon which will surely in the future merit further and more detailed study.

The training of the longwings for falconry differs slightly from the methods of training previously discussed. The manning of a longwing tends to be a great deal easier than the manning of a shortwing, and a falcon can usually be persuaded to eat from the fist within the first two days, if not immediately. They are also quick to start jumping, particularly if at all imprinted, and will progress through the early stages of coming short distances to the fist on a creance remarkably rapidly. The swing-lure can be introduced as soon as the falcon will fly four feet or so to the fist on a creance. A falcon which is pushed greater distances to the fist will invariably start chopping or slicing at the meat with her feet and carrying on, only to be pulled up short by the creance.

You must ensure that the meat on your lure is clearly visible, as a young falcon, which has been fed only on chicks and beef, will not associate feathers with food, and thus a lure not displaying meat will hold no attraction for her. Make sure too, that the meat is firmly tied on. When the time comes to introduce the lure, take things slowly and calmly, and above all avoid upsetting your falcon, as a mistake made at this juncture can lead to serious problems later on. Stand about the length of your lure line away from the bird plus three feet or so. Swing the lure and drop it out to your side at the fullest extent of the lure line, keeping hold of the lure stick. Keep the lure still; your falcon should bob her head when she sees the meat, showing her interest. She may open her wings and look as though she is about to come, and then change her mind again and look away. If she does this, twitch the line to recapture her interest. If she still will not come, take up the line and spin the lure once more, dropping it out slightly closer to her. When she eventually flies down she will not necessarily land on the lure, but will flutter down to land nearby. She will then proceed to investigate the lure by approaching it warily, and leaning over to pull at the meat, maybe footing at it. Wait, keeping completely still, until she is sitting on the lure, holding it with both feet, and eating happily. If she makes any attempt to pull the lure along the ground, let her take it a few inches and then hold it taut. She may be only trying to turn it over to pull at the meat from a different angle. While she is feeding, holding both the lure line and the creance taut to the bird, make in to her very slowly, dropping down to a squatting position when you get within eight feet of her. If she stops feeding and looks up at you, stay completely still until she lowers her head and resumes feeding once more. Making in for the first time can take as long as half an hour in extreme cases, but it is well worth the effort, for if you alarm her and she tries to carry the lure, the incident will imprint on her memory, and thereafter she will develop the habit of carrying, a vice to be avoided at all costs.

When you get within arm's length of her, making sure that both the lure line and the creance are pulled tight to you so she cannot pull the lure away from you, reach out with a small piece of beef on your gloved forefinger, and offer it to her. If she accepts it, move in a shade closer and offer her another piece. When she has taken this she will look to you for some more. Give her one more tiny piece and then slowly transfer your pick-up piece, which should be a large and easily held strip of beef, into your gloved hand, and cover the lure with your gloved fist. As your falcon bends her head to pull at the meat in your fist, let her take hold of it in her beak, but as she tenses her neck muscles to pull backwards to rip the piece off, move your fist upwards with the motion so she cannot tear at the meat. The irritation which this will inspire will cause her to lift up one of her feet to hold the fist still. The next time she tries to pull at the meat, raise your fist again, and she will be forced to step up on it. You can now pick up the lure carefully with your other hand and bundle it back into your bag. This is the object of the exercise, and your falcon will now be neatly transferred on to your fist, without even realizing that you have removed the lure. Allow her to feed up on the fist for a few good mouthfuls, while, being careful not to disturb her, you pick up her jesses and slip the swivel through your middle fingers from the back of the glove to front. After she has eaten a couple more mouthfuls, remove the pick-up piece and place her back on the post, loosening her grip if she is at all sticky-footed. Allow her to rouse and then repeat the operation, increasing the distance slightly. She should come off fairly quickly this time. Again take your time over making in. Do not give her more than four flights to the lure on the first day, and remember always to offer her the little pieces from your gloved forefinger when she is on the lure, as this will make your approach more welcome.

Continue these flights to the lure, increasing the distance as you think fit until your falcon is flying as far as she can on the creance. If she is coming the full distance as soon as the lure is produced, she is ready to be flown free. Do not fly her free for the last flight of the day when she has had nearly all her food, nor for the first flight of the day, as however well she flew on the previous day, her mood might have altered. Take the precaution of feeding slightly less on the day before you intend to fly her free, to ensure keenness. When the day arrives, give her one flight on the creance first, and if all is well, remove the creance, the swivel and her mews jesses, and insert the field jesses into the aylmeri holes. Call your falcon to the lure from a slightly decreased distance to ensure a prompt reaction. If she performs well for two flights like this, then she is ready to start making a pass at the lure. Occasionally, a falcon will start this of her own accord, chopping the lure while it is on the ground with her feet, and carrying on to circle round and take it again. This shows great promise, so do not worry about it. If she has not already done this, then now is the time to start, unless your bird is a peregrine, which you intend to fly at game. Game hawks should never be stooped to a lure as it will 'queer their pitch'. In other words, they will not, if stooped regularly at a lure, gain sufficient height to enable them to take game. The training of a game hawk, which differs at this point, will be described later.

The first time you want to make your falcon pass, drop the lure out as before, but as she approaches, whip the lure out of the way and she will continue past. With luck, she will not sit down on the ground beyond you, but will continue on and circle back towards you. At her second approach, let her take the lure on the ground. Repeat this exercise once more, and then stop throwing the lure on to the ground but swing it until she leaves her post and pass her through properly by swinging the lure towards her as she approaches, and following through in the basic underarm pass (see Chapter 4). At her next approach, let her take it on the ground. From here on it is simply a question of building up the number of stoops, one by one, never pushing your falcon too hard. I have often heard it said that a falcon should be allowed to have the lure as soon as she starts to pant. This is not correct. If an athlete stopped running every time he started to pant, he would never become any fitter. The same applies to a falcon—she must be worked 'through the pant'. However, she must not be taken to the point of exhaustion when she pitches in a tree or on the ground as this, if it happens even once, will become a habit which is nearly impossible to break. There-fore, when she starts to pant, give her only one or two more stoops and then let her take the lure. If she ever shows signs of sitting down on the ground, whistle her in and let her take the lure, as you do not want a falcon to get into the habit of sitting down. When she is doing four or five consecutive stoops to a variety of different passes, start throwing the lure up to her to let her catch it in the air. If the throw is well timed, she should manage this easily, and the combined weight of the lure and lure stick should bring her gently to the ground a little further on. If she misses the lure, she will follow it down to the ground and take it there. She may strike at the lure when it is thrown up, but not bind to it. This is nothing to be ashamed of—if the lure was a real bird it would be knocked down by such a slice, so a falcon behaving in this manner is only demonstrating a true hunting technique. If a falcon ever hits the lure unexpectedly always let her have it, for you could damage her feet if you try to snatch it away. Some falconers shout 'Ho!' or whistle to let their bird know when they intend to throw the lure up for her. It is a good idea to do this occasionally, as it can be used as a safeguard to ensure your falcon's instant return in times of trouble or disobedience. Do not, however, do it every time or else your falcon will soon refuse to come until you shout or whistle the 'you can have it now' signal. Only a rook hawk, for reasons which are discussed further on, should be trained to come instantly to a whistle. When your falcon is stooping well to a lure, and seems reasonably fit, she is, in theory, ready to be entered. If your falcon is not suitable for hunting, or if you have no desire to hunt her, then once she has reached this stage you cannot do more than continue to increase the number of stoops, making sure that you vary passes sufficiently to prevent her from becoming bored. If she shows signs of boredom, try a change of lure and even a change of flying area, when possible, to keep her amused. Here, though, for those who entertain hopes of entering their falcon, I will deal with the different species and their capabilities individually.

THE LANNER FALCON (*Falco biarmicus*)

A trained Lanner Falcon will put up a better display to a lure than almost any other trained falcon. About 30–40 consecutive stoops, which is considered good for a peregrine, is usual for a lanner. Lanners fly at 1 lb 4 oz– 1 lb 10 oz, and lannerets at 14 oz–1 lb 2 oz. On the whole, lanners have not been very successful at quarry in Britain. This, I feel, is more the fault of the falconer than the fault of the bird. Lanners are, in my opinion, underestimated. Warren Earp has taken quarry with his six-year-old haggard lanner, flying on the South Downs on a regular basis, and his bag included 40 rook, one magpie, three mallard, two lapwing, one various and one starling in a season. She also chased a rabbit. His passage lanneret took moorhen regularly, and also a collared dove and a various. Lanners should be entered in the same way as a peregrine is entered at rook. They can be considered fit for entering when they will do 30 or so stoops to a lure, keeping their height well, and without appearing tired. It is relatively easy to teach a lanner to wait on by hiding the lure when your falcon has reached a reasonable height. With the sudden disappearance of the lure, she should circle round above the falconer, waiting for it to be produced again. Waiting on is an exercise of particular value for magpie hawking, as magpies will invariably dive into cover at the earliest opportunity. The falcon can then wait on while the falconer attempts to re-flush the quarry.

Choose a fine, and not too windy, day to enter your falcon for the first time. Slip your falcon out of the hood upwind at the quarry. Obviously the easier the first flight the better, as a quick kill will give her confidence. If the quarry puts in to light cover, attempt to reflush it for her when she is almost directly overhead, as this will give her all the edge that should be necessary. Once she has killed, make in slowly, and assist her to break in to the quarry. Take her up on the fist, and allow her a medium crop of her kill, and do not fly her again that day. The following day the memory of the taste of the quarry will be fresh, and her confidence will have doubled.

If your falcon ignores all quarry and circles round looking for the lure every time you slip her, the chances are that she has been flown to the lure for too long and has become lure-bound. Occasionally this can be cured by perseverance, even by hiding so she cannot see you, but more often than not, a falcon which has reached this stage can never be persuaded to hunt.

I have never heard of a lanner taking gull or one of the more cunning members of the *corvidae* family, such as the hooded crow, but they are undoubtedly useful to a certain extent because although open country is necessary to hunt any falcon, lanners can be flown in slightly more enclosed country than peregrines. Indeed they are ideal birds for anyone who entertains hopes of obtaining a peregrine for rook hawking, as I feel that anyone who can successfully hunt a lanner is certainly capable of flying a peregrine.

79 Adult female Lanner Falcon

THE LUGGER FALCON (*Falco jugger*)

The general opinion among falconers who have worked a lugger is that in comparison to lanners, they tend to be sluggish. Females fly at 1 lb 4 oz–1 lb 11 oz, and males at 14 oz–1 lb 3 oz. They will put up a good performance to the lure—my female will wait on for up to 15 minutes—but I have never flown a lugger which would work as hard as a lanner. They are mainly useful to fly as a first large falcon to gain experience in the art of lure swinging. I must admit, though, that Robert Boucher has flown two luggers in the past which have worked exceptionally well. He used to fly them on the top of a hill, and, aided by the updrafts, they would wait on at a good height when flown to the lure. They would hunt off the fist like a hawk, and with one female he took 21 moorhen and one partridge. Perhaps, therefore, I have underestimated luggers, but I have never heard of one which would take any quarry other than moorhens on a regular basis.

THE PEREGRINE FALCON (*Falco peregrinus*)

Rook hawking

The method of entering of a peregrine out of the hood at rook is exactly the same as the entering of a lanner, which I have already described. A peregrine can be considered fit to fly at rook when it will do 30–40 or so stoops to the lure. Peregrines can become bored with the lure very quickly, and this can lead to the bird pitching in trees or ranging tremendous distances away, ignoring the lure and returning ten minutes or so later very tired. All precautions possible must therefore be taken to prevent this happening. It is a good idea occasionally to allow a young peregrine to catch the lure on a normal pass, as though you did not intend her to catch it, as she will then think herself frightfully clever to catch you out, and will redouble her efforts to try it again. A first-year falcon should be entered as soon as possible, for the earlier in the season she is ready, the younger the rooks will be, and therefore easier to catch. Never enter a peregrine in unsuitable, enclosed country, as it would undoubtedly be lost, for the distances over which a trained peregrine will travel when in pursuit of quarry are vast. When your falcon makes her first few kills, and you make in slowly to help her break into the kill, and to lift her up onto the fist, make sure that the rook is dead, for if one or other of you manages to lose your hold on the quarry while your falcon is coming up onto the fist, and the rook makes a successful bid for freedom, there will be hard feelings all round, possibly resulting in your falcon going on strike for a couple of days.

Imprinted eyass peregrines often possess an unsurpassable skill in the art of breaking feathers. The tail of an eyass falcon is considerably longer than that of a bird in adult plumage, and they tend to sit back on their train while eating off the lure, and snap off the beautiful white-tipped feathers to the extent of an inch or so. There is very little that you can do to prevent this, but should it happen, there is no point in imping the tips, so I recommend rounding off the broken ends with a pair of nail scissors to the proper shape again, so eventually, although the tail will be reduced in length, it will at least both look and operate like a complete tail once more.

Many falconers whistle every time they intend to let their falcon catch the lure in the early days of training. This is so that if the falcon, after it has been entered, embarks on a long tail chase of an old rook which is obviously going to outfly it in the end, the falconer can whistle and the falcon will immediately return to the lure, rather than waste her effort on a lost cause. Rooks are by no means easy quarry. They will often give a falcon a hard time once on the ground by stabbing with their beaks. Only large tiercels can cope with rooks.

80 Lugger Falcon   (a) In immature plumage   (b) In mature plumage

81 Peregrines in immature plumage   (a) Falcon   (b) Tiercel

Game hawking

At the time of writing I have never been game hawking. Of all the forms of hawking in Britain, it is the most demanding of both time and money, and consequently it is a pastime in which few can indulge. I cannot, therefore, write this section from my own experience but I will attempt to explain how to train and fly a game hawk from information which I have gathered.

Game hawks must not be stooped to a lure, therefore getting them fit is more difficult than getting a rook hawk fit. Normally, falcons are flown in their first year at grouse, but tiercels are given a season on partridge first. The training starts in the same manner as the training of any falcon. When the bird is flying 6 feet or so to the fist, it is then introduced to the lure while still on the creance. The lure, which is made from the wings of the intended game, is swung and dropped on the ground and the falconer shouts or whistles the call which he will eventually use on the moor to attract the young bird's attention to the game. When the falcon is coming the length of the creance to the lure promptly, she can then be flown free. Instead of making her pass or stoop to the lure, the distance she is called off is increased. At this stage the young falcons are taken up to the moors to continue their training, as the open space is now a necessity. The falcon is now hooded and given to someone else to hold on the fist, while the falconer walks the distance away which he wants the bird to fly. This distance is gradually increased up to half a mile or so. The falcon is unhooded when the falconer is in position and the lure is swung. As she flies towards the falconer, he hides the lure, causing her to circle above him looking for the lure. When she has climbed as high as she is going to, the falconer throws out the lure, shouting or whistling the signal to attract her attention. The falcon turns over and takes the lure. Care must be taken at first not to attempt to keep a young falcon waiting on for too long, in case she becomes bored and rakes away or settles, but gradually the lure can be hidden for longer periods and the falcon will begin to ring-up higher daily. She must be called off into the wind, and preferably from higher ground to help her to gain height. Above all else it must be stressed that a game hawk is *never* stooped to a lure as this will lower her pitch.

By the 'Glorious Twelfth' (12 August is the day the grouse season opens in Britain for falconers and shooting men alike) the young falcons should be ready for their first attempt at game. A pointer or a setter is used to locate the game, and sometimes a spaniel is used to flush. The falconer always has helpers to watch the ground which he cannot see and often someone to help with the dogs, if more than one dog is being used.

When the falcon is entered for the first time she is sent off from the fist when the dog is on point, and allowed to circle up while she looks for the lure. Every detail concerning wind and positioning must be correct if she is to make a kill. The grouse must be flushed downwind when she is almost directly above them. If she is very lucky, she will take one at the first attempt, but more often than not the grouse will have got up when she was badly placed, or an old bird will have moved first, and she will have attempted to fly him without standing a chance. If she misses she is called back to the lure and hooded while the game is allowed to settle. Then, if it has been accurately marked down by the helpers, she can be put off again, and the game is reflushed. This time, realizing the importance of height, she will probably wait on at a higher pitch. When she is successful for the first time, the falconer makes in slowly while she begins to pluck and break into the grouse. She is taken up on the fist when she has eaten a medium crop and is given a little more to complete her day's ration off the fist, before being hooded. In the first few weeks a falcon is given no more than three or four flights a day, and if she takes one grouse a day, she is doing

82(a) Ringing up . . .   (b) . . . to reach its pitch

reasonably well. By the third week of September, however, she will have learnt a great deal about grouse and will be muscled up and very fit. Her pitch will have improved and she will have learnt to watch the dogs. The young grouse too will be stronger on the wing, so, as the weeks go by, the quality of the flights will improve. The older falcons will now be flying game and the sport is at its best, enjoyable for falcons, falconers, spectators and dogs alike.

The partridge season opens on 1 September. Falcons are seldom flown at partridge because, partridge, being smaller than grouse, are relatively easy for a falcon to carry. The training of the tiercels is normally started a week or so after the training of the falcons, because the falconer does not want his tiercel ready to enter too soon before the start of the season lest it becomes lure-bound. Partridge hawks are trained and flown in exactly the same way as grouse hawks. Falcons fly at 1 lb 14 oz–2 lb 3 oz, and tiercels at 1 lb 2 oz–1 lb 7 oz. Peregrines fly at a higher weight at game than at rook.

In the future, due to the success rate of captive breeding of peregrines, it is hoped there will be more available for those falconers who have both the inclination and the ability to put them to good use. It is important to realize though that in inexperienced hands, a peregrine will quickly be lost.

THE MERLIN (*Falco columbarius*)

Traditionally the ladies' hawk, these little falcons are both easy and very quick to train. Their affectionate disposition soon renders them very tame, and it is therefore not necessary to make them to a hood. Unfortunately, licences to take merlins are extremely hard to obtain nowadays, so in the future, falconers will have to rely on captive breeding for a ready supply. For those who are fortunate enough to be granted a licence, however, the eyasses are usually ready to be taken during the first week in July. The nests are extremely hard to find, and you can easily spend a couple of weeks looking unsuccessfully.

Merlins are inveterate carriers of both the lure and quarry, so all possible precautions must be taken against this. If you obtain a young merlin for falconry, whether taken under licence or from an aviary, until it is hard penned you will need to turn it loose in a shed to avoid imprinting it. It is well worth taking the trouble to fix a feeding platform on the ground in the shed onto which the daily food ration can be tied down firmly by means of lengths of string. If you enter the shed after dark and tie down the food, in the morning the eyass merlin will hop down to eat, but will be unable to carry the food up onto a perch to eat it. Thus it will become accustomed to eating on the ground and in one place. Adoption of this method will not ensure that your merlin will never try to carry the lure or a kill, but it will help.

The training of a merlin to fly to a lure is almost exactly the same as the training of a kestrel. There are just a couple of extra points which must be included. Merlins love bathing, and must, like all falcons, be offered a bath every morning before flying. They like to rouse before each and every flight, and failure to do so will often lead to a disappointing performance. Education against the vice of carrying must, of course, be continued into the initial stages of training, especially when making in to your falcon on the lure. With merlins you simply cannot afford to become slap-happy and after the first few days of making in slowly, start marching confidently along the lure line.

83 Robert Boucher's male or 'jack' merlin

For a merlin your scales must be accurate to an eighth of an ounce. Jack merlins (males) fly at 5–6½ oz, and females at 6¾–8 oz. Normally you can put their weight up a little as the season progresses. The jesses must be made of extremely soft, light leather. Some falconers exercise their merlins during training twice a day to the lure, morning and evening. This is quite a good method if you have the time, only no casting must be included in the morning feed. The flying times must be regular, as even an hour or so can make all the difference to the performance. Merlins do not travel a great distance away from the lure, and are extremely quick on the turn, climbing almost vertically and sometimes appearing to loop the loop as they flip over at the top of the climb. You must, therefore, be very adept with your lure swinging if you are to stand the pace. I once saw a friend of mine attempt to fly his eyass merlin after consuming several pints too many in a local hostelry. His reactions were obviously somewhat hampered by this liquid refreshment, with the result that in his efforts to keep up with his falcon, he managed to entangle himself completely in the lure line, while the merlin sought refuge on top of his head. The moral to this story is obvious—inebriation is no aid to good lure swinging.

Merlins are flown mainly at larks (for which a permit must be obtained before they can be legally taken). They can be flown singly or in a cast. They should be ready to be entered at the beginning of August or as soon as the corn is cut, while the young larks are making their early sorties, and the old birds are heavily in the moult. Merlins are usually flown at lark over stubble, and must be flown in vast open areas, for they will chase great distances. Never fly near a field of standing corn, for if a merlin kills in such cover it will be extremely difficult to find. Ideally, for the first flight, an old lark minus a tail should be chosen, as a bird so heavily in the moult is easy meat for an inexperienced merlin. Most merlins will fly at the first lark which is put up for them, although a few take more persuasion. Early success is essential because merlins become very quickly discouraged. If your merlin is successful very quickly, she should not be given too many easy flights early in the season lest she should refuse 'ringers' later on. 'Ringers' are larks which circle or ring up very high, a feat which can only be performed by the older larks when they have almost completed the moult, and by young larks when they have become strong on the wing. Thus 'ringers' are not encountered until later on in August. For this type of flight, a good pair of binoculars is essential. The Hon. Gerald Lascelles suggests also that a falconer who has a merlin which is prone to carrying takes with him a long stick with a hook in one end, with which to pin down the lark. I have never tried this, but in theory it sounds like a practical device. The lark hawking season only lasts six weeks or so, because after this time the larks are more than capable of outflying even the best of merlins. As they have delicate constitutions, merlins must be fed up well over the winter months.

THE HOBBY (*Falco subbuteo*)

Although it was the bird of the 'young gentleman' in the Middle Ages, the hobby is rarely flown nowadays. Lascelles describes hobbies as 'perfectly docile, very fine-tempered, and very fine fliers to the lure'. He adds, however, 'Here their good qualities ceased; when tried at wild quarry of any sort they failed'. I have flown a female hobby and I consider this to be an accurate description. My female was extremely fast to the lure. She would vary her flying from long, ranging flights in search of insects, to vertical stoops from directly above my head. She would rouse on the wing, and when the lure was thrown up for her to catch, she would transfer it instantly from her feet to her mouth whilst still in mid-air, demonstrating a hobby's natural ability to eat on the wing. Possibly trained hobbies will not take quarry because they eat insects constantly whilst in flight, which takes the edge off their appetite and causes them to lose their enthusiasm for larger game. A falconer flying a hobby must remember to stop flying it in September because it will migrate.

THE SAKER FALCON (*Falco cherrug*)

These large and attractive falcons are rarely flown successfully at quarry in Britain. The two that I have trained were very second-rate. They are usually flown at rook, and, surprisingly, rabbit, and have proved more successful at the latter. Females fly at 2 lb 2 oz–2 lb 6 oz and sakrets at 1 lb 9 oz–1 lb 12 oz.

They are most widely used by the Arab falconers, who fly them mainly at the Macqueen's Bustard, which they call *houbara*. In 1979 I was fortunate enough to be invited with my husband to Abu Dhabi as guests of His Royal Highness Sheikh Zaid Bin Sultan Al Nahayan, ruler of Abu Dhabi and president of the United Arab Emirates. Sheikh Zaid had over 100 falcons that year which were, when we arrived in November, being trained for the winter's hunting in Pakistan (where the majority are released at the end of the season). We were lucky enough, therefore, to see at first hand how their training methods compare with our own.

Firstly, the equipment is somewhat different. The jesses are made of plaited cotton or silk, and are normally very brightly coloured. These are tied to the leash which is made out of three sections—the first, which is tied to the jesses, is attached to the second section by a small swivel. The third section is attached permanently to the block. The blocks are very ornate, often worked in silver, and the top is padded with leather or cloth. They are easily transportable as they can be stuck in the sand. The hoods they use are of the Bahraini design and are made of soft leather. The lures are enormous bundles of *houbara* wings, in the midst of which the meat is tied. The falconers in the Gulf States seldom wear gloves, but use *manga-lahs* or cuffs of stiff canvas or leather. The falcons themselves were all passage female sakers and peregrines. There was one falconer to every falcon. We were told that the falcons were trapped in Iran, Iraq, Syria and Pakistan, as the birds which are used in the Gulf must be able to withstand the climate. When they first arrive, the falcons are hooded immediately and left on blocks for 24 hours to sharpen their appetites. They are then taken up and encouraged to feed through the hood. For the first few days they remain hooded the whole time while the falconer strokes them and talks to them, accustoming them to the feel of his touch and the sound of his voice. Eventually, when the falcon will turn her head when she hears his voice, the falconer unhoods her for short periods. The manning of the falcons is a tireless process; the birds are taken everywhere by the falconer during the training period. After two weeks the flying begins. The falcon is hopped up to the fist for food, and after this is immediately put on the equivalent of a creance and introduced to the lure. From here on the training is very similar to the training of a game hawk. The falcons are never stooped to the lure, but the distance is increased. In Abu Dhabi they would exercise all the birds morning and evening. We would go out into the desert, and four of the falcons at a time would be taken out on the fist hooded, while their trainers would go some 300 yards away and take out their lures. Each falconer would shout for his bird, and the falcons were released one at a time, the second one leaving the fist when the first one was 50 yards ahead, so that all four would fly down, always going to the correct falconer, in staggered formation, while the falconers whooped and shouted constantly.

In the evenings, all the falconers would sit round with their falcons, and we were shown videos of the previous season's hunting in Pakistan. The straight flights at *houbara* looked very spectacular, and occasionally they ended up with a sparring match between falcon and bustard on the ground.

Sheikh Zaid told me (through his interpreter, for he speaks no English) that although peregrines are undoubtedly faster over short distances, there is, in his opinion, no better bird for hunting than a really good female saker. Sheikh Zaid himself is undisputedly one of the greatest falconers in the world. He knows all his birds individually, and every day, instead of weighing the falcons, the falconers would take them to Sheikh Zaid for him to feel the chest and breastbone, whereupon he cut a chunk of meat off a leg of lamb which was exactly the right amount to suit the individual falcon's requirements. I can only add that the accounts of the Arabs' prowess with their falcons have not been exaggerated. They have a know-ledge and skill with longwings which is unsurpassed anywhere in the western world.

THE GYRFALCON (*Falco rusticolus*)

Although few falconers in Britain are likely ever to have the opportunity to see a gyrfalcon, let alone fly one, a chapter on longwings would be incom-plete if I did not mention this species.

The gyrfalcon is the largest, fastest, and most powerful of all the falcons. It is also, arguably, the most beautiful. As such, it is and always has been, the most desired of all birds of prey, and people have gone to tremendous lengths to obtain them. Those that have been flown in Britain, however, do not seem to have performed very well. Lascelles says that although they flew well to the lure, they were very disappointing at quarry. They used to take the occasional hare, which is not as surprising as it may sound, because in their wild state they take a great deal of ground quarry, including lemmings. They were not popular for heron hawking, for the few that could be persuaded to take heron usually succeeded in crippling or killing the quarry, which was otherwise, particularly in the breeding season, always released. There is one account of Colonel Thornton taking raven with a female gyr, which must have resulted in some spectacular flights.

Gyrfalcons are very highly esteemed in the Middle East, where a great status value is attached to them. However, they are popular only for their looks, for they cannot be flown in such a climate, being particularly susceptible to heat coupled with high humidity, which seems to result in aspergillosis. Consequently, their life expectancy when introduced to a hot country is not long, even when they are kept, as some are, in refrigerated quarters.

The species is better known in North America, which forms the southernmost tip of its breeding range. Beebe and Webster, co-authors of *North American Falconry and Hunting Hawks* rate them quite highly, and reckon that in the hands of experienced falconers, they are capable of producing a performance which is unequalled. The females fly from 2 lb 14 oz–3 lb 6 oz, and the jerkins or males at 2 lb 7 oz–2 lb 10 oz. Apparently they grow attached to the falconer, are very responsive to train, and can often be entered within a week of being wild caught. A tremendous amount of space is necessary to fly them, for they will often range a mile or so away from the falconer when being flown to the lure. They need some persuasion to wait on, but can be trained to take duck, pheasant, crow and hare. It matters little if the prey is flushed when the falcon is downwind, or badly placed in some other respect, for with its superior speed, the gyr can quickly overhaul the game. Pigeon, surprisingly, is the only quarry which presents any real difficulty to gyrs, probably, Webster says, because they can outmanoeuvre the falcon by virtue of their light weight. The physical problems encountered with gyrs are firstly that they need a tremendous amount of hard exercise to keep fit, and secondly, that they are very prone to foot complaints, such as corns and bumblefoot. I am not in a position to be able to estimate whether the gyrfalcon is as valuable a falconry bird as its reputation suggests. I do feel, however, that its physical appearance has in the past accounted for much of the praise which is attributed to it.

84 Prairie Falcon

THE PRAIRIE FALCON (*Falco mexicanus*)

Prairie Falcons are native to the United States of America. Their range extends from California and Mexico to the southern parts of British Columbia. They are very highly thought of by the American falconers, who rate them as a good second best to the peregrine. I have flown both species and I agree with this. They are slightly smaller than the peregrine. Males fly at 15 oz–1 lb 4 oz, and females at 1 lb 11 oz–2 lb 1 oz. Physically they are very tough, but their individual dispositions vary enormously. Females particularly tend to be of uncertain temper, and in the early stages of manning a falconer must watch out for his ungloved hand, as prairies seem to find fingers particularly juicy. They are often slow starters, lacking the easygoing confidence of the average peregrine. After some perseverance on the part of the falconer, however, they will suddenly begin to progress quickly, and after a month to two months, they will do as many as 80 to 90 stoops to the lure, at which stage, they are ready to be entered.

They perform best when flown in the same manner as a peregrine, although they will not usually ring up and wait on like a peregrine as this is totally contrary to their method of hunting in the wild. Males are at their best when flown at magpie, and females will take rook, crow, pheasant, duck, gull, and in the States, jack-rabbits.

Many other species of falcon are flown throughout the world. Obviously I cannot devote a section to them all, but generally speaking, the basic method of training which I have described applies to all of them.

12 The Eagles

85 Golden Eagle mantling on quarry

The Golden Eagle maintains a fairly healthy population in Scotland. There are probably between 700 and 900 individuals in the British Isles, and, bearing in mind that Golden Eagles take four to five years to reach sexual maturity, there will probably be between 250 and 350 adult breeding pairs. The majority of the population is found in the Scottish Highlands, but there are a few pairs found south of the border and in the Lake District, and one pair on the Antrim coast of Ireland.

Golden Eagles are basically dark brown in colour, with a nape and crown of feathers which are straw-coloured and which give the bird its name. They are approximately 30–44 inches in length, and weigh 5 lb–16 lb and have a wingspan of about 6–8 feet. When seen in flight at a distance, they are sometimes confused with buzzards, although when seen close to their tremendous size makes them easily recognizable.

In their wild state, the eagles will take a great variety of quarry including rabbit, hare, fox, gamebirds, seabirds and even fish. They will also eat carrion. They will normally hunt in a methodical manner, soaring until they sight prey, then accelerating in a gentle downward stoop to make the kill.

Courtship displays normally start in early March. Those who are fortunate enough to witness such nuptial displays will see some spectacular flying, often including aerobatics when the female will roll onto her back to touch talons with the male. Each pair normally has two to four eyries in its territory, and often many more. They are situated on cliff ledges or sometimes in trees. The pair refurbish their chosen nest, which is often two to three feet deep and four to six feet across, in March, but all the eyries are periodically added to the whole year round. The brown marbled eggs are laid in March or early April. Usually two are laid but one, three and four have been recorded. The incubation period is 43–45 days. Normally, the female alone incubates, but a few instances of male incubation have been witnessed. The females are seldom fed by the males while sitting, but will leave the nest for short intervals to find food which has been left nearby by the males. The eggs hatch in May, usually with a three to four day gap between. This means that when the second eaglet hatches, the first one is already over twice its size. The difference in size usually has a disastrous result for the younger chick which is normally attacked and killed by its older brother or sister within the first week or so. If it lives for three weeks it stand a reasonable chance of survival, but this is seldom the case. The eaglets remain in the nest for ten to eleven weeks and make their first flight without help or coaxing from their parents, who leave them alone for longer and longer intervals while they are fledging, returning only to deliver food which they leave intact as soon as the chicks can pull for themselves. Having left the eyrie, the young apparently leave their parents' territory but stay in the general vicinity, often revisiting the eyrie site in the following winter and spring. Contrary to popular belief, there is no evidence of their being driven away by the parent birds. Unfortunately for the young birds, many landowners and gamekeepers still hold nineteenth-century attitudes towards Golden Eagles, thinking of them as vermin because of the damage to sporting interests which is unjustly attributed to eagles. Consequently, despite all efforts made to the contrary, a disturbingly high percentage of eagles are shot. The Unit of Grouse and Moorland Ecology carried out an extensive study on the Red Grouse taken by eagles, and it was concluded that the eagles normally take only the weaker, and therefore more easily caught grouse. Thus they do not do any tangible damage to the overall number of game, but take a part of the surplus stock which would die anyway. Such persecution is therefore quite unnecessary. Other landlords have told me that they are more than happy to sacrifice a few grouse each year to the eagles purely for the sheer pleasure it gives them to watch these magnificent birds on their estates. If only more sportsmen held this attitude towards the Golden Eagle, the future of the eagles in Scotland would indeed be a brighter one.

To say that the manning and training of an eagle for falconry was exactly the same as the training of other shortwings would be accurate in theory but somewhat less so in practice. Eagles present a variety of problems to a falconer, most of which are related directly to their size and power. But to train an eagle successfully, you must also understand something of their temperament which is different from that of other birds of prey. In the early stages of training most eagles are subject to quick changes of mood. One day they will welcome your presence, step politely onto your fist and fly extremely well, and the next day, for no obvious reason, you will find your bird grumpy and sulky. In such a mood, your eagle will bate away from you, or leap onto your fist and grip you nastily, yapping unpleasantly into your face, and flatly refuse to fly. They are always unpredictable, and a falconer should constantly be on the lookout for signs of bad temper.

Having said this, I must point out that I am a lover of all eagles. Many of the old falconry books advise you never to consider owning an eagle as they can seldom be persuaded to fly at all, let alone hunt, and will bring nothing but trouble and frustration. In my opinion, this paints an unrealistically black picture of eagles. I have been flying eagles since I was eight years old and I have yet to encounter one which would not at least fly to the fist. If you can cope practically with the problems of size and strength, and intuitively with those of temperament, you will be able to train an eagle in the same way that you would train any other shortwing, and if you are lucky, you will end up with a bird who will show you a single-minded loyalty wrought from a very personal understanding between the two of you. For an eagle will, if allowed to do so, become a 'one-man bird'. An eagle which develops this singularity will not fly for anyone else, and may not even sit on the fist of anyone else. It will respond only to you because it trusts you alone. I have a female Pallas's Sea Eagle who embodies nearly all the worst vices which you could ever find in a falconry bird. She is bad-tempered, sulky, extremely aggressive and a compulsive feather-breaker. Despite months of patient manning, she will refuse to sit on the fist for any length of time except when she is about to be flown, when she will sit, hunched and beady-eyed, snapping at my face and bellowing deafeningly in my ear. But, despite all her faults, she will fly extremely well. She will come instantly almost any distance to the fist. She will work at rabbit with a great deal of enthusiasm. She will gain height and circle above me, and while airborne, she is a joy to watch. Moreover, I am extremely attached to her. She may be troublesome, noisy and scruffy, but she and I have a unique understanding which I value very highly.

Theoretically, no one should consider taking on the training of an eagle until they have trained several other shortwings, particularly a large *Buteo* such as the female Ferruginous Buzzard. You must have a fair amount of open space at your disposal, a great deal of time to devote to the bird, suitable equipment and accommodation, and also the more abstract qualities of patience, perseverance, determination and strength.

Firstly, we must deal with the practicalities of the equipment. The most important item is a thick but supple glove. An eagle of the size of a Tawny upwards is quite capable of penetrating a glove which is suitable for a goshawk or a large *Buteo*. Therefore the glove to be used for an eagle must be of several thicknesses of good quality leather. Moreover, it is not just the fear of the talons piercing the leather which should worry you—it is the tremendous crushing strength of the feet which can bring tears to the eyes of the hardiest of falconers. For this reason you must have a glove which is fairly stiff around the thumb and the back of the hand. The fingers, however, must be supple, as with all gloves, so that you can feel the jesses and keep a good hold on them. For large eagles there are two additional pieces of equipment which I consider to be invaluable. The first is a leather sleeve to buckle round your gloved arm (see Chapter 3). This is necessary for those eagles which show a tendency to land on the upper arm above the glove, and also for those whose span and size of feet make it difficult for them to do otherwise. The second is an arm brace (see fig. 40 in Chapter 3). For really heavy eagles this is essential, not only for comfort but because when carrying an eagle of 5 lb and upwards for any length of time, your hand will become tired, and, whether you are aware of the fact or not, your hold on the jesses when your hand is tired will become weaker, possibly enabling the eagle to get her feet free to lash out at you. With the aid of an arm brace your hand is still at the mercy of your eagle's grip but it will not suffer from the weight. A fairly hefty lure is also a necessity, although most eagle lures, however substantial, will not last long. Imprinted eagles will frequently dab at your face, and for this reason a few people have used a fencing mask when flying them. I have never resorted to such lengths, feeling that once such a mask is used it would henceforward always be necessary when handling that bird, for its removal would encourage the bird to snatch at the face even more.

Accommodation for an eagle needs to be well thought out. There are two things to bear in mind. Firstly, eagles are particularly prone to becoming 'mewsproud'. This means that they will establish territory around their block and will vigorously attack all those who dare to venture inside that territory. An eagle thus inclined is considerably easier to deal with if it is housed in a building or weathering in which you do not have to duck or crouch to approach it. This is because taking such an eagle onto the fist involves split-second timing—as the bird lunges off the block at you, feet outstretched, you put your fist into its path and it bounces up on to the fist and grips for all its worth while snapping at your nearest cheek or biting you in the forearm. The aim then is to put the jesses gingerly into your gloved hand and untie the bird—keeping it at arm's length—with as much speed as possible so that you can get it out of the danger area. This is extremely hard to accomplish if your head and shoulders are ducked under the low roof of a weathering or mews. For one thing it brings your face closer to the bird, and for another, you cannot move as quickly or as adeptly when you are crouching, and the eagle, sensing her advantage, will redouble her efforts to get you. Thus the accommodation must be high enough to allow you to stand upright. The second point to remember about accommodation for an eagle is for those who keep cats or small dogs, or whose neighbours keep them: in such circumstances the weathering must be enclosed by perimeter fencing if you wish to avoid an incident.

The training of an eagle to fly to the fist and to the lure is the same as the training of any shortwing. The biggest problem, though, is finding the correct flying weight. As a very rough guide, I feed an eagle up to the heaviest weight that it will reach. I then mentally subtract a quarter of that total weight, and the weight that you are left with will be approximately the weight at which the bird will fly. For example, an eagle which weighs 10 lb when fat should fly at approximately $7\frac{1}{2}$ lb. Obviously this system can only be used as a rough guide, but it does help to give you some idea of the amount of weight which your bird will have to lose. Getting the weight off an eagle can be difficult. A falconer I know reduces his eagle's weight by one ounce a day. When you are talking about a total weight reduction of several pounds, this is obviously ridiculous as it will take far too long. On the other hand, you do not want to starve your eagle for a couple of weeks, for although they can withstand such treatment easily because of their powers of fasting, they will, like any human who starves himself, lose much of their appetite and become very lethargic. Thus when you come to take up your bird, when it has reached a lower weight, you will find it slow to respond and weak in flight. The best system therefore is to feed a little every day or every other day, to facilitate a gradual weight drop without loss of appetite. While the weight is coming down you must start to get your eagle eating off the fist, and jumping to the fist. Sometimes an eagle will start to come willingly to the fist while still quite fat. My husband flies an imprinted male Golden Eagle which weighed $10\frac{1}{2}$ lb at top weight and started to come 15 ft or so to the fist at $9\frac{1}{2}$ lb. He refused to come any further, however, and was quite slow to respond when called off, even at this distance. We realized therefore that this was something of a false start and indeed he did not start flying well until he was under 8 lb. This is often the case, so do not be over-optimistic if your eagle responds before you expect it to.

Once cut down to the proper flying weight some eagles, particularly imprints, will become very uncertain-tempered. If you start to have real problems with an eagle, it is often advisable to put it straight on to a lure and forget flying it to the fist at all. You must never underestimate the potential of an eagle. Sometimes you are able to interpret their thoughts—they start to raise their hackles and assume a glassy-eyed glare when they are going to go for you. At other times they will be sitting on the fist calmly, and then will suddenly lash out with such speed that you will have no time to duck your head, and they will neatly puncture your cheek. They must be instantly reprimanded by being pushed off the fist or flicked on the beak. An eagle which is allowed to get the upper hand will soon be unmanageable, rather like a dog or a child. I would never raise a finger to any other species of bird whatsoever, because it would be out of pure irritation and would destroy the bird's trust. However, with a large eagle, particularly an imprint, you must react strongly for your own safety. If you do, you will develop a mutual respect; if you don't, you will become frightened and then all will be lost.

During the training you may find that you have dropped your eagle's weight as low as you feel is safe, and it is still not coming quickly. If this happens, you have no alternative but to feed the bird right up and start all over again. Second time around, it will know what is expected of it and you may well find that it will respond at a heavier weight than you thought, and that you had gone below its flying weight last time. As soon as possible, you must get your bird flying free, and cracking onto a lure. There are three ways of hunting an eagle—off the fist, out of trees, and from waiting on. If you can get your eagle to wait on, this is easily the best method, as it is the way most eagles hunt in the wild. The best way to get an eagle to wait on is to take it to a high point on a windy day, cast it off and let it go up, keeping both fist and lure out of sight. Some eagles will not go up, but in a really strong wind, there is little they can do about it. I know a number of falconers who refuse to fly their birds in strong winds for fear of losing them. To me there are few things more magnificent than the sight of an eagle soaring and circling above me. I welcome windy days and I feel that those who refuse to risk an eagle in a strong wind should not be flying that bird at all, for it is only when up and circling that the full beauty of an eagle can be appreciated. A falconer who lives in fairly open country can hunt an eagle which will wait on by putting it up and flushing beneath it, rather like flying a falcon at game. This is by far the best way to hunt an eagle, but it can only be done in the right area, where there are plenty of updrafts. When hunting an eagle only experienced people should be invited to beat for an imprint, and they should always carry a glove. In more enclosed country you have to use one of the other two methods of hunting. I dislike flying any eagles but hawk eagles out of trees, because, being somewhat slow off the mark, by the time they have launched themselves out of the tree, the quarry is normally nearing cover. The alternative of hunting off the fist requires a great deal of effort on the part of the falconer, for to carry a heavy and keen eagle for a couple of hours is very tiring indeed. When quarry is sighted, the eagle must be given a good launch from the fist to get sufficient momentum to gain speed. It must be admitted that hunting an eagle off the fist in enclosed country is a painful business. There are few kills and a lot of hard work involved. However, to kill a rabbit with an eagle represents far more of a challenge than it does with a goshawk.

I must at this point mention a little about getting an eagle fit. This is not easy, for eagles tend to do the minimum of work necessary. They can rarely be persuaded to follow you from tree to tree as most shortwings can; they cannot of course be stooped to a lure, and even if you put them into a tree and leave them to exercise for an hour, they will normally not be far away when you return. The only answer is to increase the distance and number of flights, ensuring that you give adequate reward for effort. People are inclined to fly eagles downhill, for they gain better height and look far more comfortable in the air, but an eagle flying downhill to the fist or to the lure scarcely ever flaps its wings or puts its back into it, it merely glides. The better method, therefore, is to call your bird up a slope. It may only fly two or three feet off the ground, but at least it will be working. It may land on the ground and walk the rest of the way, but you then know that the exercise is tiring the bird and is thus having the desired effect of making it do some work. A word of warning—when casting an eagle off the fist beware in case it turns round and comes straight back at you. Any eagle, if cast into a strong wind, sometimes will turn back and hit you accidentally, purely because aerodynamically a big wingspan is difficult to control when cast off into a head wind. One final rule must be never to show food without feeding. Eagles are snappy enough without being teased with food, so you must never show food in your hand to test keenness as you might with another bird, as it will encourage them to go for your bare hands.

To train an eagle successfully, you must virtually marry yourself to it. They are a full time occupation. They cannot be manned and exercised only when work or whim permits it, and no one who cannot guarantee being able to exercise a bird at least six days a week is ever likely to get an eagle fit for hunting.

TAWNY AND STEPPE EAGLES (*Aquila rapax rapax* and *Aquila rapax nipalensis* or *orientalis*)

Either of these species is ideal as a 'first eagle', being of a reasonably manageable size (excluding female Steppes which should be avoided initially). Male Tawnies fly at approximately 3 lb–3 lb 10 oz and females at 3 lb 14 oz–4 lb 12 oz. Male Steppes fly at 4 lb 14 oz–5 lb 10 oz, and female Steppes at anything from 7–9 lb, depending on the subspecies. Tawnies and Steppes are usually described as lazy. I have found them to be the opposite. All the ones that I or my husband have flown have been slow to start with, but eventually have flown willingly and enthusiastically. We have taken quarry with both Tawnies and Steppes, and one male Steppes which we fly, regularly takes young rook which are still weak in flight. We do not encourage him to do this, because he carries them to a favourite feeding point which is the chimney of an elderly lady's cottage about half a mile away. He then proceeds to eat his rook very untidily, frequently dropping disgusting little pieces down the chimney and into her fireplace. Fortunately, he will return to the fist even with a full crop after half an hour or so. Generally speaking, though, you should avoid, whenever possible, flying any hawk at quarry which it can easily carry, for it will usually result in the bird's taking stand in a tree, sometimes for 24 hours, while it digests the contents of its crop, and you might even lose the bird completely. Most Tawnies and Steppes tend to be somewhat moody. When in a bad mood, they are grumpy and sullen, and they bark rather like a dog and raise they head feathers in a small crest. When in a good mood, however, they are delightful, almost affectionate and they squawk or chirrup cheerfully and assume a slightly fluffy posture. On the whole they are not given to rapid and inexplicable changes of mood—they either get off their block the wrong side in the morning when they will be grumpy all

86 Tawny Eagle

87 Steppe Eagle

day, or they will start the day in a good humour which will continue throughout. I find them most endearing. They have great character and are interesting to train. They can, with a little effort, be persuaded to chase quarry, and will take rabbit, squirrel, hare and various small fry according to their individual preferences.

THE GOLDEN EAGLE (*Aquila chrysaetos*)

Before ever considering taking on a Golden, a falconer must have flown a Tawny or Steppe. Male Golden Eagles fly at 5½–8 lb and females from 9½–12½ lb. There is a tremendous variation depending on which region they originate from. They are extremely powerful and have enormous feet.

In my experience, they are usually very hard to get going. They take a long time to get fit, and they quickly go out of condition if they are not flown for a couple of days. They are often unpredictable and very aggressive towards the falconer, and one must have a healthy respect for their feet which can really do some damage. Males are easier to handle because they are smaller, and are quicker and more manoeuvreable in flight.

To hunt a Golden to the best of its ability, it must be trained to wait on. Flown off the fist they are very boring and cumbersome, and will catch very little. Imprints are easier to enter than non-imprints, for they will normally bate at anything that moves. They can be flown at rabbit, hare and fox. I have heard reports that one imprinted male in Scotland even flew a deer!

To build up a working relationship with a Golden Eagle takes a very long time, but, if achieved, it is a rewarding experience.

My husband, who is very experienced with eagles, is at the time of writing flying an imprinted male Golden. This bird was very vicious when it first came to us, and it took several weeks before it would sit on the fist without snapping constantly at our faces. It is now taking quarry after months of continuous and unstinting daily effort, but it is by no means a joy to handle. I think it is fair to say that to hunt a Golden Eagle successfully, you must not only be dedicated, you must also have little regard for your personal safety!

THE IMPERIAL EAGLE (*Aquila heliaca*)

Imperial Eagles are smaller than Golden Eagles and more manageable. Males fly at approximately 5 lb 10 oz–6 lb 3 oz, and females at 6 lb 10 oz–7 lb 6 oz. I have flown only a male before, which was quite active and quick, but a friend, Rick Morant, works a female which flies as well as any trained eagle I have ever seen. She waits on at about 500–600 feet and is very obedient to both fist and the lure. She has taken rabbit, and will wait on even in quite enclosed countryside. He has, however, been flying her for a number of years, and to achieve this standard with an eagle, a falconer must think of the bird improving season by season rather than week by week.

FISH EAGLES

Fish Eagles seem to fall into two categories, those which are perfect-tempered, and those which are exceptionally aggressive. Although they are not often flown for falconry, those which I have worked and which I have heard about have been reasonably good after rabbit.

88 Golden Eagle

89 Rick Morant with his female Imperial Eagle

My husband has worked several White-bellied Fish Eagles. One particular female which flew at 5 lb 2 oz took a half-grown fox-cub. My female Pallas's Sea who flies at 7 lb 2 oz which I have already mentioned, has taken rabbit, and so have African Fish Eagles. Fish Eagles are very manoeuvreable and can therefore be worked in slightly more enclosed country than the average large eagle. They tend to be somewhat vocal and so are not the most ideal birds to keep if you have close neighbours. They are, as one-would expect, very fond of water, and should therefore be offered a bath of reasonable depth every day. I also make sure that my Fish Eagles are given fresh fish at least once a week.

SNAKE EAGLES

I have, in the past, flown only one species of Snake Eagle, namely the Bateleur Eagle, which has pictorial value rather than hunting ability. I am, however, in the process of training a Nias Island Serpent Eagle (*Spilornis cheela asturinus*), which is a diminutive race of the Crested Serpent Eagle, and which, according to Leslie Brown's *Eagles of the World* probably enjoys the distinction of being the smallest eagle in the world. For such a small eagle, she has exceptionally strong feet—a phenomenon encountered in all Serpent Eagles which need such power to hold snakes. Indeed my 7 lb female Bateleur Eagle had such a grip that she would numb my hand completely after the first few minutes of holding her.

I know of no other species of Serpent Eagle which have been flown for falconry, and I do not know, therefore, if they could be persuaded to fly anything other than snakes.

90 White-bellied Sea Eagle

91 Pallas's Sea Eagle

92 Grey-headed Fishing Eagle

93 Bateleur Eagle

94 Nias Island Serpent Eagle

THE BONELLI'S EAGLE (*Hieraaetus fasciatus fasciatus*)

I feel that Bonelli's merit a mention on their own because they are exceptionally good hunting birds. In fact, they are probably the best eagles for hunting. They behave rather like overgrown goshawks. They can be flown off the fist at rabbit, hare, moorhen and squirrel. Because of their speed, there is no need to train them to wait on; indeed, their style of hunting would be totally unsuited to this practice.

Female Bonelli's fly at 4 lb 2 oz–4 lb 8 oz and males at 3 lb 8 oz–3 lb 15 oz. Like most eagles they are aggressive and unpredictable, but Bonelli's seem to bear this aggressive streak even more strongly than other eagles. They have incredibly strong feet with which they lash out liberally. They have a little crest of feathers on the back of their heads which they raise when upset, and they have an angry glare like an accipiter.

The sexes are very different to handle. The males are slighter and quicker off the mark, while the females are impressively built with thick, powerful tarsi and have great strength of wing beat. They are suitable birds only for expert falconers, who are well used to handling large accipiters, and in whose hands their undoubted ability will be put to good use.

OTHER HAWK EAGLES

In their wild state, Hawk Eagles are 'still-hunters'. They will sit in a tree until quarry is sighted close at hand, when, with a sudden burst of activity, they will launch themselves out of the tree and on to their prey. For falconry purposes they perform most easily if flown in the same way. They are, however, extremely difficult birds to get fit as they tend, when flying free, to head for the nearest tree, and sit there, watching the surrounding vegetation fixedly and steadfastly ignoring your efforts to call them down. Although you may think that your bird is being incredibly stupid, it is, in fact, only pursuing its own hunting instincts, and boring though it may be for you, there is remarkably little that you can do about it. The answer, therefore, is to stick to open country until your bird is fit. Call it long distances to the fist and lure, and do not give it the opportunity to sit around in trees. It is best to enter it like an accipiter off the fist at a close slip, and after the first few kills, when it realizes that you too are looking for quarry, you can then start putting your eagle into trees and beating beneath it, for it will be watching you.

My female Changeable Hawk Eagle was fairly typical of her species. She had perfect manners in the mews and on the fist. She was exceptionally beautiful, with her peach-coloured eyes and her striking cream chest, streaked with dark brown. Unfortunately, though, her good qualities did not extend as far as her flying. She stubbornly refused to respond with any degree of enthusiasm to training. After weeks of intensified effort, she deigned to fly tolerably well to the fist and to the lure, but she was very slow off the mark. Her flying weight was exactly 3 lb; at 2 lb 15 oz she would be weak in flight, and at 3 lb 1 oz she was not interested.

The day came when she was ready to enter. It would have been hopeless to try to fly her off the fist because she just would not concentrate or look for quarry, so we decided to put her into a tree and beat below her. Once in the tree, she began to ladder purposefully upwards through the branches. With bated breath we began to beat the surrounding undergrowth—this was the culmination of weeks of hard work—how would she respond? She responded by diving into a nest of baby jackdaws which she had been flitting through the branches to reach. She consumed five, one after the other, and spent the next 12 hours sitting in the tree with a bulging crop.

95 Changeable Hawk Eagle

96 Philippine Hawk Eagle

Other species of Hawk Eagle which have been flown include the Blyth's Hawk Eagle, the Wallace's Hawk Eagle, the African Hawk Eagle (African Bonelli's), the attractive Ornate Hawk Eagle, and the Hodgson's Hawk Eagle (*Spizaetus nipalensis*), which is flown by the Japanese at their native hare, fox, racoon dogs and moorhens. In this country, Hawk Eagles have been flown successfully at rabbit, hare, moorhen and pheasant.

Various other eagles have been flown. Martial and Crowned Eagles are sometimes flown and they apparently behave in many respects like large Bonelli's although they are even more difficult to handle because of their size and power. Jim Fowler had a female Martial Eagle with which he took wild turkey. Wedge-tailed Eagles are flown in Australia and a few in other parts of the world, and they behave like the Golden Eagle. The occasional Bald Eagle has been flown in America although now they are so highly protected that it is virtually impossible for American falconers to get a permit to take one. There is an enormous subspecies of the Golden Eagle called the Berkut Eagle (*Aquila chrysaetos daphanea*). These huge birds are flown in Mongolia at fox and wolf, and the females are reputed to fly at over 20 lb. Last but not least, there is the celebrated Harpy Eagle, which is the largest species of eagle in the world. Stanley Brock obtained one of these birds while in South America and trained her. Her flying weight was 22 lb and she apparently concentrated her energies on the local dog population rather than on wild quarry! Many falconers, who perhaps fly long-wings or accipiters, have no desire whatsoever to own and train an eagle, and tend to be critical or even patronizing towards those who do. Everyone is entitled to his own opinion, but I feel that eagles are best left to those who have a very real and long-standing ambition to train one, for these are the people who will have the perseverance to achieve results.

13 The Unusual

97 'Hampton', a European Eagle Owl

I am including a chapter on some of the weird and wonderful birds which I and other people have flown and which cannot be included in any of the categories so far mentioned. I feel that in these days when it is often quite difficult to obtain the more traditional birds of falconry, people must be prepared to try to fly anything which is offered to them, with the exception of the smaller owls which do not generally take well to training. Who knows? You might even discover a species of outstanding hunting ability. Somebody somewhere was the first to discover the delights of the Harris' Hawk, which, with its rather bare area around its cere, you would be forgiven for thinking was largely a carrion hawk and therefore unsuitable for falconry.

EAGLE OWLS

As I have already intimated, I am not in favour of people trying to fly the smaller owls, such as the Little, Tawny or Barn Owls. In my experience, these do not often live very long when their weight is reduced for flying.

Whether this is due to the fact that they do not have crops like hawks and therefore their digestive system is not suited to training, I do not know. I feel, though, that these small owls are better kept in pairs in aviaries rather than on jesses. The larger Eagle Owls, however, are a different matter entirely. In the wild state, the European Eagle Owl takes an impressive list of quarry, including rabbit, hare, roe deer and also hedgehog—a fact which I found hard to picture until I saw my pair of Europeans eating a wild hedgehog, spines and all, which had unfortunately decided to perambulate around their aviary. It is possible to train the European Eagle Owl, the Great Horned Owl, and, presumably, similar large Eagle Owls, to hunt rabbit and hare. To achieve this, however, the owl has to be an imprint. You must get the young owl when it is no more than ten days old and hand-rear it. You can start its training even at this early stage by calling or whistling to it when you feed it, to associate the sound of your voice with food. Eagle Owls seem to be long-sighted, and they have difficulty in seeing things right under their beaks. Sometimes, therefore, you can show them food and they will not even appear to see it, or will snatch at it ineffectually. As soon as they are steady on their feet you can encourage them to walk a few steps for their food. This is not difficult as they will usually potter over to you as soon as you appear. Running across the floor for food is a natural progression from this stage—I must stress, though, that baby Eagle Owls, like all baby birds of prey, need vast amounts of food at this age, and they must not be 'cut down' in weight to encourage better performance. After a couple of weeks it is possible to get your owl to start sitting on the fist inside. It should not, of course, be jessed at this age, but it is extremely important to establish balance, as Eagle Owls have remarkably little natural balance when first taken on to the fist as adult, and will hang on grimly with their feet and wobble precariously. By the time your owl is hard penned, it should be very tame, well manned, and coming to your call for food. Now you can start the training properly, cutting it down gradually to flying-weight. European Eagle Owls vary in size tremendously, so it is very difficult to give even approximate flying-weights, but as a very rough guide, males fly at $3\frac{3}{4}$–$4\frac{3}{4}$ lb and females at 5–6 lb. The training is, in theory, the same as the training for any shortwing. There are just a couple of extra

98 One of the smaller species of Eagle Owl, the Savigny's, adopts threat posture

points which I must mention. Firstly, Eagle Owls are very powerful birds and must be handled on a reasonably thick glove. Secondly, in their wild state they are described as 'dusk and dawn hunters', and when being trained, they respond best if flown at one or other of these times. Lastly, one of the major difficulties encountered in the training of the Eagle Owl is attracting its attention. When attempting to call them to the fist, you can dance up and down and yell and whistle yourself hoarse, and it will sit—body towards you and head facing backwards, looking over its shoulder. Indeed they will look everywhere but directly at you, or sometimes they will look straight through you, seeming totally oblivious of your presence. You have to go close and show it the meat, and return to your original position quickly before it forgets about the food again.

The large owls are certainly not easy to train, but for those who aspire to handle eagles eventually, they are a useful, challenging and entertaining stop-gap.

VULTURES AND CARRION HAWKS

From the sublime to the ridiculous: a few falconers in the past have attempted to fly vultures. My husband used to fly a little Egyptian Vulture to the fist and it responded reasonably well. In France and Germany, various larger vultures are flown, such as the Griffon Vultures. When flown off cliffs or hillsides, these huge birds are extremely spectacular, but they cannot, of course, be trained to hunt.

I have a female Audubon's Caracara, who rejoices in the name of Cuthbert. Cuthbert came to me from Yorkshire. She arrived in an enormous box with steel bands around the woodwork. I had been warned by her previous owner that although her feet were harmless, her beak was like a chain saw, and she could eat her way out of everything, including jesses, and hence the steel bands. I decided that this was probably an exaggeration. I had seen pictures of these handsome hawks, trotting around their native grasslands on their long yellow legs, and I was sure that Cuthbert was not going to prove any real problem. Opening the lid of the box a fraction, we could see a pair of large brown eyes, framed by extremely long and angelic-looking black eyelashes. However, the removal of the lid was greeted by raucous yells from the interior, and Cuthbert was extracted, hanging on by her beak to my husband's sleeve. At this stage, I decided that he could train her! She progressed surprisingly quickly, but we gained scars at a rate which matched the progress. She flew at over 3 lb, and she was very attractive in flight, but she had one idiosyncrasy which was, I suppose, inherent from her natural life style; she would fly half of any distance she was called, and then drop on to the ground and run the rest of the way. She had quite a turn of speed on the flat, but she would invariably tangle her long legs and trip over. Altogether she was a very comical sight. She also adored bathing. Unlike the average hawk which approaches a bath cautiously, hops up on to the edge, and then lowers itself gingerly, Cuthbert would dive off her block straight into the middle of the bath with a tremendous splosh—soaking anyone who was within range. After scarring my husband's cheek for life with a deep and vicious blow because of an argument about sitting still on the scales, Cuthbert now resides in an aviary where she amuses herself by eating her nest box and towing her bath around the aviary with her beak. At the time of writing, we are searching for a long-suffering male Caracara who could take the strain of life with a confirmed neurotic!

On a more serious note, I have heard reports of a caracara which would actually fly rabbit, but could not hold them owing to lack of power in the feet. I do not, therefore, recommend them as falconry birds, but they are very attractive in aviaries, and apparently breed quite readily. I expect much the same could be said of the Audubon's Caracara's smaller relatives, the Red-throated Caracara and the Yellow-headed Caracara.

OTHERS

Various other unusual species have been flown in the past. I have flown a Crane Hawk, a Broad-winged Hawk, a Honey Buzzard and a Brahminy Kite to the fist, and although I could not in all honesty say that they embodied any outstanding qualities, I learnt something of use or interest from each of them. The Bateleur Eagles which my husband and I have flown would, I suppose, be classed as unusual. These eagles quickly become tame, and dog-like in that they will follow you anywhere on foot. They will croon softly to you and present the back of their heads to be scratched. In flight they are extremely spectacular, with their extended primaries and very short tail working to produce impressive displays of aerobatics.

Falconers in the past have trained ospreys to catch fish, and also cormorants. Quite often, therefore, in old works on falconry there is a section about the training of cormorants. Kites, harriers and many other classes of falconiformes have been worked too. After a few years of flying various birds most falconers decide which species they prefer, and stay with that species, and the particular type of hawking it affords. But in the years before you find your metier, my advice to anyone who is offered something out of the ordinary is take it and try it, for although it may never do more than fly to the fist, it will probably teach you something of value and thus increase your experience.

99 'Cuthbert', the Carcara

14 Captive Breeding

In recent years captive breeding has become recognized as a feasible method of producing birds of prey for falconers to fly, without drawing from the wild stocks. Every year a new species seems to be added to the already impressively long list of raptors which have been bred in captivity. Not only are falconers managing to produce youngsters from true pairs, but with the initiation of artificial insemination into the world of raptor breeding, hybrids are being produced, some of which embody the amalgamation of flying skills peculiar to the two or more species involved.

In its simplest form, captive breeding involves putting a pair of birds into a suitable but simple breeding enclosure, giving them plenty of food, and leaving them to it. If the person adopting this method is lucky, the pair of birds in the aviary will lay, hatch, and rear youngsters without additional expenditure of either time or money on the part of the breeder. This process is usually termed 'natural breeding'. In its most complicated form, captive breeding involves expensive and well equipped breeding enclosures, and the costly and complex equipment employed in artificial incubation techniques, such as candlers, incubators, brooders and generators. When chicks are to be hatched artificially and hand-reared, the breeder will need a tremendous amount of time and expertise to devote to the process.

THE BREEDING ENCLOSURE

I prefer the term 'breeding enclosure' to 'aviary'. The latter seems to imply a mesh structure, while the former more aptly describes the closed-wall seclusion compartments which are more frequently and successfully used to house pairs of raptors.

The materials for construction
Although seclusion enclosures are always preferable, certain species of birds of prey such as kestrels, owls and buzzards will breed happily and readily in open-mesh aviaries. Such aviaries are best constructed from twilweld, weldmesh or plastic-coated chain-link netting, rather than chicken-wire mesh, which although comparatively inexpensive, will cut a nervous bird's cere if it should fly against the mesh. The mesh on an aviary should be sunk into the ground as protection against predators. An open aviary ideally should have a solid backing, or be enclosed by trees or shrubs along the back wall, up against which the nest site is situated, as this will give the pair of birds some feeling of protection and seclusion, at least from one angle.

Other species, such as the large falcons, accipiters and those birds which by reputation are harder to breed, will be more likely to breed in a seclusion enclosure. Ideally, this should be constructed out of bricks and mortar on the enclosed four sides, but in practice this is extremely expensive, so such

enclosures are more commonly constructed from sheets of marine plywood, or other such heavy and practical sheets of wood. They can also be made from timber frames covered in off-cuts of wood, but if such a method is used, great care must be taken to ensure that there are no gaps between the off-cuts or the purpose of having a seclusion enclosure will be defeated. Galvanized tin sheeting should be sunk around the base of the enclosure as protection against vermin.

A seclusion enclosure can be roofed with plastic-coated chain-link, or, if the enclosure is intended for small birds (merlins, sparrowhawks etc.) mesh can be used, six inches below which a layer of Netlon should be stretched. This will have some give should the birds fly upwards and hit the roof, and it will also prevent broken feathers and cut ceres should the birds decide to behave like bats and hang from the roof.

More advanced seclusion enclosures are completely roofed over and have artificial lighting and air-conditioning. Such facilities exist in Bahrain at the Sulman Falcon Centre, run by Joseph B. Platt, Ph.D., where artificial conditioning is used to simulate the falcon's cooler, more northerly nesting grounds. With the use of artificial lighting, the photo-period (daylength) can be altered to stimulate breeding at an unnatural time of the year.

The size of the enclosure

It is obviously possible to put a pair of birds in an enclosure which is too small to enable them to breed. Equally there is a theory that an aviary can be too large to encourage birds to breed. For example, a breeder who

100 A pair of Golden Eagles in seclusion breeding enclosure

101 The huge breeding enclosure for the
Philippine Eagles on Mindanao. The birds
can be seen near the top left-hand corner

houses large falcons in relatively small enclosures has a very high success
rate, while several others who put pairs up in comparatively enormous
structures have, so far, achieved no success whatsoever. Whether this is
simply coincidence, or whether there is some truth in the theory that two
birds put in a massive enclosure will merely sit at opposite ends, I do not
know. However, the majority of people who wish to breed birds of prey are
governed by the amount of space and money that they have available to
build breeding enclosures. Thus I feel that it is most helpful to have a list
of suggested minimum and maximum sizes which have proved suitable for
the species indicated:

(The measurements are given in the order of width, length and height)

	Minimum	Maximum
Small raptors (kestrel, merlin, sparrowhawks, small owls)	6 ft × 8 ft × 6½ ft	12 ft × 12 ft × 8 ft
Medium-sized raptors (buzzards, large falcons, goshawks, large owls)	12 ft × 12 ft × 8 ft	15 ft × 20 ft × 10 ft
Large raptors (eagles, vultures)	15 ft × 20 ft × 10 ft	40 ft × 45 ft × 55 ft

(The last figures are the dimensions of the enormous enclosure in which
the Philippine Eagles are housed for the captive breeding project on Mindanao in the Philippines, run by Ron Krupa.)

Some people prefer to put birds in circular or hexagonal aviaries, believ-
ing that they can exercise more freely by flying round and round.

FURNISHINGS

Perches

Breeding enclosures must be well ventilated, but have adequate protection from inclement weather. They must have perches suited to the birds in question—injured birds will need more perches affording them easy passage from the floor to the height of the nesting area. Rather than having a series of straight bar perches criss-crossing the aviary, it is preferable to have T-shaped perches for hawks or mushroom-shaped perches for falcons. Avoid perches stretched across corners, unless at a very wide angle, for birds alighting on such perches which are placed across an angle which will not accommodate their wingspan will damage their flight feathers. Raptors prefer high perches, but all perches must allow sufficient height above them for a pair of birds to copulate. A shelf perch covered with roofing tiles and placed at one end of the enclosure will be used by the birds to strop their beaks and keep them in shape.

Nesting sites

Nesting sites can take a variety of forms. Ideally, it is best to duplicate as nearly as possible the type of situation in which the species would lay in its natural state, for example, a simulated rock ledge for a peregrine or a hollow tree stump for a small owl. It is not always practical or possible, however, to reproduce even approximately a bird's natural setting. Most species seem to breed quite happily on a ledge with a lip around it to prevent the eggs from rolling off. This should be placed in a sheltered position, as high as possible, but allowing the birds ample head height when standing upright. The ledge should always be covered over, and, if in an open aviary, protected around the outside edges for shelter and seclusion. A few inches of peat can be used as a soft covering for the ledge, and suitable nesting materials must be thrown into the aviary for nest-building birds. Ground nesters must have a similar sheltered area prepared on the ground (although many will choose their own site). Some ground nesters prefer to be able to get in behind a wooden barrier or similar. When possible, a couple of alternative nest sites, perhaps taking different forms, can be prepared. This is essential for some species which use alternate nest sites. Kestrels and small owls seem to prefer nest boxes—such as tea chests, placed side-on, with a lip on the open end top and bottom. Elaborate 'natural' rock faces have in the past induced peregrines and Golden Eagles to breed, but equally both species have been bred without this. My lanners have a stone ledge in their aviary, but prefer to lay in an old dog basket. Any nesting site must allow adequate room for the species involved to sit and to turn around.

Baths

All birds in breeding enclosures should have access to water. This should be placed in suitably sized baths, which should be positioned away from the perches to avoid rapid soiling of the water. If some pump arrangement can be included in the aviary design to refill baths regularly and to keep them clean, this will avoid the disturbance of the periodic entrance of a human to clean the bath. Some birds bath more frequently during courtship and the breeding season, and some drink more too, so water obviously plays an important part in the breeding cycle for some species.

Doors and viewing access

Ideally, all breeding enclosures should be equipped with double doors to prevent mishap when the breeder has cause to enter the aviary. All doors should have a catch on the inside so that they can be shut once the breeder has entered the enclosure.

Seclusion enclosures will need viewing access. One way glass is the best, if somewhat expensive, way of gaining this, enabling the breeder to observe unobserved. Alternatively, peepholes or viewing slots can be incorporated in the design of the structure. These should be covered over by flaps on the outside. It is possible to fix up a periscope by means of placing mirrors inside a system of plastic drain piping. This can be affixed to the inside of the aviary in such a way that the activity on the nest site can be seen. It is obviously useful to be able to see onto the ledges where the birds are nesting, and if viewing access can be arranged to accommodate this, so much the better.

Floor covering

An open aviary will probably be built on grass. This will become somewhat soiled and will grow long in the breeding season when the breeder dare not enter to tend it. Gravel is the best floor covering as this can be easily hosed clean.

PUTTING TOGETHER A PAIR

Sexing

Putting up a pair of birds for breeding is not always as simple as it sounds. Initially it is often difficult to obtain a mate for a particular bird that you want to pair up. You can guarantee that the one sex and species of bird which you need for your breeding project is the one which everyone else wants too! Sexing birds to obtain a true pair is easy with certain species, such as falcons and accipiters, but can be very difficult with others. Generally, females are larger than males in most species of diurnal raptor. This difference in size if not immediately apparent to the eye, can be determined on the scales. To record accurately the difference in weight between two birds it is important to remember that both individuals must be at their top weight. Otherwise a female bird weighed at flying weight could conceivably weigh the same as a male bird of the same species at top weight. A pair of birds should anyway always be fattened up to top weight before being introduced into a breeding enclosure so that they do not fight over food. With the species which are more difficult to sex (some of the smaller owls are especially difficult), there are several choices. You can take pot luck and put up two hopeful individuals. You can try measuring the thickness of the tarsi (lower leg) to see if there is any difference, or you can have the bird sexed by a competent vet, experienced in sexing birds. This can be done in a variety of ways. The chromosones in a blood sample can be counted. Experimental work is being carried out using this method at London Zoo but at the moment it seems inaccurate. A laparotomy can be performed. This involves minor surgery, and the bird must be anaesthetized, but it does give a positive result. Finally, sexing by faecal (mute) samples has been carried out by the avian reproductive physiologist, Arden Bercovitz. The oestrogen to testosterone ratio is determined; a low ratio usually indicates a male. This method is used to sex the Philippine Eagles on Mindanao.

102 There is often a marked size difference between the sexes, the female being larger than the male, as illustrated by this pair of Golden Eagles

Hybridization

Some people who cannot get a mate for a particular species are prepared to try a pairing with another species of similar proportions in an attempt to obtain a hybrid. Some falconers, particularly in America, cross different species in an attempt to produce a better bird which will embody the good qualities of both the species involved. This is done by using artificial insemination. Some of the crosses thus obtained include Peregrine × Lanner, Peregrine × Prairie, Peregrine × Gyrfalcon, Prairie × Shahin, Shahin × Merlin × Prairie, Peregrine × Saker and Kestrel × Lesser Kestrel. Hybridization is causing concern in some quarters lest hybrids should escape and reproduce with wild mates, thus adulterating the wild species involved. However, as many such birds would have to interbreed to represent a serious threat to the natural stocks, the risks seem slight.

Introduction and compatibility

Once you have obtained a pair of birds and have prepared a suitable breeding enclosure, you are ready to put your birds in. There are a few dos and don'ts which must be observed at this point. A female should never be put into the breeding enclosure first, and the male introduced later, as she will have established territorial rights, and, with her superior size may well attack and kill him. Both birds should be introduced into the breeding enclosure at the same time. If they fight ferociously with the female assuming the role of aggressor, and have to be separated, or if the female has already been in the breeding enclosure waiting for a male to be acquired for her, she should be taken out and the male given a couple of days in the aviary to establish territory. When the female is re-introduced, the smaller

103 For initial introductions it is sometimes beneficial if both birds are jessed

male will have the upper hand psychologically, and the pair will be better balanced. If the female is still terribly aggressive, you can try jessing her and blocking her out in the middle of the breeding enclosure for a couple of days, leaving the male loose, and thus definitely giving him the edge. After this the female can be turned loose once more with the male. If this does not work, the pair is incompatible and will, if the fighting continues, have to be separated completely to prevent a fatality. Fighting more frequently occurs if one of the pair is an imprint.

When you first introduce a pair into an enclosure, you must stay close to watch, and to split the birds up if necessary. Normally, when you put in a pair of birds, they will look around, and then fly up to the highest perches. As soon as they have spent a while looking around at the enclosure, they will start to notice each other. This is the time to be particularly vigilant. They may ignore each other, in which case all looks well, but you must stay on your guard over the next week or so, or the female may buzz the male a couple of times and then knock him off the perch on to the ground. Sometimes she will then drop on to him and the birds will spar with the feet and maybe scream at each other. Do not rush in and interfere immediately. If both birds can hold their own and do not appear to be damaged, leave them to it. The first birds that I ever put up for breeding were a pair of kestrels. When I put them together they had 23 fights in their first day, and continued to be very aggressive towards each other for the next three days. A month later they had four eggs, and hatched and reared two youngsters. Always give a pair of birds a fair trial. Do not split them up unless it appears essential.

THE ONSET OF THE BREEDING SEASON

When the pair of birds have settled together, feed them as much as they will eat, and time will pass fairly quietly and uneventfully until the breeding season. If you are unlucky, the breeding season too will pass quietly and uneventfully, but hopefully the pair will start showing signs of activity as the correct time approaches. In Britain, the breeding season is in the first six months of the year. Eagles are the first off the mark—January to February, followed by the large falcons, through February and March. The small owls follow shortly, along with the kestrels, March to April, and they are succeeded by the accipiters in late April to May. Finally come the merlins and the Snowy Owls in late May and June. The timing of the breeding season may be altered by several things. The weather plays an important part: the breeding season, which is controlled by the photo-period, can be delayed if it rains a lot and if the weather is generally poor, causing darker skies and earlier evenings. A pair of birds will often lay later than is normal for their species if it is their first year of breeding. The first signs of promise take various forms. Calling, or an increase in the frequency and occasionally in the tone of calling is one sign of courtship display. Special interest in bathing may also be attributed to courtship and other signs include mutual preening—owls will preen each other's head feathers—and food passing. This is the action of the male collecting food and giving it to the female, as he might if the female were sitting on eggs. The female may become more aggressive towards the male. There are two more positive signs, one of which is the collection of nest material and nest building, or making a scrape or hollow with the feet in which the eggs are to be laid. Ensure that plenty is available for the nest-building birds, including soft grass and leaves for lining. The other sign is mating, which will occur more frequently as the time approaches for the eggs to be laid. The female may perform practice sittings in the nest, rearranging it and making it comfortable. It is quite possible not to witness any of the afore-mentioned signs, and then suddenly to discover that the female has laid. It really depends how much time you have to observe the pair, and if you can do so without upsetting or discouraging them. Around this time every possible precaution must be taken against disturbance. A strange dog, person or lawn-mower can completely disrupt a promising pair.

Some pairs will show all the right signs, but will not lay. This is very disappointing at the time, but at least it shows promise for the following year. Do not split a pair of birds up without giving them several chances. Some pairs will produce nothing for maybe five years or more and will then lay fertile eggs. If only one of the pair appears interested during successive breeding seasons and you can obtain a replacement for the other bird, then do so. But if you only have the two individuals of a species difficult or impossible to obtain, keep on trying at all costs—you have nothing to lose.

Shortly before egg-laying, the female may look very ill. This is called egg-laying lethargy, and is to be expected, so do not rush in and remove her from the aviary. The eggs are usually laid at one, two or three day intervals. Keep a record of the date when the first egg was laid, and of the interval between the first and second eggs, so that you can gauge the incubation period. The incubation may start from the first egg—it does with some of the owls—but it normally does not start until about the third egg, or until the clutch has been completed. Keep a note of the day incubation starts. Before incubation has been started, and the egg has been 'set', a fertile egg can apparently be stored unharmed for up to ten days. Ten days after incubation has started, the eggs should be candled to check for fertility. A portable candler can be taken into the aviary to do this. A strong light is required for the eggs of medium-sized raptors upwards. If the eggs are fertile, an airspace will have started to develop at the blunt end of the egg, and blood vessels and a black dot may be visible. If natural breeding is intended these eggs can be left with the female who should not be disturbed again. If none of the eggs show signs of development, they

104 Natural breeding: a pair of kestrels with two youngsters

should be removed. This will leave time for the pair to recycle and lay a second clutch. They will usually do so if the eggs are removed within ten to fourteen days of the start of incubation. I prefer leaving them no longer than ten days to be on the safe side. It is possible that a first clutch is infertile because both birds have not come into breeding condition at the same time. By the time a second clutch is laid, they may both be in breeding condition, and thus a second clutch can be fertile while the first was not. There is some experimentation taking place at the moment with hormone implants. A small capsule is placed in an incision under the male's wing. This action is performed using the same method as that used to caponize cockerels, but this helps to induce breeding condition and leads to mating. It will be interesting to see how successful the technique is in the future.

If fertile eggs are left with the female for natural incubation, wait to see if they hatch, and take a note of the date. When they hatch, the food normally given to the parents must be increased to make sure there is always more than is necessary and vitamin supplements such as SA 37 and sterilized bone meal should be sprinkled on the food. If they do not hatch, the female will eventually desert or kick them out of the nest.

RINGING

If the youngsters are to have ABCR rings placed on their legs, care must be taken not to miss the right time. The correct size of ring must be put on when it will stay on without falling off, and the chick's leg then grows into it. The ring should be put on by putting the front three toes forward, and the back toe back flat against the leg. The timing of this has to be left largely to judgment by eye, but it should be tested from seven days onwards. After the ring has been put on, check during the next two days

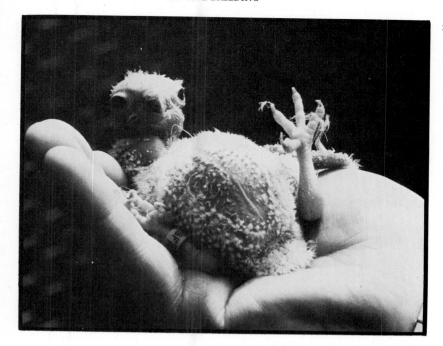

105 Eyass kestrel freshly ringed

that it does not fall off again. It is all too easy to ring a bird in the nest, and then forget about it. If the ring falls off the chick's leg may grow too large before you notice that the ring is missing. It is best to leave the young birds in the breeding enclosure with the parents until they are hard-penned.

ABCR ring sizes for birds of prey in Britain:

Size S	Sparrowhawk, Merlin, Kestrel, Hobby, Little Owl, Scops Owl.
Size U	Short-eared Owl, Long-eared Owl, Barn Owl, Tawny Owl.
Size W	Common Buzzard, Goshawk, Peregrine, Lanner, Lugger, Marsh Harrier, Hen Harrier, Caracara.
Size X	Red-tailed Buzzard.

(For supplier see Appendix). Only British raptors need to be rung, but some breeders like to ring lanners, luggers, etc. too.

ARTIFICIAL INCUBATION

The first point to make about artificial incubation and hand-rearing raptor chicks is that it is extremely time-consuming. Nobody with a standard nine-to-five job should even consider it (unless they have a wife or husband at home all day who is willing to shoulder the responsibility and the work load). Once the chicks have hatched, the task of feeding and cleaning out is a process which has to be performed relentlessly until the chicks can fend for themselves, and can be put into a nursery aviary. It is great fun to begin with; the chicks are appealing, vulnerable and helpless, and however experienced the breeder, the first chick of the season is always welcomed out of the egg with great enthusiasm. But as the weeks pass by, the novelty begins to wear off. Baby birds become tremendously demanding, and the preparation of endless tiny pieces of meat is extremely tedious. If you have a number of chicks, you scarcely seem to finish one feed and clean out before the next is due. You cannot leave the house for more than four hours or so during the early stages, as you must be back in time for the next feed, and you can certainly never risk skipping a feed, as regularity is of the utmost importance. Unless therefore you have tremendous reserves of time, dedication and patience, and also the money to buy the equipment necessary, you must remain content with natural incubation.

The main advantage of artificial incubation is that you can usually obtain a second clutch from the parent birds, and thus hope to double the number of chicks which you would have hatched naturally from the pair. You also eliminate the risk of poor incubation by the parents, as not all pairs will incubate well.

Incubators

There are many types of incubator available. Some are more reliable and suitable than others. The first point to remember is that it is advisable to have two incubators—one to incubate and one to hatch. There are two reasons for this. Firstly, an egg must be turned in an incubator, as it is during natural incubation by the parents, but the turning must cease once the chick has pipped (made the first crack or dent in the eggshell). Thus, if you have an incubator which turns eggs automatically, the eggs, once pipped, can be transferred to another incubator which does not turn them. Secondly, a hatching chick requires a higher humidity than an egg which has not reached pipping stage—so the two incubators can be set at different humidities. Even if you are only incubating one clutch of eggs, it is highly unlikely that they will all pip at the same time. It is possible to manage with only one incubator by putting the pipped egg into a small box on a bed of tissues and replacing it in the incubator. This will prevent the egg from turning in an automatic-turning incubator. The humidity is put up anyway despite the other eggs, and the incubator is then dried out after the egg has finished hatching. But as an efficient still-air incubator can be bought as a hatcher relatively inexpensively, I cannot see the point of not having two incubators.

106 Turn-X incubator

It is necessary to establish which particular features the incubators must have if they are to be suitable for hatching raptor eggs. Automatic turning is a particularly useful feature as it saves the breeder the trouble of turning the eggs by hand, and it eliminates the human element of risk due to forgetfulness. It also saves the eggs from being handled too frequently. A reliable thermometer and a means of measuring the relative humidity are essential, as are temperature and humidity control facilities. Easy viewing of the eggs is also advantageous. There are two distinct types of incubator—still-air and forced air. Forced-air is usually used for the incubation period to ensure that the temperature remains constant throughout the incubator, and still-air is usually used for hatching. The latter feature does not seem particularly important, as I have used forced-air incubators to hatch for several years without any problems. The incubators which, in my opinion, best combine all the above features are the Marsh Farms Group Roll-X and Turn-X incubators. The latter are smaller (and less expensive) than the former (see fig. 106). All experienced breeders have their own opinion about the best make of incubator to use, but Roll-X and Turn-X have an impressive track record and are used exclusively by many people. Robin Haigh has, at the time of writing, just hatched 14 chicks out of fourteen fertile Lanner Falcon eggs, seven incubated in a Roll-X and seven in a Turn-X. I feel that this leaves little doubt about the reliability of these incubators (see Appendix for supplier). A cheaper non-turning incubator of the still-air type can be purchased for hatching (see Appendix).

Candlers

A candler is essential for artificial incubation. A home-made candler can be used for small (thin-shelled) eggs, such as those of small owls, kestrels, etc. You will need a table lamp with the shade removed and a 60-watt light bulb inserted, two tins, and some insulating tape. Remove the top and bottom from one tin and one end from the other. Cut a hole approximately one inch in diameter in the remaining end, and tape the two tins together, end on end, with the hole uppermost. Place this arrangement over the table lamp, with the hole at the top, and tape in place, making sure that no light can escape from any cracks. Finally, pad around the hole with foam and insulating tape. The distance from the bulb to the hole over which the egg is placed for no more than five seconds, protects the egg from overheating. If a larger egg is to be candled, a stronger candler will be necessary to penetrate the thickness of the shell (see Appendix for supplier). Use this in total darkness.

Brooders

There are various sophisticated and expensive types of brooder which can be purchased or custom-made. They usually take the form of a sealed unit into which hot air is blown at the required temperature, controlled by a thermostat. I do not use this type of brooder. I prefer to use a simpler arrangement which can be made easily and inexpensively by anyone (see fig. 107). You will need a cardboard box, approximately 18 inches × 12 inches × 18 inches, of which half is roofed over with a cardboard lid. Through this a hole is punched, and a 40- or 60-watt green or red light bulb is suspended in the box by the flex running through the hole, with the bulb in such a position that the temperature below it at ground level is exactly 98 °F. The temperature can be altered by raising or lowering the bulb.

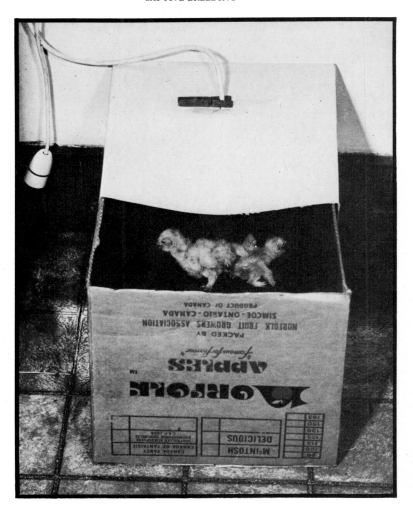

107 A simple but effective brooder box

Alternatively, a dimmer switch or an electric drill variable speed controller can be fitted to a 100-watt bulb and then adjusted. This increases the life of the bulb, and it also means that the temperature can be easily altered. The floor of the box is covered with crumpled-up and then flattened-out newspapers, and covered over with a piece of towelling. An indent is made under the bulb (for very young chicks I usually make a horseshoe shape of newspaper under the bulb, covered by the towelling to make a kind of open-ended nest). In such a box as this, the chicks can choose at which temperature they are most comfortable by moving back and forth in the box, closer or further away from the light bulb. In the purchased type of brooder previously described, the chick has no choice of temperature. Thus, if one chick pants while another is hunched and cold, the breeder is in a quandary, and to accommodate both comfortably, he really needs another brooder. If more than one species is hatched, or the chicks are of different ages, more brooders will also be necessary to accommodate the different sizes. Many cardboard-box-type brooders can be quickly and inexpensively procured, and can be changed when they get soiled, but it would be extremely expensive to obtain many thermostatically controlled brooders.

Generators and alarm systems

When you are dealing with equipment which is run exclusively off electricity, and which contains the entire product of a year's work and hope, you are extremely vulnerable to power cuts. With all your eggs in one basket, so to speak, it is advisable to have a back-up system. It is well worth while having an alarm system or buzzer which sounds if the power cuts off and a small generator which can be used to supply sufficient power immediately the alarm rings. Alternatively, a rotary converter fitted with a 12-volt battery and battery recharger can be connected to the mains input lead. A solenoid operated by the power will cut in automatically and connect the battery to run the incubator should the mains supply cut out. When the mains supply starts again, the solenoid will reverse the procedure. Those who have some knowledge of electronics can also devise an alarm system which operates if the temperature falls below the safe level, and an extra 'wafer' thermostat set in series with the regular thermostat could act as a back-up shut-off system (lest the temperature should climb) if set at a slightly higher temperature than the regular thermostat.

If equipment can fail it probably will. It should be checked and test-run before the breeding season. It is not possible to be infallible, but a breeder can sleep more easily through the breeding season if he knows that he has taken every possible precaution. It is also advisable to check with the electricity board in case there are any power cuts scheduled, and to ask for advance warning.

Artificial insemination

Although the success rate with artificial insemination is not always very high, the practice does open new doors to the breeder, as those who have a valuable egg-laying female can, if a male can be found, at least try to obtain youngsters, even if the owner of the male is not willing to put the pair together. Semen obtained from male birds may not freeze well, and cannot be kept safely for more than about one hour, so the male bird must always be brought to the place where the female is kept. Females should be inseminated several times in the week before egg-laying and preferably during the egg-laying sequence, so the male must be kept on hand to milk regularly. The technique is too complicated to be described here, and is best learnt directly from someone with experience, preferably by practical demonstration.

The time to take the eggs

There are two methods of taking the eggs. You can take the completed clutch, or you can take them as they are laid, one at a time, in a process called 'pulling'. If the whole clutch is taken, a second clutch will normally follow and this is termed 'double clutching'. If the eggs are pulled, the female will continue to lay in an attempt to build up her clutch to the normal number until her limit is reached and the last few eggs are left with her. This may result in 10–20 eggs being laid. The disadvantages with this method, however, are that the eggs have to be 'set'—the development started—in an incubator, which is usually not as reliable as the parent bird, and also that the last eggs laid may be of poorer quality with thinner shells. I therefore prefer the first method. The entire clutch should be taken five to six days after the last egg was laid. The female should then recycle. Small birds normally recycle 10–14 days after the first clutch has been removed, and large birds 15–20 days. Females laying for their first year sometimes fail to recycle.

The incubation period

The eggs, once removed from under the female, should be taken in immediately. An embryo may die if heat is withheld for more than half to one hour. The eggs should be candled to check for signs of fertility and then put into the incubator. The incubator, which should have been set up several days before the first clutch, should be running at a temperature of 99°F and at a relative humidity of around 40%. An automatic turning incubator, such as a Roll-X, will turn the eggs once every hour. If the eggs are to be turned by hand, they should be marked with two Xs on the top and bottom, with a line running between the Xs around one side of the egg. They can then be turned back and forth through the same 180° turn, three or five times a day. An egg must not be turned through 360° as the cords in the egg which support the yolk will become twisted and may eventually sever. An uneven number of turns will ensure that the embryo does not rest on the same side for two nights in a row. The blunt end of the egg should be positioned slightly higher than the pointed end. The temptation to recandle the eggs, once established as fertile, should be resisted completely. The incubation period for a particular species can be looked up in a reliable work on ornithology, or preferably imparted by someone who has already bred the species in question. To candle an egg more than twice during the incubation period is to put it at risk. The heat from a candler can adversely affect a chick, if it is left on the candler too long. A couple of seconds is all that is necessary. Eggs should not be handled for any other reason. Hygiene is of the utmost importance. Infection can travel through the shell to the embryo; therefore the eggs should be handled only with very clean hands. If the egg is infertile or development appears to have ceased, or the chick is overdue and appears dead in shell, it should be left in the incubator for four or five days beyond the final date for a possible hatch, and then removed. Addled eggs usually have no air-space, and the yolk appears to be broken up and mixed with the white of the egg. Such eggs, if left indefinitely in the incubator, will explode with a horrible smell.

The hatch

When the smallest bulge or crack appears on the surface of the shell, the egg must be immediately transferred to the incubator used for hatching. The hatcher should have as high a relative humidity as possible, preferably above 70%. This higher humidity keeps the membrane moist, and enables the chick to turn round in the egg in order to hatch. The pip will be approximately one third of the way down from the blunt end of the egg, which should be positioned so that the pip is uppermost. Now comes a long wait. Chicks can take anything from 30–75 hours to hatch, and often a chick may make no more impression on the shell from the time it pips until 30 minutes or so before hatching. It is a very anxious time. Sometimes the chick can be heard cheeping inside the shell—it may answer you if you cheep back to it. At such a time, it is a relief to hear that all is apparently well. Resist the temptation to open up the incubator and have a look at the egg. You will achieve nothing helpful, and you will let out much of the moist air. As the time for the hatch approaches, the egg can be seen rocking back and forth as the chick chips away inside. The yolk sac must be absorbed inside the chick before it hatches. This will serve as a food source during the first few days of its life. Wait until the chick has emerged, and then, with spotlessly clean hands, lift it out on to a piece of cotton wool and dry it gently, removing any mucus and little chips of shell. Powder the chick's umbilical cord with sulphanilamide powder, and place it gently in the brooder (under the light bulb in the cardboard-box-type). It is important to transfer the chick to the brooder promptly after it has emerged, otherwise it may get its leg stuck in the grid of the incubator or it may play football with any other hatching eggs! If a chick is due in the early hours of the morning, this can lead to a relatively sleepless night. Unfortunately in my experience 3 a.m. seems to be a favourite time to hatch.

Difficulties with the hatch

The hatch is always worrying because of the length of time that it takes. Human interference or 'help' is usually disastrous and should be left as a last resort. It is extremely difficult to tell if an overdue chick is really in trouble, or whether all is well and it is just taking its time. If a chick is helped from the egg, the yolk sac may not be absorbed, and the chick has thus been hatched prematurely. Some chicks will hatch without interference with the yolk sac unabsorbed. The cause of this has not been adequately established. If a chick hatches in this condition with just a small amount of yolk sac protruding, it can sometimes be pushed gently inside, and stitched in place with one suture. The area must be well dusted with suphanilamide. A chick hatching in this condition usually dies, but a few have survived. Some chicks will make a large hole in the top of the egg, and appear to be unable to turn around. Give a chick which does this time. Lots of moist air will be entering the hole to help it turn around. The only chick which I have ever helped out under these circumstances was one which got its head stuck outside the hole. It was obviously ready to hatch because it was making such efforts to get out, so the rest of it was removed from the shell carefully and safely. In an egg which is ready to hatch, the blood vessels in the membranes regress, so the shell does not bleed when chipped by the chick. If a chick is helped and the shell, when chipped carefully away, bleeds, leave well alone. The chick is alive, but not ready to hatch.

Should the decision be made to help a chick, which it only should be if the chick is *well* overdue and has already made an effort to hatch itself, pick away a tiny piece of shell at the point of pip and see if you can see the chick moving or breathing. Continue slowly, piece by piece. A sterile, blunted pin is the best thing to use. It is only rarely that chicks are saved in this way.

If a chick hatches with a lump on the back of its head, this is an oedema probably caused by too high a humidity during the incubation period. It will disperse after a few days. If a dead-in-shell chick has an oedema, death can probably be attributed to the same cause. Other than this, it is hard to establish cause of death in a dead-in-shell chick.

REARING

Feeding

Once a chick has hatched, it will be tired, and will normally sleep for several hours, during which time it will dry out and become fluffy. Cold chicks will hunch their backs towards the heat, and hot ones will pant. Most chicks will let you know when they are ready for the first feed. This may not be for 12 hours or so. If 12 hours elapse without the chick wanting food, you can tempt it with a little piece against its beak, and squeak at it like a mother would. If the chick still refuses to accept food after 24 hours, a small piece should be placed gently on the back of its tongue with blunt-ended tweezers. This should induce swallowing. Only a few pieces should be fed initially.

108 Kestrels and Barn Owls being fed with
liquidized chick

There are numerous opinions about what youngsters should be fed. I feed entirely day-old chicks. This is a list of the substance and timing of my feeding schedule:

Age of youngster	Food	Frequency		
First hatched—2 days	Leg muscle meat of day old chick	9 am	12 noon	3 pm
		6 pm	9 pm	12 midnight
3 days—10 days	Liquidized chick (see below for recipe)	9 am	2 pm	
		7 pm	12 midnight	
10 days—14 days (or until first casting is produced)	Soft pieces of chick + SA 37 and sterilized bone meal	9 am	4 pm	12 midnight
14 days onward	Small pieces of chick containing bones and a little fluff + SA 37 and sterilized bone meal	9 am	4 pm	12 midnight

The size of the pieces given should be increased as the youngster grows and the number of feeds can be gradually reduced to one a day.

109 Spotted Eagle Owls being fed from tweezers

For the first feed only four pieces of leg muscle meat—each the size of the head of a matchstick—should be given. They should first be dipped and shaken dry in cooled boiled water for moisture to aid swallowing. The youngster will usually want more, but the amount given each feed for the first two days should only be increased by two pieces per feed. The first feed on liquidized chick too should be limited as it is rich, but thereafter a youngster can eat as much as it wants. Some breeders prefer not to have a time schedule for feeding, but simply feed whenever the youngster is hungry.

Liquidized chick

Skin and de-head six chicks and remove feet and large leg bones. Remove the yolk sacs from three chicks and place all six in a liquidizer or hand-operated meat-grinder. Add a quarter of a teaspoon of SA 37 and a quarter of a teaspoon of sterilized bone flour (make sure that it is sterilized). Reduce mixture to a thick liquid and transfer to a plastic bag. Tie a knot in the end. Cut the corner and use to feed the chick like a forcing bag, removing any small pieces of bone.

The food can be kept in a refrigerator, but must be warmed slightly before feeding or it will chill the youngster. Its crop must be allowed to empty before the next feed. Remember that owls have no crops—the food passes straight into their stomachs.

Occasionally, a youngster is sick—this is usually due to over-eating or eating too quickly.

Heat

The heat should be reduced by approximately one degree a day after the first three days, until room temperature is reached. This can be done in a cardboard box by raising the bulb. When the bulb reaches its maximum height, it can be replaced by a bulb of lower wattage. When room temperature is reached, the bulb can be switched off.

Cleaning out

I use towelling on the base of brooder boxes, which is changed night and morning. The chicks need to be on a roughened surface to prevent splayed legs. This happens when the chick cannot get a grip on the ground covering, and its legs slide apart, remaining at an alarming angle and refusing to resume their normal position. Should this happen, the chick's legs should be tied together with a soft pair of jesses. This normally corrects the problem within a couple of days.

Problems and diseases in young chicks

A common ailment seems to be a mild and foul-smelling dark brown diarrhoea. This often resolves spontaneously in a few days, but a mild anti-diarrhoeal, such as Forgastrin, can be obtained from a vet and sprinkled on the food.

I have lost a few chicks from a peculiar set of symptoms, which included stiff legs, flipping on the back rather than lying on the stomach, and refusing to eat, leading to force feeding, regurgitation, and emaciation. A post mortem has revealed nothing and I am still none the wiser, although I understand that some other breeders have encountered the symptom of lying on the back and have suffered the same fatalities.

Aggressive tendencies

Some chicks become extremely aggressive towards each other. To prevent injury occurring they must be separated from each other in the brooder. The problem is particularly marked when a clutch hatches over an extended period, and there is consequently a big difference in the sizes of the chicks.

Imprinting

Imprinting is the condition which occurs when a human hand-rears a raptor chick, causing it to think of him as a parent. It occurs as soon as the eyes open. This means that to hand-reared chicks, human beings represent food-suppliers, and consequently the chick will draw attention to its desire for food by screaming every time it sees a human. This usually continues for the rest of its life. Such birds also have no fear of humans whatsoever, or of much else. Imprinting is a positive disadvantage for most birds and should be avoided at all costs. In certain species imprinting leads to loss of flying performance and loss of breeding potential, owing to aggression towards a mate. Thus it should be avoided at all costs, with a few exceptions. The exceptions are in the cases of Eagle Owls to be used for flying (see Chapter 13) and sparrowhawks. The latter are so nervy that it is advisable to imprint them so that they will not fear humans. They also breed readily if imprinted on their own kind and on humans. Various attempts are made by breeders to avoid imprinting, such as rearing a group of young birds together, hoping that they will imprint on each other, rather than on the breeder. They are then placed in an enclosed nursery aviary as soon as they can tear for themselves, and food put in for them without their seeing the food source. This method does not usually work. Secondly, James Enderson recommends the use of a glove-puppet fashioned like the head of the parent bird and used to feed the youngsters, which are prevented from seeing humans at feeding time and consequently do not associate them with food. I have never tried this method. I prefer to use, when possible, the only fool-proof method. This is fostering or replacing the chicks with the parents.

Fostering or replacement with parents

If a female lays infertile eggs, these can often be replaced successfully with chicks (or fertile eggs) from another pair of birds of similar proportions, which she will rear as though they were her own. This will obviously avoid imprinting. Alternatively, the chicks can be replaced with the parents. This works very well for timing as when the chicks from the first clutch have been rung, the second clutch will be near to pipping. The second clutch can be removed from under the parents, and replaced by the chicks from the first clutch. Although this may be worrying to do it has always worked well for me. By the time the second clutch is rung, the first clutch is branching and can be removed to a nursery aviary, and replaced by the second clutch. In this way, you can obtain two clutches of youngsters which you can guarantee are non-imprinted. Problems only occur if you want the female to recycle a third time. This will destroy the timing of the arrangement. Pairs which will not recycle at all can have dummy eggs placed under them until the first clutch are ready to be returned to the nest. Undoubtedly, techniques and equipment will be improved by experience in the years to come. Captive breeding will inevitably play an integral role in the future of falconry and thus it is important for falconers to exchange experiences, impart helpful information and generally co-operate as much as possible.

15 The Transportation of Raptors

Most falconers will at one time or another need to transport a bird. Some have to travel hawks on a regular basis to reach suitable flying or hunting ground, while others will only need to bother with travelling details when collecting or passing on birds, or when taking a bird to a veterinarian.

CAR

There are various methods of travelling a hawk in a car. Firstly, it is a distinct advantage if the bird to be travelled can be hooded. As I have explained earlier, though, this is not always possible, as certain birds will not take a hood, and some species are unsuited to hooding. If the bird can be hooded, however, it can travel perched on a suitable object. The hood must have a wide enough beak opening to enable the bird to cast, or in case it is sick. Very small birds can travel hooded on the fist. I do not recommend this method for long journeys as it is both tiring for the handler and difficult for the bird which prefers to have something firm under its feet.

110 Harris' Hawks in a Land Rover

Neither do I recommend it for birds over the size of a sparrowhawk because when being travelled a bird will, if unbalanced or unsteady, grip relentlessly, and it will also flick out its wings to regain its balance. With a larger bird, a wing tip is quite likely to catch the handler or even the driver in the ear or the eye—an uncomfortable and possibly dangerous experience. Thus a bird which is hooded is best travelled on some more permanent device such as a cadge. For this purpose, an estate car is preferable and a van or station wagon ideal. The cadge can take several forms (see fig. 111). Ideally, it should be custom-made to suit the number and size of birds intended to be carried, and to fit the back of the vehicle. The X-shaped cadge makes the best use of the available space while a simple box cadge or straight bar low screen will suffice if the question of space is not of paramount importance. Care should of course be taken to ensure that birds cannot reach each other when on a cadge. An alternative to a cadge framework is a heavy base which will wedge across the width of the floorspace. On to this block perches can be bolted (see fig. 112). The blocks should be high enough to accommodate the length of the tail, padded on the top with carpet, and have straight, rather than tapered, sides to enable the hawk to brace her tail against them for balance. Alternatively, a single bird up to the size of a large falcon can be travelled on a seat perch (see fig. 113). This is not a method which I would recommend for accipiters, for while falcons only need the area immediately under their tail protected from mutes, an accipiter slicing from seat height would need the whole of the vehicle interior covered with protective sheeting. In fact you would be well advised to add a mackintosh and so'wester to your list of travelling requirements!

A well manned and steady bird can travel unhooded in any of the above ways. For those that will not sit still when unhooded, there are several choices. The bird can be boxed. The box should be tall enough to allow the bird to stand, plus at least six inches so that it does not feel cramped, and wide enough to enable the bird to turn round. The air holes must be placed at regular intervals round the sides of the box at a height of about three inches from the base. If they are placed higher up the sides or in the lid the bird will jump up to get to the light. If they are placed right at the base of the sides, the floor covering of the box might restrict the air flow. The box should have no perches inside, thus enabling the bird to lie down if it wishes, and to prevent it from being thrown off a perch against the side of the box by violent motion. The floor covering can be of newspaper, carpet or similar. I prefer carpet as the bird can grip into it. For journeys with nervous birds, a wooden box with padded sides and roof is preferable to prevent damage to the bird. Obviously, the type of material from which the box is made should depend on the type of bird to be carried in it. For small birds, cardboard is fine, where it would be totally unsuitable for a large eagle. Wooden boxes designed for big birds are best equipped with handles to facilitate easy carrying. I have found a tea chest with a hinged door on the front and handles on each long side to be ideal. Some of my birds have become so used to this form of transportation that they will step off the fist into the box quite happily without needing to be cast. The swivel and leash can be removed if the bird is to be taken out at the journey's end inside a building, but if the purpose of the journey is to go hunting or similar and the bird is to be taken out of the box out of doors, the swivel and leash should be left on, with the leash protruding from the box and secured outside to enable the hawk to be taken out of the box and on to the fist without risk of loss. A bird should never be travelled unaccompanied in a box with a leash and swivel on.

I have devised another method of travelling a bird unhooded which I have found extremely useful. The bird is cast and an old sock with the toe

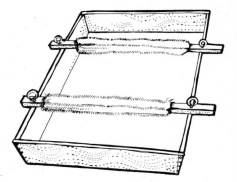

111 A simple cadge

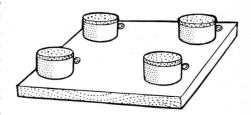

112 A block cadge

113 A seat perch

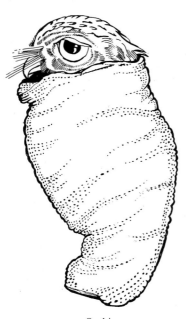

114 Socking

cut open or nylon stocking (which is cooler for longer journeys) is slid from the beak down over the body, leaving just the head protruding (see fig. 114). The bird is thus gently restrained with its wings folded and can be wedged into a comfortable position with cushions, or some other form of padding. Although the bird may struggle a little at first, it will soon lie still, content to be able to see everything that is going on around it. The sock is removed by sliding it down towards the tail at the journey's end. There are two major advantages with this method of travelling a bird. Firstly, you can keep your eye on it all the time, without having to listen to it banging about in a box, and secondly, there is no risk of broken feathers. A bird which is too large to be 'socked' can be wrapped in a length of material which can then be taped into position with wide sticky tape round the shoulders, central body and wings, and round the tail and feet (see fig. 115). Care must be taken to ensure that the wrapping and taping is not tight enough to cause the bird discomfort, but is firm enough to prevent it from wriggling out. This method is dangerous for long journeys because of the risk of overheating.

Occasionally you will encounter a bird which suffers from car-sickness. For this reason a bird should not be fed before travelling. In falcons, car-sickness leads to the appearance of the bird being about to cast. I have a female peregrine which will try to be sick in a car when hooded, but will be perfectly all right as soon as the hood is removed. In hawks, car-sickness is a retching motion which is obviously as uncomfortable for the hawk as it is for humans. Any bird which is habitually car-sick is best not boxed or hooded, and should be given plenty of fresh air by means of a slightly open window. A bird which has been sick will not normally be very enthusiastic about flying at the journey's end. Plenty of air is extremely important when travelling on a hot day. It is of even greater importance if the car is parked and the hawk left inside. The window must be left slightly ajar, for to be left hooded in a hot car must be excessively uncomfortable for a bird, and can be fatal. A hawk must not be left unattended, however, in a parked car with the windows wide open lest it is interfered with by a curious passer-by who decides to offer it a piece of cheese sandwich. Sadly too, there are still those who are hostile towards falconry who will administer unwanted attentions through an open window such as cutting a hawk's jesses in an attempt to turn it free.

It is possible to hunt a well trained bird direct from a vehicle. To do this, two people are required—one to drive, and the other to hold the hawk on the fist in readiness to be pitched out of the window when quarry is sighted. The updraft caused by the motion will help a falcon to gain height quickly. This method of hunting is more commonly used in America than in Britain.

When travelling single-handed a bird of any sort in any manner other than in a box, it is well worth the driver's while to wear a pair of light leather driving gloves to enable him to give instant assistance to the bird should it

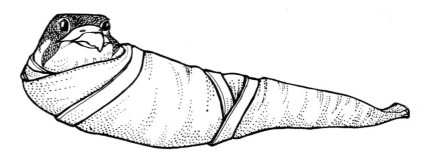

115 A different method of socking a hawk, using a length of material

be required. When a passenger is present, he or she should do likewise, taking care that the bird is not in a position to upset or endanger the driver. Car travelling on a cadge or perch is something which should be practised with a bird, starting with short journeys close to home. To have a bird which is a good and experienced traveller is a distinct advantage, rather like having a horse which is good to box.

My Changeable Hawk Eagle was so used to car travel that she would go to sleep on the cadge hooded, correcting her balance automatically to suit the motion of the vehicle. To achieve such a relaxed passenger, a falconer must remember that loud music, clouds of cigarette smoke, and jerky driving will not make the trip a pleasant one from the hawk's point of view.

A bird has no choice about whether it travels or not, and so every effort should be made to make the journey as comfortable as possible.

TRAIN

The first thing which must be done for any bird which is to travel by train is to tape its tail. Indeed, all birds which are to be crated or boxed should have their tails taped if they are to stand any chance of their tail feathers surviving the journey unscathed. This can be performed in several ways with a variety of materials. A roll of brown gummed paper—the sort which you lick to make it sticky—is most commonly used. This can either be taped from the top right down to and slightly beyond the bottom of the tail, or it can be put in one or three bands, at the middle, or at the top, middle and bottom respectively (see fig. 116). The bird must be cast and held with its tail folded rather than fanned and a second person can stick the tape. Alternatively, a piece of thin cardboard can be folded round the tail and stuck at the top to the over tail coverts, and bound with sticky tape. I do not like this method as the bird finds such an appendage extremely cumbersome. When I had run out of gummed paper once, I tried paper masking tape and, to my delight, I found it worked extremely well. It is sticky enough to hold well but also very easy to peel off the tail. A female sparrowhawk was sent by train to me with her tail taped with masking tape, on my recommendation, and she sat quite happily on the fist while the tape was removed with ease, to reveal a perfect tail. Generally speaking, I find it easier than the traditional gummed paper, but it is purely a matter of personal preference as either will suffice.

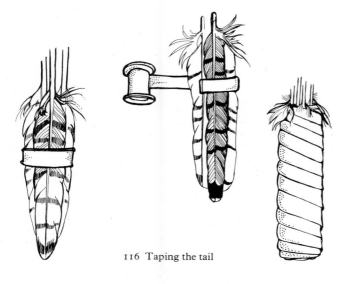

116 Taping the tail

When you wish to send a bird by train, the first point to check is that both the station from which you want to send it and the station at its eventual destination will handle livestock, as not all stations do. Secondly, the person who is receiving the bird should be informed of its departure time and must then contact his receiving station to inform them of the bird's forthcoming arrival and to ask to be telephoned immediately the box arrives. In my experience, railway staff are extremely helpful and interested if you tell them that you are expecting a hawk to arrive in their station. They also tend to be extremely keen to dispatch the box to you as quickly as possible when it arrives! A point to bear in mind is that livestock will not be accepted over weekends, and on a long journey when a change of trains is necessary it will not be possible to give an exact arrival time.

The box in which the bird travels will normally be charged for by weight and the length of the journey, but if it is a very large box, it may be measured and charged for by the cubic foot. The same criteria apply to the box as in the section under car travel. The substance on the floor of the box must not be sawdust, shavings or anything similar as the motion of the train might cause it to be disturbed and get into the hawk's eyes. The box must be clearly labelled, leaving space on the top for the railway's own label. You must put a 'This way up' label where it can be seen at a glance, and also mark it 'Livestock—with care please'. You must, of course, put clearly the name of the destination station, and the name and address of the person who is to collect the bird. Lastly, you will need a label to say 'Please ring (insert telephone number) immediately on arrival'.

If the journey is going to take less than a day to complete, then food need not be put in the box. If, however, it is a longer journey, then some food can be put in so that the bird can eat if it so wishes.

Should the box fail to arrive within a couple of hours of when it was expected, you must first ring the sender to check that it left on time, then ring the station from which it was sent and get an exact list of all the stations where it will have had to change trains, so that you can trace its route by contacting those stations to see if they remember the box passing through their hands. I once had a Little Owl which was 'lost' by British Rail in London for seven hours. After a search, however, it turned up eventually, having been sent on a detour to the wrong station, and was none the worse for the adventure. On the whole, birds seem to travel very well by train. I have never encountered a bird which was 'train-sick', and I feel that provided the box is suitable and the air holes sufficient, you are unlikely to run into any problems with this mode of transport.

AIR

As with shipment by train, it is extremely important to check with the airline involved that they will accept live birds. Although the boxing and labelling will be the same as described under train travel, there are certain additional significant points to note. When a hawk is being sent by air into another country, veterinary certificates will almost undoubtedly be required by the receiving country from the country of origin. Such a certificate is also required by certain American states when a hawk is being shipped from one state to another. Where a licence is required to import or export a hawk, this documentation must be shipped with the bird as well. All airlines conform to IATA regulations and specify the type of material from which the travelling box or crate must be constructed and its size, and the shipper must conform to such regulations or the bird will not be accepted. Some countries will not admit any birds of prey whatsoever, so once again this should be checked beforehand. All information should be double checked one day prior to departure for confirmation as regulations have a habit of altering from day to day and different officials will sometimes give different stories.

Downy young, eyasses and trained hawks with taped tails, all travel reasonably easily in a darkened box of suitable size. Wild-caught birds are more worrying to ship. The chances of a wild-caught raptor arriving without a number of broken flight feathers after an air journey in a normal box are very slight indeed. Thus such hawks should be shipped either in well padded boxes with thoroughly taped tails, or they can be socked in nylon hosiery or jacketed. Socking is only suitable for very short air journeys, as a bird which is prevented from standing for more than ten hours or so will become extremely sore and stiff. Most hawks are also incapable of passing mutes while socked and this will make them extremely uncomfortable and constipated if the journey is a long one. Birds which are to be socked must not, therefore, be fed before travelling. They should be wedged firmly but comfortably into position in a well ventilated compartment in a crate. I would definitely recommend this method for wild-caught birds on short air journeys, but for longer journeys with wild-caught raptors, the jacket is the best device to use in conjunction with a hood (see fig. 117). A jacket made out of hessian or light padded canvas, or a strong cotton material can be slipped over the bird's head, and with its legs inserted through leg holes, it can stand up when the jacket has been stitched into position. The stitching can be done rapidly with big stitches. The jacket, cut approximately to fit the size of the bird, must not be pulled tight, but left loose enough for the bird to breathe comfortably. Similarly, the leg holes must be large enough to allow easy movement of the legs. With the tail taped, a hawk thus prepared can be put into a smallish box to prevent it from turning round and to support it should it be unbalanced by the motion of travelling. For extremely nervous birds, a mild sedative can be administered safely. Advice on the type and dosage is best obtained from your vet, but check first because some airlines may refuse to accept a sedated bird. On journeys of a couple of days or so, food can be sent for trained birds. Wild-caught hawks will have to do without. If food is to be sent, it can be sent frozen or semi-frozen—according to when it is to be fed—in blocks of the right amount. These well-wrapped blocks can be attached to the outside of the crate with clear instructions about timing, stating that no water is necessary, and that there must be sufficient light for the hawk to be able to see to eat. On the whole, air travel is nothing to worry about from the hawk's point of view, provided that it is made as comfortable as possible. From the sender's point of view it is complex to organize, and everything must be double-checked down to the last detail to prevent mishap.

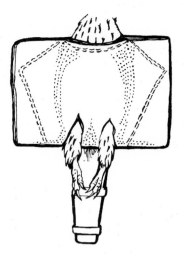

117 The jacket

BOAT

I have had but two occasions to travel a hawk by boat. One of the hawks was made very sick by the motion of the boat, while the other was perfectly all right. For a journey on a ferry or similar, a trained bird is best taken across hooded on the fist. (The hood must, of course, be removed should the bird attempt to be sick.) If the bird is to be sent unaccompanied, it can be boxed in the method already described with clear labelling. I imagine that sailing affects only certain birds adversely, as it does only certain humans.

16 Lost Hawks

Every falconer will lose a hawk at some time, as inevitably as every horse-man will periodically fall off a horse.

As your hawk disappears towards the horizon, stand still. Do not start running after it, for the first time that you pause to climb a fence or a gate you will lose sight of it, and consequently will not know if it has changed course and you are running in the wrong direction. If possible, mark it down—take note of the approximate position of where it disappears from view. Wait for a while to give it the chance to return. Often when a hawk disappears unexpectedly, it will return to where it left you a short while later. If you have disappeared, it will be confused and may pitch in a tree close by, or it may go off again. If, however, you have spent a short period swinging the lure, or jumping up and down waving the fist (depending on whether you are flying a longwing or a shortwing), whistling and shouting yourself hoarse without the hawk putting in a reappearance, then you must give chase, heading towards the position where you last saw your hawk. If your hawk is wearing telemetry, you only need to collect your aerial and receiver and start tracing the bleeps, but falconers who do not possess telemetry units will have to follow a more complicated procedure.

If the distance merits transport in a vehicle, quickly equip it with all the necessary retrieving aids (binoculars or preferably a telescope, plenty of meat, lures, a creance, a landing net, traps etc.) and set off. If you are going on foot, you will have to carry anything that you feel is necessary. Any help in the form of extra people to look for the bird is both useful and encour-aging for the falconer. Search methodically as much as possible on that day, listening for bells, and looking for crows, rooks or other flocks of birds which might draw your attention to your hawk by mobbing it. Many little clues can help—the warning cry of a blackbird, or the sudden exit of a few birds from a tree. Hawks often seem to prefer to perch in dead trees so inspect any dead trees carefully. If you spot your bird, see if it has a full crop—it may have made a kill. If it has not, try to call it down to the fist or lure, showing plenty of meat as an incentive, and choosing an easy path for it to fly down—do not make the angle too steep. If it totally ignores you, you can then really start to worry (if you have been careless enough to lose an untrained hawk you will have been really worried long before this point!). Stay as close to the bird as possible for the rest of the day, attempt-ing to mark it down when it takes stand for the night. Diurnal birds of prey do not like to move after dusk, so if your hawk is in an accessible place on a dark night, you might be able to climb up and grab it, or net it with a landing net. If you cannot do this, stay beneath your hawk for the night, or go home and return before first light. A trained bird at flying weight will be more hungry by the following morning and, after it has cast, if it needs to, you might persuade it to come down to the fist or to the lure at dawn.

If you search unsuccessfully for the remainder of the day when you lose your hawk, you should return home at dusk and notify the police, local animal welfare organizations such as the RSPCA, and any falconers who

live in the vicinity. These are the people who might be contacted if a hawk
was spotted or found. It is also worth talking to your milkman and postman
as they might spot or be told of a loose hawk. If you have not regained your
hawk in a few days, you can draft an advertisement for a local newspaper,
offering a reward for the hawk's safe return or for information leading to
its capture.

Most birds of prey will remain tame towards humans and will respond
according to their training for several days and even weeks. The exceptions
are the accipiters. A goshawk once lost will become completely wild within
two or three days. Thus, the time limit for finding and retrieving a lost
accipiter is considerably less than with most other species of raptor. When
tracking and calling to the fist or lure fail to induce a hawk to return, the
only alternative is trapping.

TRAPPING

There are various forms of traps and methods of trapping which can be
used for hawks. Traps are seldom used in Britain as the trapping of passage
or haggard birds of prey is illegal, so the British falconer will have no need
for a trap except to retrieve a lost hawk or a bird at hack. On the continent,
and particularly in America, they are widely used to trap passage hawks,
and consequently the average American apprentice falconer is far better
acquainted with the use of traps than an experienced British falconer.

The noose-jacket

In America these are widely used for trapping passage falcons. They are put on a live pigeon and are consequently called pigeon-harnesses. In Britain it is illegal to use captive quarry to retrieve hawks, just as it is to use baggies, or 'bagged quarry', so a noose-jacket can only be put on dead quarry. The jacket itself is made out of soft leather or canvas. It is made to tie round the quarry and is covered in nylon nooses. The quarry is staked out in an open space as near to the hawk as possible. Dead quarry will have to be twitched, jerked or pulled along the ground to attract the hawk's attention. In theory, the hawk should fly down to take the quarry and its feet should become entangled in the nylon nooses enabling the falconer to rush in and grab it. In practice, this usually works quite well, but the timing is critical. If you rush in too quickly, the hawk may not be sufficiently entangled, and on your approach may break free.

The bow net and flying hawks at hack

The bow net was most frequently used for trapping hawks at hack. The practice of hacking is seldom adopted nowadays in Britain, partly because it is no longer considered necessary, but mainly because with valuable birds in such short supply, it is considered too risky. I will briefly explain the principles of flying hawks at hack, however, as it is a practice with which all falconers who value the traditions of falconry should be at least vaguely familiar.

A group of eyasses are placed in a hack shed or in a similar arrangement, such as a pigeon loft, which will afford easy access for the eyasses to enter and leave the hack house at will. The group is put into the hack house just before they can fly. Their food is tied down twice daily on to a hack board. The eyasses become accustomed to eating off the hack board. When they can fly, they are able to leave the hack house and exercise freely, returning each day to eat off the hack board. Thus the eyasses can fly freely, exercising and playing together, building up their muscles, and learning all the skills of flying in connection with coping with different wind and weather conditions. The falconer must time his recapture so that the eyasses get the maximum time free that is possible, but trapping them before they start making kills on a regular basis, whereupon they would no longer be in need of the food on the hack board and would thus cease to return to the hack house.

In a group of hawks which are flying at hack, one or two will often be lost. Nowadays, there is always the risk that hawks flying at hack will be shot, and fewer falconers live in a quiet and secluded stretch of countryside which is suitable for flying hawks at hack.

Hacking-back is a similar process which is used to rehabilitate hawks. The process is exactly the same, except for the obvious difference that the hawks are not trapped when they start to make kills.

To return to the bow net, this trap was most frequently used to recapture hawks flying at hack. It was positioned close to the hack house, trapping the eyasses when they returned for food. Originally, it was made from a circular net of light but strong mesh, of approximately three feet in diameter. A light iron rod is bent to a semicircle on a diameter of three feet and it is covered with half of the net circle which is secured firmly to its circumference. The other half of the net is stretched out and pegged down on the ground. The bow is hinged to the ground by two large staples and bent over flat against the ground so that the net forms a circle, half attached to the bow and half pegged to the ground. A piece of tough beef is tied securely in the middle of the circle, and a long piece of cord is tied to the rim of the bow from whence it runs to the falconer who is hidden from the hawk's sight. The net can be concealed by laying tufts of grass over it. When the hawk lands on the net to take the meat, the falconer waits until she is positioned in the middle of the trap, eating unconcernedly, pulls the cord and the trap closes smartly, capturing the hawk in the net. The cord must be secured and then the falconer can go in and remove the hawk. The bow net has now been improved by the addition of a spring, triggered by the falconer's pulling away a strut which holds the bow flat.

The dho-gazza

This trap is only used in countries where live bait can legally be used to attract a falcon. It is a black mesh net strung with spring clips between two poles from just above ground level up to a height of about seven feet. The net is designed to collapse on impact. The live pigeon is staked out, close to the net, allowing it some movement to catch the falcon's attention. When she stoops, she will hopefully miss the pigeon which can move out of the way, but collide with the virtually invisible net which will pull free from the poles and entangle the falcon. The dho-gazza can be made more efficient by using two nets placed at right angles to each other.

The bal-chatri

This is basically a wire mesh basket which is covered in nylon nooses and inverted over meat or live quarry. The hawk becomes entangled in the nooses in the same way as it does in the noose jacket.

Winding up

This refers to a method of recapturing a trained falcon, rather than to a trap. If a falcon which has been lost for some days will come to a lure but will not allow the falconer to make in towards her, she can be 'wound up'. This involves staking one end of a creance in the ground so that it is held approximately one-and-a-half inches above ground level. The lure is staked out and when the falcon flies down to take it, and has started feeding, the falconer can walk around the bird with the other end of the creance in large circles, wrapping the line around her ankles. The circuits must be completed carefully, at the time when the falcon's tail is raised as she bends to eat. When a few turns have been taken around her ankles, she will be caught, and, keeping the line taut, the falconer can make in quickly and take up his falcon.

The problem with this method is that if the grass is too long it will snag the creance. This problem can sometimes be alleviated by putting the lure on a small hand-constructed mound of grass, so that the falcon's ankles will not be obscured by grass.

To lose a hawk in fair flight after quarry is no disgrace, although this might be small comfort to the falconer at the time. When a bird is lost owing to inaccuracy of weighing, flying in unsuitable conditions, or, worse still, faulty equipment, it is entirely the fault of the falconer. Should the latter reason mean the bird flies off with swivel and leash attached, the result will probably be a fatality unless the hawk is recovered quickly. The importance of thoroughly checking a hawk's equipment daily cannot be over-emphasized.

17 Conservation and the Law

119 ABCR Barn Owls breed readily in captivity

I have often encountered individuals and organizations who believe that falconers are the enemies of wild birds of prey. This is not true. The majority of falconers are sensible enough to realize that in order to perpetuate the sport the conservation of the wild population of raptors is of the utmost importance. There is a minority of people (many of whom are not falconers but dealers) who bring the sport of falconry into disrepute by taking protected birds of prey illegally from the wild, just as there are some gamekeepers and 'sportsmen' who shoot raptors, but this does not necessarily mean that all falconers, gamekeepers and sportsmen behave in this disgraceful manner. It is falconers who, by trial and error, have established captive breeding as a realistic way of conserving the wild populations of birds of prey. Now falconers in several countries are nearing the stage where they can breed sufficient numbers of raptors in captivity to satisfy their own demands. Over and above this, the outstanding success of American schemes to breed and release endangered species proves that the many falconers who have expert knowledge of captive breeding techniques can really make a positive contribution towards conservation.

120 Philippine Eagle: Ron Krupa, a falconer, runs a breed and release project for these rare eagles in the Philippines

121 A Little Owl

In addition, many falconers rehabilitate injured birds of prey which are brought to them. This is usually done at the expense of the individual who personally meets the veterinary and other expenses involved. At our School we have a constant stream of injured raptors, suffering from varied ailments, ranging from gunshot wounds to the effects of poisoning. Over 50% of those which survive can be rehabilitated after treatment and convalescence, while the others are paired up and used in breeding programmes.

The taking of wild birds of prey in Britain is governed by the 1954 Protection of Birds Act. This prohibits the taking of wild birds without a licence. Licences for English and Welsh birds of prey are granted by the Department of the Environment, Tollgate House, Bristol, and for the Scottish raptors by the Scottish Home and Health Department, St Andrew's House, Edinburgh. The successful applicant is permitted to take one eyass bird of the species applied for. In Britain licences are never granted to permit the trapping of a passage or haggard bird. Only one licence is granted within a year to a successful applicant. A licence is also required to import or export a bird of prey. A bird obtained under licence can only be transferred to another falconer after permission has been obtained from the authority who originally granted the licence. Generally speaking, licences are not easy to obtain.

British birds of prey can be bought and sold if they are ABCR—aviary bred, and close-ringed. It is illegal to sell any British raptor which is unrung, and it is also illegal to be in the possession of a recently taken bird of prey without a licence. Currently, there are no restrictions in Britain as to who may buy an ABCR bird of prey. It is left to the discretion of the person offering the bird for sale, and thus, all too often, birds of prey end up with unsuitable and ignorant people.

At the time of writing the Wildlife and Countryside Bill is before Parliament. This contains certain proposals concerning the keeping of birds of prey in captivity in Britain. When these proposals are implemented into law a system of registration will be introduced for all diurnal captive birds of prey in Britain. This will mean that every legal captive raptor will have a band put round its leg and the bird will be registered to its keeper. Thus if the bird is sold or passed on, the authorities must be informed and the registration transferred to the new keeper, similar to the manner in which a car is registered to its owner. To keep in captivity any bird of prey which is not registered will be illegal. This system will help in several ways. Firstly, nobody could claim to have bred a certain species of British bird of prey without a pair of parent birds of that species registered in their name. Secondly, if a captive bird was stolen from a falconer (something which happens all too frequently nowadays), there would be more likelihood of the bird being traced by the number on its registration ring. Thirdly, it should discourage people from taking birds of prey illegally from the wild if they know that the bird will not be registered and consequently would be valueless. When these proposals become law, there will obviously be a great deal more relevant information with which a falconer must become familiar. Information regarding the laws relating to birds of prey at any time should be obtained from the Department of the Environment in Bristol.

It is the responsibility of all falconers to respect the laws relating to birds of prey, and to the taking of certain protected quarries. Similarly, falconers must respect the land and property of those who are kind enough to allow them to work their hawks over it. Any misconduct on the part of a falconer serves only to threaten his sport. The future perpetuation or condemnation of falconry rests largely in the hands of those who practise it.

122 A lecture and demonstration for a group of children. It is important to educate people in the ways of birds of prey

18 Falconry Worldwide

123 The Peregrine Falcon is highly acclaimed worldwide for falconry

The number of countries in which falconry is practised is surprising. In some countries there are only a handful of falconers who train native species and who are little hindered by legislation concerning the practice of falconry and the taking of birds of prey from the wild. In other countries, falconry is totally controlled by the government or local authorities who organize every aspect of the sport and strictly protect their native raptors by limiting the number which can be owned for the purposes of falconry. In my efforts to find out more about the various laws, practices and individuals concerned with falconry throughout the world, I have written to as many falconry organizations and individuals abroad as I could find addresses for. The majority have been exceptionally helpful and forthcoming and it is with their assistance, therefore, that the following information has been accumulated.

AMERICA

In America, the laws vary from state to state. However, the federal regulations under the title of Wildlife and Fisheries lay down certain minimum standards for the various states to follow in the issuing of falconry permits. Thus in some states falconry is exceptionally well organized and controlled, while in others it is illegal, largely because of the very high cost involved in organizing falconry to the requisite standard.

The main points of the American law are as follows. Anyone who wishes to practise falconry must first apply for a permit. The minimum age for a falconer is 14 years. To be granted a permit, the applicant must achieve over 80% in a written examination devised by the state, relating to basic biology, care and handling of raptors, literature, laws, regulations and other appropriate subject matter. The applicant must also prepare raptor housing facilities and equipment to suit the requirements of the individual state. The facilities and equipment must be inspected and approved by a member of the State Wildlife Department before a permit will be granted. There are three classes of falconer, the apprentice class, general class, and master class. Apprentices must practise for their first two years under the guidance of a general or master falconer. A falconer is not allowed to have more than three apprentices at any one time. Apprentices are allowed only one bird— either an American Kestrel or a Red-tailed Buzzard, and they can only replace it once during a period of 12 months. General falconers must be at least 18 years old and are allowed a maximum of two raptors. They must have a minimum of two years' experience in the practice of falconry at the apprentice level or its equivalent. Master falconers must have at least five years' experience at the general class level or its equivalent. They are allowed a maximum of three raptors. Raptors must be trapped as passage birds. Only general and master falconers are allowed to take eyasses. It is illegal to sell birds of prey. It is illegal to retain feathers for any purpose other than imping.

These are the basic requirements of the Federal Law. However, many of the states in which falconry is practised include in their legislation certain additional requirements which embellish the federal laws. Although there are approximately 1400 falconers in the USA and Canada, their distribution among the various states is by no means even. For example, in Colorado there are approximately 150 falconers, and in New York 200, while in Virginia there are only 22, and in Maine a mere four individuals who are licensed falconers. In New York people who are interested in getting a licence for falconry will receive on request from the State Department of Environmental Conservation a comprehensive selection of informative advice sheets about all aspects of falconry, even including a list of prices to help the prospective falconer gauge approximately how much it will cost him to maintain a raptor to the requisite standard. All states where falconry is legal have a club or society, membership of which is not obligatory for practising falconers within the state. There is a national falconry club in the USA—the North American Falconers' Association. NAFA produces a journal, *Hawk Chalk*, and has a membership of approximately 1500, including foreign members.

Certain states have stricter restrictions than are required by Federal Law. In Maine a general falconer is only allowed to sponsor two apprentices rather than three. In several states the age limit for falconers is 16 or over, rather than 14. In New York, if an eyass is taken from a nest, the tree from which it is taken must, by State Law, have a tree guard attached by the falconer to protect the other youngsters in the nest from racoons and other predators. Most states charge a fee for the issuing of a falconry licence, normally in the region of ten dollars. It is also common practice to have a falconry advisory board to advise the licence-issuing authority in the state. These boards normally consist of five or more individuals who may be master falconers, ornithologists or environmentalists. When a bird is taken from the wild it must have a band attached round its leg bearing a serial number which is logged by the licensing authority. The authorities can revoke a licence if a hawk is improperly maintained.

Importation and exportation are controlled by licence, and quarantine is usually mandatory, unless a bird is imported under the Pet Bird Law from another country in which the falconer has been staying for 90 days or more. At the time of writing, quarantine is even imposed on the transfer of a falconer's bird from one state to another, so it is perfectly all right for a hawk to cross a state boundary under its own steam, but if it does so in the company of a falconer it must serve a quarantine period. This seems a somewhat harsh ruling as it deprives falconers of being able to fly their hawks at a national falconry meet in another state. Generally speaking, the USA are fairly well off for native species suitable for falconry, the most widely used being the Red-tailed Buzzard, so there are comparatively few imported species flown. Of the few that are imported, the Lanner Falcon is the most frequently encountered, and the occasional Lugger Falcon, Saker Falcon and exotic eagle such as the Crowned or Changeable Hawk Eagle.

To breed raptors in the USA written permission must be obtained from the relevant authority. Much of the progeny produced by captive breeding is released, as the youngsters cannot be sold and consequently breeding on a commercial basis for personal profit is legally impossible. Cornell University operates a large and successful captive breeding project, and releases captive-bred peregrines annually. The facilities are open to the public.

Although the average British falconer might find the legislation in the USA somewhat over-restrictive, the system has many benefits which are lacking in British law. Firstly the method of testing and inspecting applicants for falconry permits prevents ignorant and ill-qualified individuals from obtaining and subsequently mismanaging hawks. Secondly, prevention of the sale of raptors renders them valueless in monetary terms. Thus the incentive to steal raptors either from other falconers or from the wild is absent. Falconers in the USA are therefore dedicated individuals who practise falconry purely for the love of the sport.

ARABIA

There is little or no legislation in Arabia relating to falconry, the taking of native birds, or to the import and export of raptors. There are few raptors native to Arabia. Despite the particular Arabic interest in falcons, there are few species which breed in Arabia. The only nesting falcon in the Gulf region is the Sooty Falcon, (*Falco concolor*). The Saker Falcon is frequently referred to as an 'Arabic falcon', but in fact sakers do not breed in significant numbers in Arabia, but are found from central Asia and southern Russia across Turkey, the Balkans and eastern Europe. So the sakers which the Arabs fly are nearly always imported.

The Arabs prefer sakers for several reasons. Firstly they can withstand the tremendous temperatures and high humidities of Arabia. Secondly they are robust, but have very soft feathers which, unlike the more brittle feathers of many other falcons, can withstand the knocks and scrapes involved in taking quarry which would cause other feathers to break. Also, although the Arabs normally fly their falcons at Houbara (Macqueen's Bustard) sakers will also take desert hares when other quarry is lacking.

This is something which a peregrine, the other falcon flown by the Arabs, will not do. When I asked Sheikh Zaid of Abu Dhabi for his personal opinion on a comparison of merit between peregrines and sakers he replied that although the peregrine was faster over shorter distances, a really good saker combined all the best qualities of a peregrine but had more staying power and was thus matchless. The Arabs normally fly only passagers, and falcons rather than tiercels or sakrets; Lanners are sometimes flown, but they are not regarded very highly. The occasional gyrfalcon is also encountered from time to time, but they are known as 'drawing-room hawks', for they cannot be maintained in flying condition in the Arabian climate.

Captive breeding is, to the best of my knowledge, only taking place successfully at the Sulman Falcon Centre in Bahrain, under the guidance of Joseph Platt. The Centre has pairs of peregrines, sakers, prairies, and gyrfalcons. In 1981, 13 peregrines, sakers and prairies were produced. The youngsters are used for flying by HH The Crown Prince Sheikh Hamad bin Isa Al-Khalifa, who set up the Centre in 1977.

A great deal has already been written about falconry in Arabia, and most people are familiar with the Arabians' love of falcons, and their dedication to the sport. Mark Allen's excellent book *Falconry in Arabia* (Orbis, London, 1980) is a comprehensive and fascinating work which I would recommend to anyone particularly interested in Arabic hawking.

AUSTRALIA

It is illegal to take birds from the wild for the purpose of falconry in Australia. It is also illegal to import or export hawks. This obviously presents problems to falconers but the few keen individuals who are

124 Egon Russell, an Australian falconer, with a European Sparrowhawk

practising falconry seem quietly to bypass the difficulties and fly mainly Brown Falcons, Black Falcons, goshawks, peregrines and Wedge-tailed Eagles. Brown Falcons are apparently somewhat buzzard-like in their nature. The Black Falcons, however, will fly splendidly, waiting on for extended periods, and taking a variety of game. The Wedge-tails will work off the fist at quarry, or can be persuaded to wait on at a good pitch. The large females fly at 10–12 lb.

Some captive breeding is starting. At the moment it seems uncertain whether the eyasses will be able to be flown legally for falconry.

BELGIUM

There is very little legislation about the keeping of hawks in Belgium, but a special authorization is necessary to take them from the wild. This is usually granted only to scientific organizations and to falconers. The permits are not transferable, and in theory only one bird of prey is granted per falconer, but in practice a falconer usually has two or three. The number of permits granted is fixed at 25 for the whole of Belgium. The falconers hope to increase this number, and to divide the number amongst the individual regions, Brussels, Flanders and the Walloons.

At the moment it is permissible to import, to detain, and to transport non-indigenous species, but this may change under the Convention of Washington. There is no quarantine in Belgium, although a veterinary certificate is often required by the Customs. Native species suitable for falconry include peregrines, which are very rare, merlins, which are also rare, goshawks (150–200 pairs), and sparrowhawks. The gyrfalcon is still on the Belgian list of indigenous raptors, but in reality it has only been seen occasionally in the past by an ornithologist. Imported Saker Falcons, Lanner Falcons and Shahins (sub-species of peregrine) are also flown, and so, occasionally, are Red-headed Merlins, Shikras, Red-tailed Buzzards, Prairie Falcons, a Steppe Eagle and an Ornate Hawk Eagle. There are comparatively few species of quarry to hunt in Belgium. A hunting licence is not necessary for falconry. Bagged quarry is permitted, but only during the hunting season.

There are 50–60 members of the two falconry clubs, of which only 25–30 possess birds. To join the *Club Marie de Bourgogne* a person must have two sponsors. He then becomes an associate member for two to three years, during which time he must learn from the experienced members, and cannot vote within the club. His premises and area are inspected to ensure that he has adequate facilities to keep a hawk. The other club, *Belgische Verenigingvan Vlaamse, Valkeniersen Havikeniers*, uses the Flemish language only, while *Club Marie de Bourgogne* uses both Flemish and French. In the latter, the membership fee is 500 Belgian francs per annum; members under 18 years of age can join for nothing. The club organizes several field meets a year and usually holds one at the time of the annual general meeting. Newsletters are sent out regularly to the members.

Some captive breeding successes have occurred with peregrines, Sakers, goshawks and kestrels, and also with hybrids, which have apparently proved extremely good falconry birds. The members of the club co-operate to put together mature pairs for breeding. Some initial attempts are being made in the field of artificial insemination.

FRANCE

To practise falconry in France you have to be a member of one of the two falconry associations in the country. The Minister of the Environment is responsible for authorizing both the usage and the transportation of birds of prey used for falconry. Peregrines, goshawks, sparrowhawks and kestrels are the native raptors most commonly flown. Lanner Falcons are bred in captivity and are also used; they are flown mainly at partridge. Beginners must start under the guidance of an experienced falconer before they are allowed their first bird, which is usually a kestrel, but occasionally a lanner. Both clubs, ANFA and GFASO organize falconry meets, which are sub-divided into a meet for *les autoursiers* who, like the British 'austringers', fly short-winged hawks, mainly *l'autour* (the goshawk) and *l'epervier* (the sparrowhawk), and a meet for *les fauconniers*, who fly longwings—mainly peregrines and lanners.

There is much interest in the conservation of raptors, particularly the peregrine. Projects to breed peregrines in captivity have recently been started. Lanners are bred frequently, and projects to breed sparrowhawks and hybrids—lanner × peregrine—have been set up.

Although there are considerably fewer falconers in France than in Britain, (ANFA has a membership of 80) they are keen and well organized, concentrating their energies purely into hunting, and breeding only those species which are suitable for falconry.

GERMANY

Falconry is very popular in Germany. Goshawks, peregrines and several species of large eagle are flown. There is no shortage of quarry and consequently the sport flourishes. There is a large centre open to the Public at Hellenthal where there are many species on display, ranging from gyr-falcons to vultures.

IRELAND

The law in Ireland concerned with licences for possession and importation of raptors differs in Northern Ireland and the Republic. Generally, licences are only granted for sparrowhawks and kestrels, and consequently these are the two species most commonly flown in Ireland. There are also a few peregrines, Red-tails, and European Goshawks used for hawking but the largest single collection of raptors in the country is held at the National Falconry Centre of Ireland, Robertstown, Co. Kildare, which is open to the public. The birds on display include a Bateleur Eagle, a Griffon Vulture, a Golden Eagle, a Lanneret, several Common Buzzards, and a couple of Snowy Owls. The Irish Hawking Club has approximately 57 members. The club suffers some pressure from the Irish Anti-Blood Sports League who are apparently quite active in their efforts to ban falconry altogether. All Ireland's native raptors are strictly protected. Peregrines, although still scarce, are gradually regaining their previous numbers. There is great interest in captive breeding amongst the falconers, and pairs of several species including peregrines have been put together. Some successes have been achieved, notably the pairing of the Hon. Mr John Morris's saker with Mr Ronald Stevens's tiercel peregrine to produce hybrids.

In the past Ireland was a stronghold for falconry, particularly famous for magpie hawking. Now a practising falconer is indeed a rarity, and the need for a degree of revitalization is apparent.

ITALY

The *Circola dei Falconairi d'Italia* has a mere six or seven practising members. Far from wishing to increase the number of falconers in the country, the club actively resists advances from interested individuals hoping to take up the sport, preferring to restrict the numbers to those who are well qualified to keep hawks. Thus it is only a very persevering individual indeed who succeeds in taking up falconry in Italy.

There have recently been some new laws passed in certain regions of Italy which seem to aim at repressing the few falconers left. Falconry is now only permitted with birds bred at authorized centres. As there are no such centres in Italy, Italian falconers are being forced to look outside the country for captive-bred hawks. An additional difficulty is the shortage of game. Some of the falconers, notably Dr Umberto Caproni di Taliedo, now come to Scotland annually to fly game hawks, and they also go to Spain to hawk Red-legged Partridge.

Although, therefore, falconry could scarcely be said to be flourishing in Italy, the standard of hawking is obviously very high.

JAPAN

Hawking in Japan is restricted in several ways. Scarcity of game is perhaps the most unfortunate of these. The traditional quarry in Japan were geese and cranes. The latter are now strictly protected, while the former are no longer encountered in great numbers. Goshawks and Hawk Eagles are most frequently trained, but peregrines and sparrowhawks are also flown. The use of bagged quarry is legal in Japan, and this is used not only by the falconers in urban areas, but also occasionally for public demonstrations.

With the establishment of a mews at the State Gardens of Nagroya, interest in falconry has apparently revived in Japan in recent years. Dr E. W. Jameson has written a well-researched book entitled *The Hawking of Japan* which is both comprehensive and extremely interesting.

THE PHILIPPINES

There are no laws relating to falconry in the Philippines. Threatened or endangered species such as the Philippine (Monkey-eating) Eagle are in theory protected, but the law is seldom enforced. However, falconry is not practised in the Philippines.

The only falconer, on the island of Mindanao, is Ron Krupa, who is in charge of the Philippine Eagle breeding project, which is supported logistically by the Philippine Government. He believes that many of the 24 species of diurnal raptors found in the Philippines are suitable for falconry. At his Centre, which is open to the public, he is also attempting to breed Grey-headed Fishing Eagles, Philippine Hawk Eagles, and Philippine Horned Owls. A White-bellied Sea Eagle is flown at hack from the Centre. The Philippines are beginning to show a glimmer of interest in the conservation of their endangered native raptors, particularly in the Philippine Hawk Eagle, and the Giant Scops Owl, as well as the Philippine Eagle. Ron Krupa is also involved in an educational drive aimed at forest conservation for the forests are being cut down at an alarming rate and this threatens the raptor populations which decrease as their habitat is destroyed.

The future success of the breeding project depends largely upon whether the Philippine Government continues to give the Centre its full support. Ron Krupa, worried about the future of the Centre, points out that the programme needs financial as well as moral support if it is to succeed.

125 Tawny Eagle: these birds seem more popular for falconry purposes in Britain than in their native Africa

SOUTH AFRICA

Falconry is only practised in the Transvaal and Natal. Elsewhere it is illegal, or there are no practitioners. There is a system of grading based on exams and practicals. Learners are apprenticed to a practising falconer until they are considered competent to take their own bird, which is often one intended for rehabilitation. Lanner Falcons, Black Sparrowhawks and African Hawk Eagles (African Bonelli's) are most frequently flown, but Shikras, kestrels, Red-headed Merlins, Gabar Goshawks, Pale Chanting Goshawks, Ovambo Sparrowhawks, Red-breasted Sparrowhawks, Little Sparrowhawks, African Goshawks and White-eyed Kestrels are also flown. Peregrines are too rare to be permitted regularly to falconers. Lanners are mainly flown at francolin and doves, as are Black Sparrowhawks and African Hawk Eagles, which also take guinea-fowl and hare. The taking of quarry is controlled by the relevant hunting seasons.

SWEDEN

Originally falconers in Sweden were allowed to fly only goshawks. Special permits were needed and special hunting seasons existed. Since 1972, however, falconry has been illegal in Sweden.

Some captive breeding projects exist for scientific research. Peregrines and Eagle Owls have been bred successfully. The youngsters are hacked back to the wild, or used for other breeding projects. Any native ex-falconers or falconry-orientated individuals are unpopular with the ornithologists. My correspondent felt that this was unfortunate because falconers' experiences are needed in Sweden for the breeding projects.

Of Sweden's native birds of prey, the goshawk continues to dominate numerically. Peregrines are threatened—there are only six pairs left. Gyr-falcons are maintaining a reasonable footing—somewhere between 30 and 60 pairs. The Golden Eagle is also doing well—there are approximately 300 individuals in Sweden. Their situation has been improved by winter feeding by the nature societies. There are fewer White-tailed Sea Eagles, but the population is increasing. Merlins are far from plentiful, but kestrels and hobbies are faring better. Rough-legged, Common and Honey Buzzards enjoy a fairly stable position. Of the owls, the Little Owl is the rarest, while the Eagle Owl is recovering largely owing to the success of captive breeding projects.

SWITZERLAND

The laws in Switzerland are somewhat confusing as the country is divided into 26 cantons, each of which has its own laws about hunting and the preservation of wildlife. In most of the cantons, falconry is possible. Goshawks and peregrines are normally flown, the latter at crows and magpies. There are only between 20 and 30 falconers in the country, who belong to the Swiss falconers' association—*Schweizerische Falkner Vereigigung*. All the native raptors are heavily protected. Some captive breeding has been attempted, but so far without success.

TURKEY

There are no laws in Turkey relating to falconry. The only laws with any possible relevance pertain to import and export, which apply mainly to 'pets'. There are several falconers in Turkey but without any system of registration, and noting the absence of any falconry clubs and societies, it is very hard to estimate the number of individuals who actually practise falconry.

The raptors in Turkey are varied because it is on a major migration route. Thus the birds of prey in (or passing through) Turkey include ospreys, White-tailed Sea Eagles, Red Kites, Black Kites, Short-toed Eagles, sparrowhawks, European Buzzards, Shikras, Levant Sparrowhawks, goshawks, Long-legged Buzzards, Honey Buzzards, Bonelli's Eagles, Booted Eagles, Golden Eagles, Imperial Eagles, Greater and Lesser Spotted Eagles, Steppe Eagles, Marsh Harriers, Hen Harriers, Pallid Harriers, Montagu's Harriers, Saker Falcons, Lanner Falcons, Peregrine Falcons, Eleonora's Falcons, hobbies, merlins, Red-footed Falcons, Lesser and Common Kestrels, Egyptian Vultures, Black Vultures, Griffon Vultures, Barn Owls, Scops Owls, Eagle Owls, Brown Fish Owls, Little Owls, Tawny Owls, Long-eared Owls, and Boreal Owls. It seems surprising, therefore, that there are only two birds normally flown for falconry—namely goshawks and sparrowhawks.

Most of the falconers are in the Eastern Anatolian region, where they fly sparrowhawks at quail and goshawks at rabbits, pheasant, duck and partridge. Occasionally a Booted Eagle is trained and flown at rabbit.

Considering the noticeable lack of regulations about trapping, quarry and usage of hawks it seems astonishing that falconry in Turkey is not more popular, and that a wider variety of species, particularly among the longwings, are not trained. Apparently, however, the average person in Turkey has not the resources, time, or know-how to indulge in the sport, and so falconry in Turkey now, as in the past in so many countries, is mainly a sport for the elite.

ZIMBABWE

In Zimbabwe falconry is controlled by the Department of National Parks and Wildlife Management. There are three grades of falconer—the novice Grade C, Grade B and the highest Grade A. Grade C falconers are not registered with the Department of National Parks, and can fly only non-Royal Game Hawks listed in Part III of the Department's Schedule of native raptors, which includes Shikras (Little Banded Goshawks) Gabar Goshawks, Pale and Dark Chanting Goshawks, African Goshawks, Red-breasted Sparrowhawks, Ovambo Sparrowhawks, Little Sparrowhawks, Wahlberg's Eagles and Augur Buzzards. Grade C falconers are advised to join the Zimbabwe Falconers' Club (PO Box 8564, Causeway, Zimbabwe) where they can benefit from association with experienced registered falconers, although membership is not obligatory. To become a Grade B falconer, a Grade C falconer must be verbally and practically examined by an examiner (an experienced falconer or honorary officer of the Department appointed for the purpose). The examination is based on the condition of the applicant's hawk, its response to stimuli offered by the falconer and the general relationship between the hawk and the falconer in other respects, and on answers to informal questions put to the falconer by the examiner, which satisfies him that the issue of a permit for a Part II hawk will result in the hawk being properly housed, fed, trained, exercised and hunted. The recommendation of the examiner is sufficient for the Department to upgrade a falconer from Grade C to Grade B. Grade B falconers are permitted to fly a maximum of two Part II raptors, which are Black Sparrowhawks, Lanner Falcons, and African Hawk Eagles. Grade A and B falconers must sign the Falconer's Code of Conduct and they are registered by the Department. Grade A falconers are those permitted to fly Part I hawks—namely Peregrine Falcons. There are many excellent Grade B falconers who do not wish to fly peregrines and are thus content to remain with a B grading. However, those who aspire to fly peregrines must achieve a high standard of hunting proficiency with the Lanner Falcon. They must also use suitable hunting dogs to assist them—locally bred pointers are used and occasionally English setters. The reclassification must be acceptable to at least three registered Grade A falconers and to a qualified senior officer of the Department. A Grade A falconer can possess a maximum of three Part I and II raptors, which includes a maximum of two peregrines. There are eight Grade A falconers and approximately 40 registered Grade B falconers, although only about 20 are practising.

The birds most popular for falconry are therefore the Royal Game species Part II raptors—Black Sparrowhawks, African Hawk Eagles, and Lanner Falcons. Taita Falcons, Ayres' Hawk Eagles, Crowned Eagles, Martial Eagles and Verreaux's Eagles (Black Eagles) can also be obtained under special permit. However, the large eagles are not considered suitable for general falconry, and permits are therefore only issued to those who can justify flying and hunting them. There are no foreign birds of prey in Zimbabwe, and import and export is strictly controlled. The exportation of Royal Game species is usually prohibited. The control of the taking of quarry is vested in the landowner. Tiercels and lannerets are flown at doves, snipe, larks, rollers, francolin and occasionally teal. Falcons and Lanners are flown mainly at francolin and teal. Black Sparrowhawks take francolin, quail, larks, and occasionally guinea-fowl. African Hawk Eagles are flown at hare, especially at night with the aid of a spotlight. They are also hunted at francolin and guinea-fowl in the same manner as Black Sparrowhawks.

DDT is still used in Zimbabwe, although the Government is moving towards a ban of this and other residual pesticides. While DDT is still actively in use, raptors are threatened. Peregrines, Lanners and Black Sparrowhawks are considered to be particularly at risk, and the levels in their eggs are being monitored by Ron Tomson, Officer of the Department and a Grade A falconer. He is actively supported by the falconers. A captive

126 A hooded Steppe Eagle

breeding programme has been set up within the Zimbabwe Falconers' Club, and includes four pairs of peregrines, three pairs of lanners, and a pair of Black Sparrowhawks. The first two peregrines to be bred in captivity in Africa were reared in 1981. The Club publishes a newsletter entitled *Talon* twice yearly and an annual journal called *Footnotes*.

Eyasses, passage hawks and haggards (except haggard Black Sparrowhawks) can be flown, although the seasons for taking the former and the latter are controlled. A hawk can be hacked back and replaced at any time by a falconer. Aylmeri jesses are obligatory with flying jesses when the hawk is being flown free. If the falconer does not maintain and hunt his hawks to the requisite standard his permit can be revoked.

Thus it can be seen that falconry in Zimbabwe is extemely well organized, with the emphasis admirably placed on hunting.

OTHER COUNTRIES

Falconry is also practised in several other countries, including Holland, Austria, Spain, Tunisia, India, Pakistan and New Zealand, and in Russia and Turkestan where Berkut Eagles used to be (and still may be) flown at wolves which threatened flocks of sheep.

Savigny's Eagle Owl

A Miscellany of Points to Remember

Always cast your bird into the wind.

Do not cast a bird in a strong wind towards a bank of trees, for if it goes up over the top, you will lose sight of it.

When walking with a bird in a wind or breeze, always face it into the wind.

Beware of flying a bird free in a strong wind.

Indigenous species can be flown in light rain, but do not fly in heavy rain.

Do not fly a bird in mist or fog.

When flying a bird initially in snow, put it on a creance for the first few flights.

Never tether your bird out in hail

Do not block your bird in hot sun for any length of time or leave it in a hot vehicle.

Do not fly your bird in very hot weather, particularly falcons as they will climb to cooler heights and will possibly stay up there and drift off.

Do not approach a bird with strong sun behind you as it will not be able to see you clearly and will bate away from you.

Always carry spare jesses, swivel, leash and a hood in your falconry bag, but not bells as you will constantly mistake their ringing for your bird.

Always carry a pair of 10×50 binoculars when you are flying a longwing which ranges.

Do not wear big flappy coats or wide bottomed trousers when handling birds.

Make sure that you can run easily in your footwear. Wellington boots can sometimes hamper you in this respect.

Wear country colours when you are out hawking.

Always give your bird a warm-up flight before you take it out and expect it to hunt.

Do not fly your bird close to a river as it will invariably chase something on the other side. If you are hawking moorhen or similar on a river bank, make sure you know the crossing points.

Avoid flying shortwings when the leaves are on the trees in case you lose them.

When hunting, always observe the country code.

Always have a brightly coloured lure and creance stick so that you can see it easily in the grass.

Make sure that the swivel can rotate easily and that its rotation is not blocked by a jess slipping down.

Make sure that two or more birds in the same mews cannot reach each other.

Do not tie your bird near to a wall or some object which it will try to bate towards to sit on.

Make sure that the rings on your perches can rotate freely.

Always make sure that your bird cannot knock its flight feathers against the walls of the mews or any other solid object.

Never tie your bird under a fruit tree, in case a fruit falls down and hits it.

Check your equipment daily for wear.

When walking with a bird and another person, always tell your companion to walk on your right (or on your left if you are a right-handed falconer) so that the bird can see the person.

Never take any risks with a bird by flying for friends in unsuitable conditions. Something will invariably go wrong.

When passing a bird from fist to fist, always take hold of the jesses and leash first, and then pick it up with your fist behind the bird's legs.

Always grease your jesses regularly.

Do not fly your bird free less than three-quarters of an hour before dusk, in case you lose it and darkness falls before you can retrieve it.

Beware of hawks which have previously been trained to fly to the fist opposite to the one you use. Such birds will often sit the wrong way round on the fist, and may even attempt to fly to the wrong side.

When hawking with companions always ensure that they too have the wherewithal to retrieve a lost hawk.

If you lose a hawk when flying it, check the wind direction, as the hawk will normally go downwind.

Checklist of Flying Weights

Please note that these weights are intended only as an approximate guide.

	IMPERIAL		METRIC	
	MALE	FEMALE	MALE	FEMALE
Kestrel	5½ oz–6½ oz	6½ oz–8 oz	149 g–177 g	177 g–227 g
European Buzzard	1 lb 8 oz–1 lb 12 oz	1 lb 14 oz–2 lb 2 oz	680 g–794 g	850 g–964 g
Red-tailed Buzzard	1 lb 14 oz–2 lb 5 oz	2 lb 6 oz–3 lb 3 oz	850 g–1 kg 49 g	1 kg 79 g–1 kg 446 g
Ferruginous Buzzard	2 lb 3 oz–3 lb 2 oz	3 lb 4 oz–4 lb 12 oz	992 g–1 kg 417 g	1 kg 474 g–2 kg 155 g
Harris' Hawk	1 lb 2 oz–1 lb 8 oz	1 lb 12 oz–2 lb 8 oz	510 g–680 g	793 g–1 kg 134 g
European Sparrowhawk	5 oz–7 oz	10 oz–11 oz	142 g–198 g	283 g–312 g
Sharp-shinned Hawk	3¼ oz	5¼ oz	92 g	149 g
European Goshawk	1 lb 4 oz–1 lb 15 oz	2 lb–3 lb 8 oz	567 g–879 g	907 g–1 kg 588 g
Shikra	4 oz–5 oz	5 oz–8 oz	113 g–142 g	142 g–227 g
Cooper's Hawk	10 oz–12 oz	15 oz–1 lb 2 oz	283 g–340 g	425 g–510 g
Hobby	6½ oz	8 oz	177 g	227 g
Lanner Falcon	14 oz–1 lb 3 oz	1 lb 4 oz–1 lb 10 oz	397 g–539 g	567 g–737 g
Lugger Falcon	14 oz–1 lb 3 oz	1 lb 4 oz–1 lb 11 oz	397 g–539 g	567 g–765 g
Peregrine Falcon	1 lb 2 oz–1 lb 7 oz	1 lb 14 oz–2 lb 3 oz	510 g–652 g	850 g–992 g
Merlin	5 oz–6½ oz	6¾ oz–8 oz	142 g–177 g	191 g–227 g
Saker Falcon	1 lb 9 oz–1 lb 12 oz	2 lb 2 oz–2 lb 6 oz	709 g–794 g	964 g–1 kg 77 g
Gyrfalcon	2 lb 7 oz–2 lb 10 oz	2 lb 14 oz–3 lb 6 oz	1 kg 106 g–1 kg 191 g	1 kg 304 g–1 kg 531 g
Prairie Falcon	15 oz–1 lb 4 oz	1 lb 11 oz–2 lb–1 oz	454 g–567 g	765 g–935 g
Tawny Eagle	3 lb–3 lb 10 oz	3 lb 14 oz–4 lb 12 oz	1 kg 361 g–1 kg 644 g	1 kg 758 g–2 kg 155 g
Steppe Eagle	4 lb 14 oz–5 lb 10 oz	7 lb–9 lb	2 kg 211 g–2 kg 551 g	3 kg 175 g–4 kg 82 g
Golden Eagle	5 lb 8 oz–8 lb	9 lb–12 lb 8 oz	2 kg 495 g–3 kg 629 g	4 kg 309 g–5 kg 670 g
Imperial Eagle	5 lb 10 oz–6 lb 3 oz	6 lb 10 oz–7 lb 6 oz	2 kg 551 g–2 kg 807 g	3 kg 6 g–3 kg 289 g
Bonelli's Eagle	3 lb 8 oz–3 lb 15 oz	4 lb 2 oz–4 lb 8 oz	1 kg 588 g–1 kg 786 g	1 kg 871 g–2 kg 41 g
European Eagle Owl	3 lb 12 oz–4 lb 12 oz	5 lb–6 lb	1 kg 701 g–2 kg 155 g	2 kg 268 g–2 kg 722 g

Checklist of Names of Sexes

FEMALE	MALE
Sparrowhawk	Musket
Hobby	Robin
Falcon (Peregrine)	Tiercel
Gyr	Jerkin
Lanner	Lanneret
Merlin	Jack
Saker	Sakret

Places of Interest to Visit in Britain

THE BRITISH SCHOOL OF FALCONRY
Stelling Minnis
Canterbury
Kent CT4 6AQ
Tel: Stelling Minnis (022 787) 575

*The School run by the author and her
husband (not open to the public).
Falconry courses available
(residential and non-residential) at
beginners' and advanced level. All
aspects of falconry covered.*

THE BIRD OF PREY CONSERVATION
   AND FALCONRY CENTRE
Newent
Gloucester GL18 1JJ
   Tel: Newent (0531) 820 286

*Open from February to November.
10.30 am–5.30 pm except Tuesdays.
Regular flying demonstrations,
weather permitting.
Breeding section open.*

THE WELSH HAWKING CENTRE
Weycock Road
Barry
S. Glamorgan
Wales CF6 9AA
   Tel: Barry (0446) 734687

*Open all year round except Christmas
Day. 10.30 am–6 pm.
Regular flying demonstrations, weather
permitting.*

THE HAWK CONSERVANCY
Weyhill
Andover
Hampshire SP11 8DY
   Tel: Weyhill (026477) 2252

*Open from March to November, every
day of the week. 10.30 am–4 or 5 pm.
Regular flying demonstrations, weather
permitting.*

LONDON ZOO
Regents Park
London NW1 4RY
   Tel: 01 722 3333

*Open all the year round, except
Christmas Day, every day of the
week. 9 am–6 pm.*

WELSH MOUNTAIN ZOO
Colwyn Bay
Clwyd
Wales LL29 5UY
   Tel: Colwyn Bay (0492) 2938
   & 31660
*Open Summer, 9.30 am–6 pm. Winter,
10 am–6 pm.
Falconry displays 11.45 am–3 pm.*

Equipment Suppliers

Furniture, incubators (Roll-X and Turn-X), comphrensive list of falconry books:

ROBIN HAIGH
Abbey Bridge Farm House
Colonel's Lane
Chertsey
Surrey
England KT16 8RJ
Tel: Chertsey 60236

Equipment, books:

MARTIN JONES
The Lodge
Huntley
Gloucester
England GL19 3HG
Tel: Gloucester 830629

JOHN COX
Taly Coed Court
Nr Monmouth
Gwent
Wales
Tel: Llantilio 294

Acorn bells:

YE OLD BELL MAKER
Peter Asborno
4530 W. 31st Ave
Denver
Colorado 80212
USA
Tel: (303) 667-4717

Telemetry:

TELONICS
1048 East Norwood
Mesa
Arizona 85203
USA

EFFECTIVE TELEMETRY
750 Bonair Place
La Jolla
California 92037
USA
Tel: (714) 454-2321

CUSTOM ELECTRONICS
2009 Silver Court West
Urbana
Illinois 61801
USA
Tel: (217) 344 3460

Candlers (cool light testers) and hatchers (Hova-Bator incubators):

BAR HATCH EQUIPMENT
Enhurst Road
Cranleigh
Surrey
England GU6 7NG
Tel: Cranleigh 71660

ABCR rings:

A. C. HUGHES
1, High Street
Hampton Hill
Middlesex
England TW12 1NA
Tel: 01 979 1366

Clubs and Societies Worldwide

THE BRITISH FALCONERS' CLUB
c/o P. T. Fields
3, Orchard Lane
Longton
Preston PR4 5AX
England
Publication: *The Falconer*

THE WELSH HAWKING CLUB
c/o Ann Shuttleworth
21, North Close
Blackfordby
Burton-on-Trent
Staffordshire DE11 8AP
England
Publication: *The Austringer*

NORTHERN ENGLAND FALCONRY
CLUB
c/o B. Thelwell
2, Fourlands Drive
Lolle
Bradford
Yorkshire BD 10 9SJ
England

ASSOCIATION NATIONALE DES
FALCONNIERS ET AUTOURSIERS
c/o Barnard Prevost
Quartier de Bruys
Route de Comillan
73300 Salon de Provence
France
Publication: *Chasse au Vol*

SCHWEIZERISCHE FALKNER-
VEREINIGUNG
c/o F. Michel
Birkenweg 24
2800 Matten B Interlaken
Switzerland

OSTERREICHISCHER FALKNERBUND
c/o Heinz Pils, Vizeprasident
A4421 Aschach/Steyr
Saab 38
Austria

ZIMBABWE FALCONERS' CLUB
P.O. Box 8564
Causeway
Salisbury
Zimbabwe
Publications: *Talon* biannually;
Footnotes annually

CLUB 'MARIE DE BOURGOGNE'
c/o Patric Morel
Rue Kievit 23
3070 Kortenberg
Belgium

NEDERLANDSH VALKENIERS
Verbund 'Adriaan Mollen'
c/o Heer W. P. J. Lammers
Vincent V. Goghstraat 21
Lisse 1660
Holland

THE NORTH AMERICAN FALCONERS'
ASSOCIATION
c/o Brian J. Walton
Rm. 231 Clark Verr Hall
University of California
Santa Cruz 95064
California
USA
Publication: *Hawk Chalk*

ALASKA FALCONERS' ASSOCIATION
P.O. Box 81239
College
Alaska 99708
USA

ARIZONA FALCONERS' ASSOCIATION
c/o Kristy Anderson, Secretary
1218, E. La Jolla Drive
Temple
Arizona 85282
USA

BRITISH COLUMBIA FALCONRY
ASSOCIATION
  c/o Colin Trefry, President
  157, Graham Drive
  Delta, BC N4W 2J2
  Canada

COLORADO HAWKING CLUB
  1029 E. 8th Ave
  No. 307
  Denver
  Colorado 80218
  USA

FLORIDA HAWKING FRATERNITY
  RT. 2, Box 266-8
  Bradenton
  Florida 33508
  USA

GREAT LAKES FALCONERS'
ASSOCIATION
  c/o George Richter, Secretary
  P.O. Box 121
  Warrenville
  Illinois 60555
  USA

IDAHO FALCONERS' ASSOCIATION
  c/o Wm. Smith, Secretary
  14989 Bear Island Drive
  Idaho Falls
  Idaho 83401
  USA

INDIANA FALCONERS' ASSOCIATION
  c/o James Wills
  16655 Gerald St
  Granger
  Indiana 46530
  USA

KENTUCKY FALCONERS' ASSOCIATION
  9112, Maple Road
  Louisville
  Kentucky 40229
  USA

MARYLAND HAWKING CLUB
  P.O. Box 125
  Garrett Park
  Maryland 20766
  USA

MASSACHUSETTS FALCONRY & HAWK
TRUST
  c/o Scott Keniston, L.O.
  RT. 2, Box 456
  Winterport
  Massachusetts 04496
  USA

MICHIGAN HAWKING CLUB
  D. D. Steere, Secretary/Treasurer
  532, Rich St
  Ionia
  Michigan 48846
  USA

MINNESOTA FALCONERS' ASSOCIATION
  c/o Frank Taylor
  420 Liberty St N.E.
  Fridley
  Minnesota 55432
  USA

NEW JERSEY RAPTOR ASSOCIATION
  1390 Whitebridge Road
  Willington
  New Jersey 07946
  USA

NEW YORK FALCONRY ASSOCIATION
INC.
  c/o Frank Porcari
  8-22 College Place
  College Point
  New York 11356
  USA
  Publication: *Mews News*

PENN FALCONRY AND HAWK TRUST
  c/o Marek L. Plater
  Box 22
  Kintnersville
  Pennsylvania 18930
  USA

POTOMAC FALCONERS' ASSOCIATION
  c/o Michael J. Johnson
  908 Frederich St S.W.
  Vienna
  Virginia 22180
  USA

WYOMING FALCONERS' ASSOCIATION
  L. Warren Higby
  RT. 63, Box 390
  Lander
  Wyoming 82520
  USA

Glossary of Falconry Terms

ABCR Aviary bred, close-ringed.

Accipiter A short-winged hawk identified by short, rounded wings, long tail and light eyes.

Arms The legs of a hawk from the thigh to the foot.

Austringer One who keeps and hunts accipiters, compared with a falconer who trains falcons.

Aylmeri's Leather anklets through which field or mews button jesses can be put.

Baggy See **Train.**

Bate To attempt to fly off the fist or perch when held or tied, in fright or at the lure or quarry.

Beam feathers The primary or phalangeal feathers of the wing.

Bechins Morsels or mouthfuls.

Bells Small bells, usually of brass, nickel or monel

Bewits Short thin strips of leather by which the bells are fastened to the legs.

Bind To grab and hold onto quarry in the air with the feet.

Bird of the fist A bird trained to come to the fist only, not to the lure. Only shortwinged hawks are trained in this way, not falcons.

Block A truncated cone or cylindrical piece of wood, having a ring in it for the attachment of the leash, and placed out of doors, whereon the hawk is set to 'weather'.

Blood feathers New feathers not yet fully grown, whose shafts contain blood at the top.

Bob Up and down movement of the head made by falcons when especially interested in something.

Bolt, to fly at Said of a short-winged hawk; to fly straight from the fist at the quarry.

Bowiser A young hawk able to fly from bough to bough.

Bow-perch A semicircular perch with a padded top, used for hawks out of doors.

Bowse To drink.

Braces Leather straps used to open or close the hood.

Brail A narrow strip of thin soft leather, with a long slit in it, used for tying one wing of a restless hawk that bates too much.

Brancher A young bird of prey that has left the nest and which is still learning to fly and is fed by its parents.

Break into The act of breaking through a kill's skin—usually starting at the soft underbelly.

Cadge A portable perch used to carry a number of birds hooded. It is slung from the shoulders by straps and is rectangular, the cadger walking in the centre.

Cadger The person who carries the cadge, the cadge-boy.

Call-off To call a hawk or falcon from a perch to the lure or to the fist.

Canceleer To make two or three sharp turns in the descent when stooping.

Carry When a hawk attempts to fly off with the quarry in her foot on being approached.

Cast, a Two birds, not necessarily a pair, flown together.

Cast, to To impel a hawk gently forward off the fist to get it airborne.

Cast, to The act of disgorging a pellet of the undigested parts of a meal—fur, feathers, bone etc.

Cast, to To hold a hawk in a cloth between the hands for imping, putting jesses on, etc.

Cast gorge To throw up the meat that is in the crop.

Casting   The pellet of feathers or fur disgorged by a hawk after completing the process of digestion.

Cawking-time   Pairing time.

Cere   The bare, wax-like skin above the beak.

Check   To change from one quarry to another during flight, or to hesitate because of sighting another quarry.

Clutch   To seize the quarry in the feet.

Come to   To begin obeying the falconer.

Condition   The hawk is in high condition when it is fat, too high when it is over-fat and not keen. In low condition the hawk is thin, and when it is too low it is too thin.

Cope   To file, and so shorten, the beak and talons of a bird.

Cowering   Quivering or shaking the wings, observed in young hawks.

Coystril   An old name for a kestrel.

Crab, crabbing   When hawks seize each other, either in the air or on the ground.

Cray   A disease in hawks like a form of constipation, namely a stoppage of the tewell so that the bird cannot mute.

Creance   A light line attached to the swivel of a partly trained falcon before she is allowed to fly loose.

Crines   The short hair-like feathers about the cere.

Croaks or kecks   A disease of the air and lung passages, analogous to a cough and so called from the sound the bird makes during any exertion such as flying or bating.

Crop, a   The amount of food a bird is given at a single meal.

Crop, the   The vascular sac above the breastbone which serves as the first receptacle for the food taken by a hawk before it is passed or 'put down' to the stomach.

Crop, putting over   The action of a hawk when she writhes with her neck, and squeezes a portion of the contents of her crop downwards into her stomach.

Crop, put away   When all the food in the crop has been passed downwards into the pannel.

Crossing flight   When another bird flies between the hawk and her quarry.

Deck feathers   The two centre feathers of the tail.

Disclosed   Said of hawks that are just hatched, now obsolete.

Diurnal   Day-time hunter.

Draw the hood   To draw the braces which close the hood.

Drawing from the mews   To withdraw a hawk after she has moulted.

Endew   To digest.

Enew or inew   See **Put in.**

Enseam   To purge a hawk of superfluous fat, and so render her fit for flying.

Enter   To give a bird its first flight at prey.

Eyass   A nestling, or young hawk taken from the eyrie.

Eyrie   The bird of prey's nest, usually used in conjunction with eagles.

Falcon   Term originally used to mean the female peregrine, and sometimes used for females of the other species of *falconidae*, but now generally used as a term to cover all longwings.

Fall at mark   To land on the ground and wait there for the falconer.

Feak   To wipe the beak clean on the perch with a stropping action after feeding.

Feed up   To give a bird extra meat in order to increase its weight.

Fetch   To reach and turn the quarry in pursuit.

Filanders   Intestinal worms.

Flags   The secondary or cubital feathers of the wing.

Flights or flight feathers   The main feathers used in flight, the primaries.

Fly on head   To miss the quarry and check.

Foot, to   To strike with the feet, and clutch or bind. A 'good footer' is said of a hawk that clutches well and holds.

Frounce   A canker or sore in the mouth and throat, often fatal, usually seen as a coloured coating on the tongue.

Fully down or full-summed   When a hawk has got all her new feathers after moulting.

Gentle   An old name for a peregrine.

Get or go in To approach the hawk as soon as she has caught the lure or quarry.

Gleam The substance thrown up after casting.

Gorge To allow a bird to eat as much food as she can at a single meal.

G.S.P. German short-haired pointer.

Gurgit To choke with too large a mouthful.

Hack A method of rearing young hawks completely free for a few weeks until they are old enough to train.

Hack back To hack a hawk that is no longer wanted and so ensure that it can fend for itself in the wild.

Hack-bells Large heavy bells put on hawks to hinder them from preying for themselves while 'flying at hack'.

Haggard An adult hawk in mature plumage, after having moulted in the wild state.

Halsband Literally, neck-band; a cord of soft twisted silk placed like a collar round the hawk's neck with the end held in the hand; used by Indian falconers, when flying the sparrowhawk, to steady the bird when cast off.

Hard down or hard penned When the new feathers are full grown and the shafts have hardened off to a quill.

Havock A cry raised by falconers in the hunting field. Now obsolete.

Hawk A most confusing term. Strictly speaking, a hawk is a short-winged, yellow-eyed bird of prey, as opposed to the long-winged, dark-eyed falcon. But the word is often used to cover both hawks and falcons, and hawking is done with either.

Hey or heye Term used by old authors meaning in good or high condition.

Hood A close-fitting leather cap, often tooled and decorated, used to blindfold a bird.

Hood block The wooden block on which some types of hoods are blocked to shape them.

Hood off To pull off the hood and slip a hawk at the quarry.

Hood-shy A hawk that dislikes being hooded, generally through a fault of the falconer, is hood-shy.

Imp A method of repairing broken flight feathers by replacing the broken portion with part of a feather from a previous moult.

Imping needle A bamboo splint used to join the two parts of a feather. They are oval or triangular.

Imprinting The action of a young hawk associating humans as its parents and responding accordingly.

Inke The neck of the quarry, now obsolete.

Intermew To moult a trained hawk in the confinements of the mews.

Jack A male merlin.

Jerkin A male gyrfalcon.

Jesses The narrow strips of leather fastened round a hawk's legs to hold her by.

Jokin A term used by old authors meaning 'sleeping'.

Keen, to be Willing, even anxious, to fly or hunt.

Leash A long narrow thong or strap of leather or nylon with a falconry button at one end, which is passed through the swivel and used to tie a bird to its block or perch.

Lines, lewns, loynes, lunes Antiquated words for the leash.

Longwings A term used to cover all falcons, who have long, pointed wings and dark eyes.

Lure An imitation bird or animal used to entice the hawk back in flight. It is usually made from a pair of wings or the skin of the type of quarry at which the bird is to be flown, and sometimes has raw meat tied to it.

Lure-bag Usually made of canvas, contains the lure and other equipment.

Lure-line Long string to which lure is attached.

Lure-stick Stick to which lure-line is attached.

Mail The breast feathers of a hawk.

Mail To wrap a hawk in a cloth either to tame her, or to keep her quiet during an operation such as coping or imping.

Make-hawk An old, experienced hawk flown with an eyass, when training, to teach or encourage it.

Make in   To approach a hawk on the ground with care, in order to take it up.

Make point   To rise perpendicularly in the air over the place where the quarry has 'put in'.

Man   To man a hawk is to make it tame by accustoming it to man's presence, usually achieved by holding the wild bird on the fist for the requisite period of time. Manning a hawk is *not* training it.

Mantle   To stand over a kill or food with wings lowered and slightly spread out to hide the food. Basically a belligerent attitude. Young hawks do this in the nest and they tend to continue to do so if they are handled too young. The habit is lost in the wild after leaving the nest, and passage or haggard hawks rarely mantle.

Mantle   The act of stretching a wing, leg and the tail, in one movement to one side of the body; generally repeated on the other side.

Mar-hawk   One who spoils a hawk by clumsy handling.

Mark   A call used by the falconer as a request to onlookers to watch where both hawk and quarry go.

Mark, to fly at   Generally said of a goshawk when, having 'put in' a covey of partridges, she takes stand, marking the spot where they disappeared from view until the falconer arrives to put them out to her.

Mark down   To pin-point the spot where hawk or quarry has gone.

Marrow   With old falconers 'mary', e.g. mary of beef or mary of goose; given as a remedy, or to envelop medicine.

Mew   To moult.

Mews   The building or room where hawks are kept. Also the place in which they are put away to moult.

Mites   The parasites that infest the head and nares of a hawk.

Musket   The male sparrowhawk.

Mutes   The droppings or excrement of hawks.

Nares   The nostrils of a hawk.

Nocturnal   Night-time hunter.

Nyas   An eyas or eyass—a nestling hawk taken from the eyrie or nest.

Ostringer   Another way of spelling austringer.

Pannel   The stomach or lower bowel of a hawk.

Pantas   A disease in hawks akin to asthma.

Passage   A line of flight in relation to birds.

Passage hawk or passager   A bird caught on passage or migration and still in its immature plumage.

Paster   Plaister, used medicinally; now obsolete.

Pelt   The dead body of the quarry.

Pendant feathers   The feathers behind the thighs of a hawk.

Pennes   Flight feathers—the feathers from which quill pens were made.

Perch   That on which you put your hawk when you put her off the fist. Originally the perch was used in the house, and the block out of doors.

Petty singles   The toes of a hawk.

Pick-up piece   The piece of meat held in the gloved hand, used to cover the meat on the lure to entice the hawk from the lure or quarry onto the fist.

Pill or pelf   What is left of the quarry after the hawk has been fed upon it.

Pin and web   A disease of the eye in hawks causing dimness and a film.

Pitch, to   To land on a perch.

Pitch, the   The height at which a hawk 'waits on', having risen in the air by ringing up.

Plumage   Another word for 'casting'.

Plumage   The feathers of a hawk.

Plume   To pluck the feathers off the quarry.

Point, to make her   When a hawk rises perpendicularly in the air over the place where she has 'put in' the quarry.

Pounces   The talons of a falcon or the claws of a hawk.

Preen   To clean and dress the feathers with the beak.

Primaries   The longest main-wing feathers, ten outermost in each wing.

Principals   The two longest feathers in the wing of a hawk.

Put in   To drive the quarry into cover; to take refuge in cover.

Put out   To flush the quarry out of cover in which it has taken refuge.

Put over   To empty the crop into the digestive system, an action performed with a back and forth motion of the body, and particularly with the neck.

Quarry   The game at which a bird is flown. Earlier usage meant the entrails of a kill.

Quick   Alive.

Rake away   To fly wide of the falconer, or of the intended quarry, or even away from it, possibly after a different quarry.

Rake   To fly close to the ground.

Ramage-hawk   See **Brancher.**

Rangle   Small stones given to hawks to aid digestion. A hawk may pick them up and eat them of its own accord if they are put within reach.

Reblock   To reshape a hood by soaking it in water and drying it on a hood block.

Reclaim   To 'man' a hawk, or to retrain a hawk that has been idle for a period.

Red-hawk   A peregrine in the red or immature plumage, sometimes used to mean a first-year bird.

Ring-perch   A modernized form of a bow-perch. The hawk sits on top of a padded circle, which in turn is attached to a stand.

Ring up, tower   To climb spirally in flight.

Ringing flight   A flight that necessitates a falcon ringing up after the quarry.

Robin   The male hobby.

Rouse   To raise the feathers slightly before shaking the plumage back into position.

Ruff   To hit the quarry and make the feathers fly, without trussing it.

Rufter hood   A plain, easy, leather hood, used by hawk-catchers but not by falconers, with the back cut away to fit hawks newly caught, and a large beak hole through which they can easily feed; used when a hawk is being tamed, and superseded by the proper hood when she is trained. The absence of a plume prevents her from pulling it off.

Rye   A disease in hawks which shows itself by a swelling in the head.

Sails   The wings of a hawk.

Scouring   Purging.

Screen-perch   A perch on which hawks are kept indoors. The screen hanging from it stops the hawk tangling itself round the perch and helps it to regain the perch if it bates off. Now this perch is considered dangerous, and is not used by good falconers.

Seare, sere   See **Cere.**

Secondaries   The feathers used for flight next to the 'primaries', but slightly shorter, and usually wider across.

Seeling   An old method of obscuring the sight of a newly caught hawk by passing a thread through the eyelids to stitch them together. This practice has long been superseded in this country by the more humane use of the hood, though still adopted by some falconers in India.

Serve   To put quarry out of cover for a hawk.

Set down to moult   To put into the mews for moulting.

Shaft   The central hollow strut of a feather, giving it its support.

Sharp set   Very hungry, and keen to fly (used of longwings).

Shortwing   Term used to cover eagles, hawks and buzzards, who have rounded ends to their wings when seen silhouetted in flight.

Slice   The action employed by eagles, hawks and buzzards of evacuating mutes.

Slight falcon   An old name for the peregrine.

Snite   To sneeze.

Soar   When a hawk takes to the air and enjoys flying for the sake of flying, by gliding on thermals and other air currents, rather than flying at quarry.

Sore-hawk   A hawk of the first year.

Spring   To flush the partridge, pheasant or other bird to be flown at from the covert.

Stoop   The rapid descent of a falcon from a height, at quarry or lure, with wings nearly closed. The meaning is similar to that of swoop.

Strike the hood   To pull the braces open of a hood, so as to be in readiness to take off hood the moment the hawk is to be flown, or quarry is sighted.

Swivel   Two rings, connected in a figure of eight fashion with a bolt or rivet. Used to connect the jesses and the leash when a hawk is held or tied on the perch, to prevent them from getting twisted. Also known as a 'tyrrit'.

Take the air   To mount.

Take the lure   To catch hold of the lure.

Take stand   To pitch on a tree or perch and wait.

Tarcel   See **Tiercel.**

Tarsus   The leg of a hawk.

Tassel   See **Tiercel.**

Tercel   See **Tiercel.**

Tewell   The lower bowel, affected by the disease termed 'cray'.

Tiercel, tarcel, tassel, tercel   The male peregrine, from the French *tierce*, meaning third. The tiercel is a third less in size than the falcon (female peregrine). The term is widely used to mean the male of any type of falcon, but this is wrong as by no means are all male birds of prey a third less in size.

Tire   To pull at a tough piece of meat.

Tiring   Any tough piece, such as the leg of a fowl, with little meat on it, given to a hawk when in training to pull at, in order to prolong the meal, and exercise the muscles of the back and neck.

Tower   See **Ring up.**

Train   The tail of a hawk.

Train   Live quarry, also known as the 'baggy', given on a line to the hawk when first entered. The use of bagged quarry is illegal in Britain.

Truss   To clutch and hold the quarry in the stoop without letting it go, instead of striking it to the ground.

Trussed   Live prey seized by the feet and held.

Tyrrit   See **Swivel.**

Unreclaimed   Wild.

Unstrike the hood   To loosen the braces so that the hood may be easily pulled off.

Unsummed   A hawk is said to be unsummed while moulting, before her new feathers are grown up.

Urines   Nets to catch hawks.

Wait on   To circle round high up over the falconer, waiting for him to flush the quarry or throw out the lure.

Various   A term used in quarry lists to cover any small fry which may have been inadvertently caught by a trained hawk.

Varvels   Before swivels were invented a metal ring was sewn on to the end of each jess, and the leash put through. The rings were flat, like washers, and often had the arms of the bird's owner, or his name engraved upon them. Sometimes they were made of silver, or even gold.

Wake   To tame a hawk by keeping her on the fist day and night, keeping her from sleeping. Also 'watch'.

Warbile, warble, warbel   To stretch both wings upwards over the back till they nearly touch, and at the same time to spread the tail.

Watch   See **Wake.**

Weather   To place the hawk on her block in the open air during the day.

Weathering ground   The area where the hawks are kept on blocks through the day.

Webbing   The soft strands each side of the shaft of a feather.

W.H.Y.   Abbreviation often used in advertisements for raptors meaning 'What have you?'

Yarak, to be in   A term which originated in the East, usually applied only to shortwings, 'sharp set' being the correct synonym for longwings. It means fit, keen and ready to be flown. A bird which is out of yarak should not be flown as it is not in the right condition.

Bibliography

BEEBE, F. L. and WEBSTER, H. M., *North American Falconry and Hunting Hawks*, published privately 1964. Reprinted 1976: Box 1484, Denver, Colorado 80210.

BLAINE, G., *Falconry*, Neville Spearman, London, 1970. First published 1936.

BROWN, LESLIE, *British Birds of Prey*, Collins, London 1976. Reprinted 1978.

COOPER, J. E., *Veterinary Aspects of Captive Birds of Prey*, Standfast Press, Saul, Gloucestershire 1978.

GLASIER, PHILIP, *Falconry and Hawking*, Batsford, London 1978.

JAMESON, E. W., *The Hawking of Japan*, University of California, Davis, California, 1962. Reprinted 1976.

McELROY, H., *Desert Hawking*, published privately 1977, Box 896, Tuber City, Arizona 86045.

LASCELLES, GERALD, *The Art of Falconry*, Neville Spearman, London 1980. First published 1892.

SALVIN, F. H. and BRODRICK, W., *Falconry in the British Isles*, Windward, Leicester 1855. Reprinted 1980.

UPTON, ROGER, *A Bird in the Hand*, Debretts Peerage Ltd, London 1980.

WOODFORD, M. H., *Manual of Falconry*, A & C Black Ltd, London 1960. Third edition 1977.

Index